IMMEDIATIONS

A *Camera Obscura* book

Immediations

THE HUMANITARIAN IMPULSE IN DOCUMENTARY

Pooja Rangan

Duke University Press / Durham and London / 2017

Printed in the United States of America on acid-free paper ∞
Typeset in Arno Pro and Meta by Graphic Composition, Inc.,
Bogart, Georgia

Library of Congress Cataloging-in-Publication Data
Names: Rangan, Pooja, [date] author.
Title: Immediations : the humanitarian impulse in
documentary / Pooja Rangan.
Other titles: Camera obscura book.
Description: Durham : Duke University Press, 2017. | Series:
A camera obscura book | Includes bibliographical references
and index.
Identifiers: LCCN 2016056543 (print)
LCCN 2017004585 (ebook)
ISBN 9780822363552 (hardcover : alk. paper)
ISBN 9780822363712 (pbk. : alk. paper)
ISBN 9780822373100 (ebook)
Subjects: LCSH: Documentary films. | Documentary films—
Social aspects. | Humanitarianism.
Classification: LCC PN1995.9.D6 R364 2017 (print) | LCC
PN1995.9.D6 (ebook) | DDC 070.1/8—dc23
LC record available at https://lccn.loc.gov/2016056543

Cover art: Production still from *L'Enfant Sauvage*, 1970. Courtesy of Photofest.

FOR MY FAMILIES, OF HEART AND MIND

CONTENTS

ILLUSTRATIONS

ACKNOWLEDGMENTS

The project that became *Immediations* began when I was a graduate student at Brown University in the Department of Modern Culture and Media. The brilliant cohort of peers that I met there were some of my earliest interlocutors and remain a continual source of inspiration. I am grateful for the many discussions I have had about this book with Ani Maitra, Tess Takahashi, David Bering-Porter, Julie Levin Russo, Sarah Osment, Gosia Rymsza-Pawlowska, Paige Sarlin, Michelle Cho, Marc Steinberg, Yuriko Furuhata, Maggie Hennefeld, and Josh Guilford. Ani, Tess, and David, in particular, have read and commented on several chapters of this book at various stages. There isn't a day that passes when I am not grateful for these dear friends, and for the faculty at the MCM department, who brought us together and trained us with such commitment and rigor.

It was also at Brown that I met Rey Chow, who became my graduate advisor. Rey has shaped this project, and my mind, in ways I cannot measure. Beyond her ideas, whose mark on this book will be clear, I have learned so much from her about intellectual community, professional generosity, and what it means to be a teacher. I would not be the person I am today if it weren't for Rey. At Brown, I was also privileged to study with Mary Ann Doane, Wendy Chun, Phil Rosen, Lynne Joyrich, Michael Silverman, Nancy Armstrong, and Elizabeth Weed. Susan McNeil and Liza Hebert, the department administrators, were my home away from home, and I thrived thanks to their kindness.

The groundwork for this project was laid at the "Visions of Nature: Constructing the Cultural Other" Pembroke Seminar in 2008–2009, led by Leslie Bostrom, in which I participated as a graduate fellow. A dissertation award from the Pembroke Center for Teaching and Research on Women provided a much-needed boost of confidence as I began shaping this project into a book. I send my warmest greetings to my fellow participants in the "Visions of Nature" Pembroke Seminar, as well as to the members of the Speculative Critique Colloquium, whose astute questions helped me to see the larger shape of this book. Special thanks are due to the Graduate International Colloquium Fund at Brown, and to the Andrew W. Mellon Foundation, whose grant support made this colloquium possible and brought me into contact with Lisa Cartwright and Bishnupriya Ghosh, both of whom have enthusiastically welcomed me into their scholarly networks.

I have had the immense fortune to have Lisa Cartwright and Fatimah Tobing Rony, two scholars whom I hold in the highest regard, as readers of my manuscript for Duke University Press. Their generous and generative reader reports helped me to discover the book's argument and its relationship to feminist media studies. My own shortcomings aside, this book became a better one because of their feedback. Courtney Berger has been a patient and kind editor, providing encouragement and vision in equal measure. Sandra Korn and Lisa Bintrim, at Duke University Press, have been a pleasure to work with, and Kim Miller's copy edits brought coherence to my writing. I am grateful to Mark Mastromarino for producing an excellent index. Dilshanie Perera, Olimpia Mosteanu, Miu Suzuki, Margaret Banks, and Zachary Yanes all provided valuable research assistance.

Several others have contributed indirectly and directly to the completion of this book. Many of my strongest ideas came from late-night conversations with Toby Lee, Danya Abt, Michelle Materre, Ann Neumann, Lauren Berliner, Paromita Vohra, Veronica Pravadelli, Leslie Thornton, and Tom Zummer. Keya Ganguly's notes on early drafts of the first two chapters have been a tremendous resource throughout the writing process. At the New School, I was lucky to be taken under Dominic Pettman's wing. Dominic's infectious curiosity encouraged me to pursue some of the book's more obscure leads, as well as to understand its central claims about the human. I also met Genevieve Yue while at the New School, and she has become a cherished collaborator and friend. Genevieve read through the entirety of this book at the final hour, and helped me to see the big picture again through her own intelligent eyes. Sarah Osment helped me through the weeds when I was proofreading and patiently answered every query. Amelie Hastie has been an incredible mentor and reader during the final stages of the book's completion, and her love of film has helped me to find a way to my own. My partner, Josh Guilford, has seen this project through from beginning to end. His innate kindness has smoothed out its pointy edges, and I rest easy at night knowing that

I can rely on his steady presence and intellectual companionship. To Josh, and to my parents, Sheela and Girish Rangan, I owe everything. They provide the daily life support, humor, and love without which no work would ever get done.

This book was written with the assistance of a Copeland Postdoctoral Fellowship at Amherst College, which gave me a leave from teaching in 2013–2014. I am grateful to Amherst College for the gift of time, both during this fellowship year and in the well-timed sabbatical leave shortly after I began teaching there. I thank Austin Sarat and the members of the Copeland Colloquium on Catastrophe and the Catastrophic, especially Christopher Dole, for their camaraderie during the Colloquium, and the film and media and English faculty at Amherst for welcoming me so warmly into their midst. I am lucky to have Lisa Brooks as my departmental mentor and have enjoyed many stimulating conversations with her about this project.

Individual chapters of this book have substantially improved as a result of being worked over at a number of workshops over the years. I thank the participants of the Vulnerability and Innocence in Humanitarianism workshop at the New School, especially Miriam Ticktin, Lisa Cartwright, Thomas Keenan, and Andres Henao Castro, for their feedback on chapter 2. Chapter 4 benefited greatly from being workshopped at the Visual Culture Lab (I especially thank Orit Halpern, Vicky Hattam, and Julie Beth Napolin). Chapters 3 and 4 were workshopped at the Animation and Forms of Life workshop at the New School and the subsequent Media Crossings workshop at McGill University; I thank Deborah Levitt and Thomas Lamarre for including me in these conversations.

Several parts of this book began as conference papers at Visible Evidence, the Society for Cinema and Media Studies, and the World Picture Conference. I have met some of my most encouraging supporters at these venues, including Patty White, Alisa Lebow, Meghan Sutherland, Brian Price, Jennifer Horne, and Jonathan Kahana. I am also thankful to audiences at Penn State's Department of Women's, Gender, and Sexuality Studies, Pratt University's Aesthetics and Politics series, MIT's Feminisms Unbound series, and Colgate University (especially Emilio Spadola) for their insightful questions during invited talks. Jennifer Wagnor-Lawlor, Gabeba Baderoon, Stephanie Boluk, Jonathan Beller, Kimberly Juanita Brown, Ani Maitra, and Mary Simonson are to thank for these invitations. I was incredibly moved by their hospitality, and by the vitality of the affective and intellectual communities they foster. The Flaherty Film Seminar, which I began attending in 2007, is another important community without which I would be bereft, and I cannot thank Chi-hui Yang and Elizabeth Delude-Dix enough for asking me to become a board member in 2014. Anita Reher and Sarie Horowitz, who run this organization, are two of the hardest-working people I know. Much of the thinking that went into this book has been sustained by their labor.

Finally, I would like to thank the members of the Camera Obscura collective for inviting me to publish this book as part of their relaunched book series at Duke University Press. Their recognition of this project's resonance with their own means the world to me, especially since my first peer-reviewed publication was an article in *Camera Obscura*.

Sections and earlier versions of some of the chapters were previously published in the following journal issues: an early version of chapter 1 in *Camera Obscura* 25, no. 3 75 (2011): 143–77; an early version of chapter 2 in *differences* 24, no. 1 (2013): 104–36; an excerpt from chapter 2 in *Shoppinghour Magazine* 9 (2012): 58–61; and a brief section of chapter 3 in *Feminist Media Histories* 1, no. 3 (2015): 95–126.

IMMEDIATIONS

THE HUMANITARIAN IMPULSE IN DOCUMENTARY

What does endangered life do for documentary? As practitioners, critics, and spectators of documentary, we rarely ask this question. Instead, we commonly believe that documentary works on behalf of disenfranchised human beings by "giving a voice to the voiceless." This book argues the opposite. I argue that endangered, dehumanized life not only sustains documentary, but supplies its raison d'être. This is especially true, I propose, of participatory documentary, whose guiding humanitarian ethic—giving the camera to the other—invents the very disenfranchised humanity that it claims to redeem.

François Truffaut's *The Wild Child* (*L'Enfant Sauvage*), a film set in Enlightenment-era France, poignantly dramatizes the follies of this humanitarian ethic. The film's protagonist, Dr. Jean-Marc Gaspard Itard, has rescued a mute and seemingly feral young boy, hoping to educate him and thereby reveal his latent humanity. The experiment is not going well. Itard's attempts to socialize and educate the "wild child" are met with hostility, violence, and several escape attempts. More than once, the boy collapses during Itard's unrelenting language lessons, flailing in distress and bleeding from the nose. Paradoxically, it is when the boy successfully demonstrates his humanization (he has returned to Itard after a failed escape attempt, having lost his survival instincts) that Itard experiences his deepest doubts. He longs to return the boy to his "innocent and happy life." Realizing that his rescue mission has created a prison from which there is no escape, Itard steels himself in his task, and resolves to redeem the boy's lost innocence—his humanity—through further education.

Itard's dilemma is a perfect allegory of the internal contradictions of participatory documentary. The fantasy of the wild boy's lost humanity not only allows Itard to embrace the misguided reasons for his humanitarian intervention, but reinforces the intervention's importance. The gesture of giving the camera to the other is motored by a similar fantasy. Participatory documentary views its beneficiaries as deprived of both humanity and its latent essence—a latency that fuels the humanitarian impulse to redeem and evidence their humanity by giving them a voice.

I aim to produce a critical and philosophical understanding of this humanitarian documentary impulse. I focus on contemporary humanitarian rescue missions in which documentary serves as a humanizing prosthesis for dehumanized subjects: photography workshops among the children of sex workers in the film *Born into Brothels*, live eyewitness reporting by Hurricane Katrina survivors, therapeutic attempts to facilitate autistic speech, and the rehabilitation of Asian draft elephants as painters. I ask, How does the perception of humanity at risk drive the production of humanist aesthetic forms that *produce* the "humanity" that they claim to document? How does the urgent ethical imperative of representing lives at risk lead to new formal innovations in the "creative treatment of actuality"? Why does the dubious pursuit of humanity reinforce documentary's reputation as a progressive, reflexive discourse, and what do the so-called beneficiaries of this discourse stand to gain or lose from this pursuit?

Questions such as these begin to suggest how disenfranchised humanity is repeatedly enlisted and commodified to corroborate documentary's privileged connection with the real. They also return us to the unfashionable historical connections between documentary and immediacy, which documentary scholars have been at pains to undo. The word *immediate* derives from the Latin *immediātus*, meaning "without anything between." The *Oxford English Dictionary* defines the adjective *immediate* as indicating a direct relation or action between two things or persons that can be spatial ("involving actual contact or direct relation: opposed to *mediate* and *remote*"; "having no person, thing, or space intervening") or temporal ("occurring, accomplished, or taking effect without delay or lapse of time; done at once; instant").[1] Both senses of *immediate* are encapsulated in the documentary values of directness and urgency championed by the Scottish filmmaker, critic, and theorist John Grierson, who is credited with coining the term *documentary*, as well as the phrase "creative treatment of actuality," as a definition of the genre.[2] The son of a schoolteacher, and a student of moral philosophy, Grierson envisioned documentary as a form of cinematic pedagogy for drawing public attention to contemporary social problems such as unemployment, homelessness, poverty, and hunger.

The goal of documentary for Grierson was "social not aesthetic"; he believed in propaganda first, and art second.[3] In an essay titled "The Documentary Idea: 1942," Grierson elaborates: "the documentary idea was not basically a film idea at all. . . . [T]he medium happened to be the most convenient and most exciting available to us. The idea itself, on the other hand, was a new idea for public education."[4] A few pages later, he adds, "It is not the technical perfection of the film that matters, not even the vanity of its maker, but what happens to the public mind. . . . [Good propaganda must] create a sense of urgency in the public mind, and gear it in its everyday processes to the hardness and directness which make for action and decision."[5] Grierson wished to innovate a form of cinematic mediation in which the role of the aesthetic was to refer the spectator to urgent social realities in a direct, immediate, and didactic fashion. As Jonathan Kahana puts it, documentary, for Grierson, was "always about something more or other than what it depicts."[6]

The interwar and wartime context in which Grierson developed his ideas regarding documentary, as well as his subordination of documentary's aesthetic and creative potential to the higher goal of social purpose, indicates that documentary came about as part of the modern ethical imaginary that Elaine Scarry and Craig Calhoun have named "emergency thinking."[7] *Emergency thinking* (a term I will soon elaborate on) institutes a humanitarian order of priorities in which saving endangered human lives takes precedence over all other considerations, including the aesthetics and politics of representation. The humanitarian mandate demands action over thinking, ethics over aesthetics, and immediacy over analysis. Grierson's prescription of these priorities as ideals for the emerging genre of documentary can be read as an impulse toward humanitarian media intervention at a moment of disillusionment regarding the integrity of global democratic structures: as Brian Winston notes, the "suffering humanity" of "social victims" is the most powerful legacy of the Griersonian school and remains a staple of the realist documentary to this day.[8]

Immediations argues that contemporary participatory documentary interventions that seek to immediately empower dehumanized subjects are the heirs of Grierson's humanitarian mission. My goal is to theorize the aesthetic and political implications of the audiovisual tropes that are mobilized when documentary operates in the mode of emergency—that is, when it seeks to redeem dehumanized lives as a first-order principle. I call these tropes *immediations* in order to emphasize the mediated quality of their emphasis on immediacy. The neologism is a call to theorize the medial frames that are at work precisely when mediation seems to disappear or cease to matter. I ask, How does documentary render suffering humanity *immediate*? What aesthetic, formal, and narrative tropes does it invent to generate the sensations of temporal urgency and direct spatial presence? How are the effects of these representational conventions made to seem immaterial, secondary, or even irrelevant when it comes to the ethical mandate of saving lives? By posing such questions, I aim to understand how the concept of the human fuels documentary's investments in narratives of social and representational progress. I insist on the circular quality of these seemingly emancipatory narratives, as well as the openings that result from a documentary ethic that is oriented not toward the human, but toward all that it excludes as other.

The language of documentary immediacy is most insidious when it is employed by disenfranchised subjects representing themselves. This is why I focus on tropes of documentary immediacy—or immediations—in the context of participatory documentary. The immediations that I examine include the photographic aesthetic of innocence employed by non-Western children (chapter 1), the televisual codes of "liveness" used by disaster victims as a testimonial strategy (chapter 2), the use of the first-person voice-over to give voice to nonverbal autistics (chapter 3), and the self-portrait as evidence of animal intelligence (chapter 4). These tropes share a common feature: they rely on the truth effects of documentary, invoking its status as actuality rather than creative artifact, to guarantee the humanity of the dehumanized subjects who deploy them. The time-sensitive predicament of human lives at risk legitimates and even calls for the documentary rhetoric of immediacy. I argue that the endangered humanity of these lives is a red herring: it demands that we ignore the discursive work of the immediations (such as the self-portrait or the first-person voice-over) that are actively involved in regulating the meaning of the human even as they present the appearance of truth or self-evidence.

I aim to undo the mutual reinforcements of documentary's claim to an unmediated encounter with reality and the humanitarian appeal to the ambiguous and elusive concept of humanity. The emergence of the child as a humanitarian emblem of innocent and pure humanity is a paradigmatic instance of these reinforcements. Truffaut's film about the wild child dramatizes the persuasive power of this emblem despite all evidence to the contrary. The purported innocence of children also prompts one of the maxims of participatory documentary: that placing a camera in children's hands will allow us to "see through their eyes," free from the defilement of mediation. This is the central conceit of the film *Born into Brothels* (2004), discussed in chapter 1. The photographic aesthetic of "feral innocence" adopted by the children who star in this film contains the threat that these children, whose mothers are sex workers in Calcutta, pose to the humanitarian fantasy of childhood innocence by flattening the embodied position they allegedly speak for into a fetish. The discourse of photographic spontaneity thereby affirms the belief that children exist outside discourse and productive economies even as it enlists non-Western children in the production of humanitarian commodities. Such an appeal to humanity as a form of documentary proof obliterates the historical specificity to which documentary aspires, and which documentary scholars identify as the basis of the genre's political and ethical potential.[9]

The analytical work of this book consists of articulating how the aesthetic of feral innocence and other humanist tropes of documentary immediacy exploit the concrete material circumstances and labors of disenfranchised individuals—and do so in a manner that reinforces their status as other. This effort extends the tradition of feminist critics of documentary like Trinh T. Minh-ha and Fatimah Tobing Rony. In the 1990s Rony and Trinh mounted important critiques of documentary that centered on the realist tropes of "romantic naturalism" (Trinh) and "romantic preservationism" (Rony) frequently employed in ethnographic depictions of the non-West.[10] Even when they were not explicitly racist in intent, these scholars argued, the use of "objective" or "neutral" conventions (such as long takes, wide-angle shots, and explanatory third-person commentary) to represent non-Western and indigenous cultures nonetheless marked them as authentic, timeless, and untouched by civilization—that is, as other. Little has been done to update these critiques of documentary humanism in the past twenty-five years. Instead, documentary scholars agree that the genre has achieved a certain reflexivity and sophistication, in part because technical and social advances have enabled documentary's others to represent themselves (in *Introduction to Documentary*, Bill Nichols includes the "participatory mode" in his schematic of enlightened documentary approaches). Much of the recent work in documentary studies, although excellent in its own right, regards the tendencies critiqued by Rony and Trinh as an unfortunate historical misstep and focuses on the documentary genre's redeeming interests in irony, spectacle, subjectivity, and avant-gardism.[11]

This book challenges this consensus and its investments in technological and representational reflexivity. I argue that the practice of othering has not abated with the advent of participatory documentary. Rather, it has found new sites, moving from indigenous cultures to the figures I discuss in each of my chapters, including the child, the refugee, the autistic, and the animal. It has also taken on supple new forms that operate not through exclusion and setting apart but through inclusion, participation, and empowerment. I show how the documentary tropes that I call immediations exclude these figures as other but do so through the seemingly inclusive gesture of inviting them to perform their humanity. In this regard, I subscribe to Michel Foucault's theory that modern power operates through affirmation and not negation, and that its logic is proliferative, not conservative.[12] Foucault and his interlocutors, who have mobilized his insights to identify large-scale shifts in the dynamics of labor, subjectivity, and difference in modernity and postmodernity, are foundational to the book.

I see the humanitarian impulse in participatory documentary as an example of what Rey Chow calls the "inclusionist, liberalist cultural logic" of dealing with difference in the post-Enlightenment West.[13] Chow explains this logic using the example of the term *ethnic*: in modernity, an open, inclusive attitude has replaced the premodern, discriminatory attitude toward ethnic difference. And yet, although *ethnic* is used to connote a universal humanity ("we are all ethnic"), the term is deployed to discriminate against cultural particularity ("those ethnics over there") whenever political, economic, or ideological gains are at stake. For Chow, the predicament of ethnicity is symptomatic of the internal violence that is endemic in the affirmative logic of multicultural liberalism. The impulse to valorize the humanity of all seems at first to be democratic and modern. However, when humanity is upheld as a primary principle and imperative, it can turn into an alibi for discriminatory and violent acts—all performed in the name of humanity. Ethnics pay the highest price for this modernizing narrative, in the form of painful psychic and material losses: the liberatory practice of claiming their humanity inevitably entails the abjection and exclusion of the particular, embodied facts of difference, which are seen as a primitive form of captivity.[14] Humanitarian tolerance thus operates as a softer version of what Foucault dubs racist bio-power. Ethnicity serves as a line of inclusion as well as exclusion for expunging difference from the social field, such that some are made to suffer while others are made to thrive.[15]

Ethnicity is not the only site of difference through which this narrative of covert exclusion is currently being played out. Childhood, refugeehood, disability, and animality are all boundary conditions that have risen to prominence in contemporary critical and popular conversations as emblems of a universal human condition. The humanitarian preoccupation with the child as a symbol of universal humanity is one example of the contemporary fascination with liminality. Another, from academic quarters, is Giorgio Agamben's protest that we all share the bare, exposed condition of the refugee, who can be killed but not sacrificed ("we are all virtually *homines sacri*").[16] Similar assertions of this type have also recently been made regarding the conditions of disability and animality. I ask, What do these universalizing claims share with the humanitarian ethic of benevolent inclusion? Under what circumstances does this ethic turn corrosive and exclusionary?

Participatory documentary offers a unique opportunity to examine the stakes and the casualties of the liberal, humanitarian ethic described above. The act of giving the camera to the other is intended to resolve the discriminatory paradigm of representation discussed by Trinh and Rony. This gesture, which acknowledges the other's humanity, makes it clear that participatory documentary partakes of the ongoing critical and popular investments in otherness as a litmus test for humanity. The turn to society's others to locate the essence of humanity also reminds us that humanity—as the signifier of both an ambiguous collectivity and the equally ambiguous traits proper to the human—is always "defined by its breach," to quote Ruti Teitel.[17] We would do well to pay close attention to these breaches and to their perception as breaches. It is only in the *perceived* absence of humanity, I argue, that we can pinpoint the ideological work that goes into defining its attributes, which can otherwise appear perfectly natural, transhistorical, and self-evident. I focus, therefore, on various humanizing attributes, such as liveness and voice, that are attributed to dehumanized subjects who are thought to have been denied them.

Immediations, I propose, are the documentary tropes of evidencing these attributes of humanity in all their immediacy. If humanity is the "ultimate imagined community," as Dominic Pettman puts it, then documentary immediations can be regarded as part of the ritual, tropic performances of belonging to this community.[18] Through them, we begin to grasp the normalizing calculus that goes into defining the benchmarks of humanity in the liberal West, the complicity of documentary media in regulating these definitions, and the unevenly distributed costs of achieving these benchmarks. In each of my chapters, I show how the ostensible goal of humanitarian intervention—that is, mitigating the impacts of a hostile or absent state—leads participatory documentary initiatives to function as makeshift humanitarian entities to which disenfranchised subjects must appeal using the tropes of immediation. My analyses of these tropes examine what ethical, perceptual, and relational modes are excluded from the definition of humanity, and how the formal conventions of documentary representation are implicated in naturalizing these exclusions. I also attempt to paint a picture of the humanitarian documentary conventions, networks, and institutions that are made to thrive as a function of these very exclusions. At its core, *Immediations* argues that documentary, especially in its most benevolent, humanitarian guises, is thoroughly implicated in the work of regulating what does and does not count as human.

In *The Open*, Agamben offers a compelling insight: he argues that the human is an entity with no positive attributes other than the ability to recognize itself as human. His insight emerges from symptomatic readings of a variety of philosophical sources, including the founder of modern taxonomy, Carl Linnaeus. Linnaeus's enigmatic taxonomic classification of *Homo sapiens* lists no specific qualities but rather an imperative: "Know thyself." Agamben interprets this to mean that the human is not a clearly defined species or substance. Strictly speaking, *Homo sapiens* has no fixed meaning; rather, it is an "optical machine" or "device for producing the recognition of the human."[19] Agamben differentiates between two iterations of the "anthropological machine": an ancient version, which operates by humanizing the animal, that is, by incorporating an outside; and a modern version, which operates by animalizing the human, or isolating and excluding the nonhuman within the human. Either way, the device functions by producing a caesura within the spectating entity that has ripple effects across the social field—looking in this device, the not-yet-human entity (mis)recognizes itself as human by isolating and casting out those elements that do not correspond to the image of the human.[20]

Immediations are a potent example of such an optical device through which the human is manufactured. My analyses of these devices suggest that the two versions of the anthropological machine described by Agamben may be productively considered as simultaneous interpellative operations facilitated by participatory documentary interventions. The trope of the first-person voice-over in documentary films produced by and starring autistic protagonists (chapter 3) offers a striking illustration of how immediations simultaneously expand the community of humanity and expunge it of difference: this seemingly self-evident convention of "having a voice" not only holds up a mirror to so-called voiceless autistics, calling on them to express their interiority in a normative way, but also hails humanitarian spectators to recognize and connect with their humanity, conceived in the same normalizing terms. In this way, autistics are taught to speak the language of human personhood and intersubjectivity—they are humanized—while in the very same movement autistic modes of communication and relationality are excluded and coded as nonhuman.

I respond with a two-pronged critical approach. First, I identify how the ethic of immediation gives rise to humanitarian genres of participatory documentary, such as child-produced photography or the animal self-portrait. I trace how humanity is coded in the audiovisual and narrative language of these different documentary forms, and how their legitimating claims, exhibition sites, and political economies are bound up in the effort to separate "us" from "them." Second, I propose strategies of reading that denaturalize the coded interpellations that I call immediations, revealing that what is constructed as self-evidently human is both cultivated and calculated. The "other" often suggests these strategies; frictions inevitably ensue when familiar forms find themselves in unfamiliar hands. What is more, evidence of these frictions can often be found hiding in plain sight. Amplifying them requires close, careful formal analysis, for which I draw on vocabulary from documentary studies as well as media and cultural studies more broadly. In sum, I aim to cultivate an attunement to the contradictions that emerge from the liberating encounter with difference before they are smoothed over by the ideological glue of humanism.

These twin critical tasks share a philosophical goal: to find ways of realizing the radical potential of giving the camera to the other, even if this means letting go of the human, or, at the very least, of what we think the human is. Throughout the book, I confront mediation as an ethically fraught but dialectically generative process at the heart of the humanitarian encounter. Although I begin with documentary, the scope of my pursuit spills over its canonical domain: some of my main interlocutors do not write about media but about child labor, human rights, autistic perception, and animal ethology. My engagement with them does not indicate my disinterest in the traditional pursuits of documentary studies so much as my investment in its interdisciplinary openings. This book is not addressed solely to documentary film scholars but rather speaks more broadly to those who are interested in the social issues to which participatory documentary seeks to give voice. It is my hope that this address will suggest the vitality of documentary for broader conversations in which the meanings and limitations of humanity are being debated, and vice versa.

Reading Emergency

One of this book's aims is to theorize how emergency is mediatized and to reinforce the notion that *reading* emergency against its humanitarian justifications is a political act. Calhoun defines *emergency* as a particularly modern imaginary engendered by the human suffering caused by the escalating incidence of catastrophe, war, conflict, and state violence. The temporality of emergency is that of a sudden, unpredictable event that emerges against a background of ostensible normalcy, demanding an urgent response. The claim of emergency, to cite Scarry, is that one must act *now*, for there is no time to think.[21] The implication is that lives hang in the balance: since the casualties of emergencies are often subjects who have been deprived of their civil rights and protections, emergency calls for a humanitarian, not political, response—a "sense of ethical obligation based on common humanity, rather than on citizenship or any other specific loyalty."[22]

Emergency has become a pervasive theme in the political and critical theory of the last several decades. In part, this is a response to current events such as the war on terror, disasters related to climate change, and the overall shift toward emergency rule, that is, nonconstitutional and nondemocratic modes of governance, across the globe over the last sixty years. However, as Bonnie Honig points out, the thematization of emergency may be a symptom of its thoroughly discursive character rather than a response to empirical events. The reality of emergency is more and more difficult to tell apart from its perception, Honig notes, thanks to "the media tendency to market everything as urgently exceptional and as, therefore, worth watching."[23] I argue that we need to read the medial frames of emergency in order to theorize how emergency is produced as a mediatized spectacle. Lisa Cartwright's work on the technical and political transformations that produced an emergency imaginary around the figure of the orphaned child in postdictatorship Romania is a model for my own analysis of the children of Calcutta sex workers in chapter 1.[24] I am also indebted to Lilie Chouliaraki and Mary Ann Doane, both of whom have theorized and critiqued the mediatization of emergency described by Honig in their studies of television news.[25] I aim to extend these scholars' approach in relation to the reality effects of participatory documentary.

I refer to participatory documentary as a "humanitarian media intervention" in order to highlight the role of documentary representations in the discursive construction of emergency. Participatory documentary often evokes the logic of emergency as a justification for its rhetoric of immediacy: media exposure is positioned as an urgent, humanizing remedy for subjects who have been deprived of various rights. To cite an example from my second chapter, "live and direct" eyewitness images of destitution are sought from poor African American victims of Hurricane Katrina who have lost everything but their lives. I argue that the humanitarian demand for referentiality and immediacy consolidates a particularly apolitical discourse of human rights that is grounded in abstract, essential characteristics of humanity (e.g., "life itself").[26] In such a context, participatory documentary exhorts destitute individuals to showcase the very bare humanity whose lack it purports to remedy as a mediatized spectacle—the ultimate drama of the real. When we decline to read images of immediacy as an extension of the discursive conditions under which they were produced, I argue, we participate in and exacerbate this spectacle.

The challenge of reading emergency may also be stated as a question: what does it mean to *read* a human rights speech act, that is, an urgent speech act produced under conditions of emergency? The discourse of human rights, which can be conservative in practice, is in principle potentially radical, and the difference between the two lies in approaching human rights speech acts not as self-evidences but as representational acts that require interpretation. Jacques Rancière and Thomas Keenan locate the radical potential of human rights discourse in its rhetorical structure, which operates through a counterintuitive claim: human rights speech acts insist that those who do not stand for humanity may speak for humanity.[27] These acts exemplify what Honig calls "the paradox of politics" in that they appeal to an imagined community of humanity that does not yet exist but that they hope to remake in their own excluded image.[28] The human in this discourse is invested with political and not merely ontological significance: it is an open space that remains to be defined—for better or worse—through an unending process of discursive struggle (this is why I do not argue in favor of a posthuman position: as a placeholder for a political subject yet to come, the human is just as adequate and flawed).

I focus on participatory documentary as an important site of this discursive struggle, in which the meaning of the human is constantly being redefined and radicalized through human rights claims. But, like Keenan, I am also convinced that we cannot take these communiqués for granted. The most radical speech acts are not immediately legible; they require their audience to take a leap of faith into the unknown. Part of the work of this book involves developing a critical and analytical vocabulary that makes these acts legible without rendering them fully transparent or immediate. How do human rights speech acts use the language of documentary immediacy to transform it? How do they remake the structure of the documentary devices and tropes that produce a recognition of the human and, in the process, change what counts as human?

Ethics after Humanism

The work of reading emergency that I have just described problematizes the Levinasian ethical framework that preoccupies contemporary debates regarding humanitarian response. The ethical turn spearheaded by Emmanuel Levinas displaces the ontological investment in being-for-itself by positing the superior moral priority of being-for-the-other. Levinas argues that the primary relationship that constitutes being is the relationship with the other, whose essential vulnerability, which he famously designates as the *face* of the other, suspends the natural right to self-survival, replacing it with the moral obligation to respond. In his words: "To expose myself to the vulnerability of the face is to put my ontological right to existence into question. In ethics, the other's right to exist has primacy over my own, a primacy epitomized in the ethical edict: you shall not kill, you shall not jeopardize the life of the other."[29]

The gist of this ethical principle, if not its source, is often evoked in support of humanitarian response. In an essay criticizing the complicity of humanitarian and military intervention, Didier Fassin reserves the following praise for its underlying ethic: "one has to be reminded that in the humanitarian ethics, the potential sacrifice of one's life reasserts the sacredness of others' lives, which is precisely denied by the military necessities."[30] The theological bent of Levinasian ethics is evident in Fassin's rendition of the vulnerable other, who represents killability as well as a divine prohibition against killing. Fassin's point is that even though humanitarianism can, in practice, perpetuate undemocratic modes of governance, its ethical mandate is humanizing and democratic: humanitarian agents reassert the worth of human lives that have been stripped of their political value in their willingness to sacrifice their own (politically significant) lives. What is more, Fassin regards the importance of "bearing witness," that is, representing the humanity of dehumanized lives, as being on par with physical acts of relief and rescue.[31]

In her book *Precarious Life,* Judith Butler considers the defacement of the face, understood in the Levinasian sense, as one of the most devastating representational and philosophical consequences of the permanent warfare inaugurated by the events of 9/11.[32] Butler clarifies the stakes of Levinas's work for media scholars in some important ways: she notes that the face, as Levinas defines it, is not literally a face or even exclusively human, even though it is a condition for humanization. Rather, the face is an abstract and wordless "cry" that confirms the inadequacy of representation for conveying the essence of the human, which can only be glimpsed at its limits.[33] For Butler, the framing of specific faces as human at the cost of others, who are depicted as inhuman and therefore killable, is an instance of war being carried out through representational means. She concludes her analysis by calling for reform of the normative schemes of intelligibility through which the human is understood. The task, as she puts it, is to "establish modes of public seeing and hearing that might well respond to the cry of the human within the sphere of appearance, a sphere in which the trace of the cry has become hyperbolically inflated to rationalize a gluttonous nationalism, or fully obliterated."[34]

On one hand, Butler sets forth an undeniably valuable critique of humanitarian ethics in the vein of Fassin. She identifies representation as the ground and battleground of ethics but also warns that the tactic of humanizing the other by "capturing" their humanity in some representable trait (e.g., the face, the eyes) is just as problematic as the dehumanization that warrants it: both locate the essence of the human in some foundational quality. Butler's critique of humanitarian ethics resonates with my own in that she situates its problems and prospects squarely in the domain of representation. On the other hand, this critique is an uneasy fit with Butler's own humanism of the other. Like Levinas, Butler operates within an ethical frame in which the other's relational modes and motivations can be understood only in terms of the rational, humanist goal of self-preservation. To put it another way, the cry of the other can only be heard by Butler in terms of suffering, and that suffering can only be interpreted as being inflicted from outside. Butler naturalizes self-preservation as the grounds for an ethical understanding of the human, and, in doing so, she engages in the very foundationalism that her work critiques.[35] This normative turn in Butler's thinking, which has caused much consternation among her critics, is less surprising when we consider her concern with self-preservation—or saving lives—as a symptom of emergency thinking. The consequence of such emergency thinking is that Butler cannot imagine relational modes that lie beyond the purview of self-preservation and that may appear on the surface to be irrational, illogical, or even self-destructive.

But what happens when the cry of the other challenges every basis of what it means to be human, to relate to others, and even what it means to be alive? How do expressions such as these reconfigure the humanitarian representational codes of documentary, and how are we to respond to them? These are the kinds of questions I pose by focusing on encounters with alterity that exceed or frustrate the Levinasian ethical paradigm. I am interested in subjects whose relational modes and motivations are at odds with their self-preservation as well as with the humanitarian ethic of participatory documentary—such as the working child, the hurricane victim turned volunteer, the autistic who rejects human faces, or the suicidal animal. This line of inquiry has already been advanced substantially by feminist and postcolonialist scholars (Gayatri Chakravorty Spivak's groundbreaking essay "Can the Subaltern Speak?" is one example) but has recently been taken up in new and exciting ways in areas such as childhood studies, disability studies, and animal studies. Scholars like Olga Nieuwenhuys, Erin Manning, Lisa Cartwright, and Laura U. Marks, who work at the intersection of these areas, issue important challenges regarding the nature of the interhuman bond that is taken as a given in discussions of humanitarian ethics and human rights media. These scholars are some of my closest allies: I value and emulate their commitment to examining the specificity of relational modes that place humanity, as we know and inhabit it, at risk.

This is a risky scholarly path, because it can appear at first to support ethically fraught practices such as child labor and animal abuse. I willingly take this chance with a larger goal in mind: evolving an approach to media practice and analysis that is perpetually oriented toward what resists definition as human. Ultimately, I argue, this is a more capacious and far-reaching approach to media ethics that opens up the horizons of humanity rather than presuming them in advance.

Mediation and Beyond

I enact my commitment to a nonhumanist ethic of mediation in the way I approach media analysis. I approach the author, spectator, and medium of documentary as dynamic contingencies that are coproduced in the event of mediation and that do not precede or follow from it in any predetermined manner. This open-ended approach to mediation as a multisited encounter is not typical among my fellow travelers who write about images of immediacy and the spectatorship of suffering. Although these scholars are ostensibly engaged with the same topic as this book, their analytical focus on the figure of the spectator leads them to pursue different lines of questioning.

As an outcome of the aforementioned ethical turn in discourses of humanitarianism, it is now widely acknowledged that human rights are articulated through acts of representation and spectatorship. There has been a corresponding surge of attention over the last decade to the spectatorship of distant suffering, instigated by and responding to Luc Boltanski's landmark book *Distant Suffering*. One of the important themes Boltanski introduces (although he treats it as salutary, not problematic) is the obliteration of distance by televisual images that invite compassion, a sentiment typically associated with proximity and immediacy, for the suffering of distant and unknown victims of war, disaster, and the like. The consequences of normative moral and emotional states, and the forms of action associated with these states, have subsequently become a prominent theme in analyses of the news media and photojournalism. Disappointingly, the bulk of this literature focuses on the decline of spectatorial response in the form of denial, moral atrophy, or "compassion fatigue."[36] Others, like Cartwright and Chouliaraki, have challenged this tendency, critiquing the consequences of the presentist politics of compassion cultivated by images of immediacy. I join these scholars in objecting to instrumental approaches to humanitarian mediation that view the documentary image as a means of engineering humanist sentiments.

What is needed, to quote Cartwright, is an analysis of "the nature of the real in all of its mediated forms including the visual, and with all of the troubling immediacy of impact that the visual brings."[37] Sharon Sliwinski, Leshu

Torchin, and Wendy S. Hesford have all recently responded to Cartwright's call in their respective monographs on the visual culture of human rights.[38] I share these critics' belief that images of suffering are crystallizations of, and a site of contention regarding, the historical and representational norms that shape the recognition of rights. I do, however, diverge from their concern with the public (or its representative figures, the witness and the spectator) as the primary target that is reshaped by such contentious images. Keenan theorizes human rights images as "operations in the public field," adding that the "public" should not be understood in the Enlightenment tradition as a preexisting community or people. For Keenan, the public is "something that comes after the image, a possibility of response to an open address. The public, we could say in shorthand, is what is hailed or addressed by messages that might not reach their destination. Thinking about the images at hand, we could even say that what defines the public is the possibility of being a target and of being missed."[39]

I propose that the hailing described by Keenan should be theorized in terms of not only the encounter between the spectator and image but also the encounter between the producer and the medium. If Keenan is interested in what comes after the image, I am interested in what comes *before* documentary. What "message" is sent to society's others when they are asked to document themselves and claim their human rights? To what extent is this message embedded in the conventional language, narrative norms, and itineraries of documentary media, or even, at a more fundamental level, in the bodily comportments that such conventions presume and invite? What happens when the message is missed, rejected, or misrecognized—can this lead to new engagements with the medium that transform the kinds of encounters it can facilitate?

I approach the discourses surrounding participatory documentary with these questions in mind. These have led me to often surprising and instructive answers. In chapter 2, I examine how a celebrated theoretical model of participatory media, Michael Hardt and Antonio Negri's account of communicative biopolitics, fails to examine the coded norms of documentary technologies that are deemed democratic, and therefore what comes before them. In chapter 1, I find an antidote to this tendency in an early and much-derogated anthropological experiment in giving the camera to the other. Despite (or perhaps because of) its acknowledged problems, Sol Worth and John Adair's Navajo Film Themselves Project offers valuable lessons regarding the aforementioned norms' potential to be misinterpreted or subjected to a foreign logic even before they materialize in an image. What is more, Worth and Adair are attentive to the acts of translation required to apprehend the socioeconomic valences of this logic, and to the new vistas of mediation that such attention can bring about.

The idea that documentary may be encountered as something other than a representational medium becomes a central theme in the second half of the book. In chapters 3 and 4, I introduce alternative concepts of medium and communication derived from autistic and nonhuman modes of being in the world, drawing on Erin Manning's and Mel Baggs's accounts of autistic perception and Roger Caillois's and Laura U. Marks's accounts of mimesis. These accounts suggest that mediation need not be understood strictly in terms of a representation designed for interpretation by a human subject, and that documentary therefore need not be apprehended as a force intervening between subject and object, or spectator and reality. In these chapters, I move beyond the representational mandates of voice and visibility that define the humanitarian impulse in documentary and explore nonverbalization and surrender as modes of mediation. These two chapters pose the question: can there be a noninterventionist mode of encountering the other?

A Note on Method and a Summary of the Chapters

The challenge of evolving a noninterventionist mode of encountering the other also confronts this book at the level of method. My suggestion in chapter 4 that surrender can be an alternative to intervention may be read by some as an acknowledgment of the impossibility of this challenge, and hence of the conceptual limits of my project. As one reader, responding to an early draft of this book, put it, "If taking a picture of a needy other is a form of domination, and giving a needy other a camera is a form of humanitarian resistance doomed to lead to cooptation, the only thing left is to refuse to treat the image as a viable tool or weapon of politics." It may seem paradoxical, therefore, that the theoretical interventions of the book emerge from close readings of images and other media texts, rather than from a counterhistory or genealogy of participatory documentary.

I do not see this as a paradox, but as a dialectic that propels and emerges from this book's methodology. To clarify, I do regard representing the humanity of suffering others and inviting them to do so themselves as two sides of a misguided problematic. The problems of these twin stances are revisited in each chapter, and in chapter 3 I dub them the "dominant" and "resistant" voices of documentary in order to signal their ubiquitous presence across the landscape of humanitarian media. I am, however, invested in the possibility of a third, *autistic* voice that exceeds the dualistic horizons of humanity defined by the other two and that persists in its alterity—a voice that may initially seem unintelligible. I glean the conditions of possibility and the itineraries of this voice through close, careful reading. My aim is not to enable this autistic voice to speak authentically, or to prescribe how and when such a voice might speak; the former would locate it outside discourse, while the latter would predetermine the time and place of politics. I aim instead to locate such a voice within existing immedial conditions that are already fraught, but that are nonetheless the precondition for an encounter with alterity that can shift our sense of the possibilities of images beyond the interventionist metaphors of "tool" and "weapon."

The movement from the first two voices to the third voice is also the logic governing the movement of the four chapters, from child media advocacy and live eyewitness reporting by disaster victims to autistic voicing and animal art. Each chapter iterates a classic scene of humanitarian mediation: the scene of taking the other out of the jungle and humanizing them by giving them a camera. The parts of "other," "jungle," and "camera" are played by different characters in chapters 1 through 4: child–brothels–innocence; refugee–disaster zone–liveness; autistic–"prison of silence"–voice; and animal–zoo–self. Over the course of the book, I slowly unravel this scene until we arrive at its inverse: the scene of dehumanizing the camera by surrendering it to a nonhuman logic. The opening two chapters deconstruct the logic of participatory documentary, while the final two chapters aim to construct an alternative to the humanitarian media intervention. In chapters 1 and 2 I read the "resistant" voices of documentary's others as symptoms that make visible the internal contradictions of the "dominant" humanitarian vision of their humanity, whereas in chapters 3 and 4 I focus on minoritarian existences that challenge the very notion of resistance or speaking out as a politically reflexive act. I employ a variety of approaches to reading that are sometimes referred to as "critique"—these include deconstruction, symptomatic reading, and discourse analysis—in an effort to work against the emphasis of immediations on surface reading, face value, and self-evidences. I do not dispense with these methods of reading in chapters 3 and 4, but these chapters raise questions about the limited meanings of mediation that are reinforced by their emphasis on disillusionment and defamiliarization as the bedrocks of reflexive critique. These final two chapters evolve new approaches to mediation by reading with the grain of dissenting, autistic voices that speak in what may seem to be an incomprehensible idiom. Only by engaging with the limits of political and formal reflexivity am I able to identify the liminality of these voices in relation to the medium, and the reasons the position to which they are addressed can be difficult to inhabit.

A final methodological note: the practices and texts to which this book is devoted are defined by their immediacy and crude realism. They are usually considered unworthy of critical attention, let alone sustained theorization. At best, they are scrutinized for their faithfulness to the reality they represent, and, at worst, they are treated as tools, significant only for the actions and responses they catalyze. The academic attention they are afforded is usually of the historical and technical variety reserved for what Nichols calls "the discourses of sobriety."[40] *Immediations* resists this self-fulfilling prophesy of documentary. The chapters emphasize rigorous analyses of emblematic cases leading to theoretical proposals, rather than broad overviews of scores of films culminating in a taxonomy of documentary genres and conventions, a tendency that dominates writings on documentary. This is a calculated choice: I insist that the tropes of documentary immediacy not only should be read closely but can be a portal to compelling speculations regarding the meaning of the human. My approach is not straightforwardly historical but works diagonally, across disciplines and media forms, to locate the theoretical antecedents—and futures—of current practices of participatory documentary. Thus, I prioritize oblique connections and polemical reframing over historical depth and fidelity to the letter of the extant critical literature. What this approach loses in precision, I hope it makes up for in vitality.

In chapter 1, "Feral Innocence: The Humanitarian Aesthetic of Dematerialized Child Labor," I connect contemporary child media advocacy with two of its precursors: cinematic representations of "wild children" and early experiments in shared ethnographic filmmaking. The chapter revolves around the film *Born into Brothels* (2004), which documents the efforts of photojournalist Zana Briski (also the film's codirector) to save the children of prostitutes in Calcutta, India, from a future in sex work by training them to produce and sell photographs of their lives in the brothels. I spend a lot of time analyzing the self-effacing visual devices of Briski's film and photographic pedagogy. I introduce the concepts of "pseudoparticipatory documentary" and

"feral innocence" to describe how the film enables its audiences to take pleasure in the savage eroticism of the children's photographs while still regarding them as spontaneous creative expressions of their inner innocence (or
"prisms into their souls," to cite a phrase commonly mentioned in praise of
these photographs). These two concepts serve as pivots in my analysis of the
humanitarian impulse to salvage childhood as a state prior to culture, mediation, and labor. I consider both the media-historical contexts and ideological
ramifications of this impulse, concluding that the practice of child media empowerment dematerializes the concrete role of child labor in the production
of humanitarian commodities.

The concept of dematerialized child labor offers one way of thinking about
how the labor of the dispossessed supplies an electric charge of urgency and
immediacy to humanitarian documentary images. Chapter 2, "Bare Liveness:
The Eyewitness to Catastrophe in the Age of Humanitarian Emergency," approaches the problem from another direction, focusing on the televisual
rhetoric of liveness and documentary representations of catastrophe. *Liveness*
refers to a set of rhetorical conventions designed to convey the technical capacity to transmit events in real time. I examine the humanitarian emergency
as a special genre of live media event in which liveness has added currency as
a testimonial code of unmediated exposure to death, or what Agamben calls
bare life.[41] I look closely at the tropes of liveness performed by professional
television reporters to establish their presence at disaster scenes and propose
that these tropes are both inspired by the bare lives of disaster victims and
subsequently imitated by these victims as a means of leveraging their eyewitness status. My case studies include a performance art project mounted by a
Haitian youth collective in the aftermath of the earthquake in 2010, Anderson
Cooper's coverage of Hurricane Katrina for CNN, and *Trouble the Water* (dir.
Carl Deal and Tia Lessin, 2008), a documentary acclaimed for its inclusion of
eyewitness footage shot by Katrina survivor Kimberly Roberts. Reading these
texts in conjunction, I ask what it means that the precarious circumstances
of disaster victims inform the documentary codes of the humanitarian emergency, and sustain its spectacle.

The guiding mission of participatory documentary is to "give a voice to the
voiceless." This adage, which invokes documentary's commitment to enabling
marginal social subjects to express themselves, also refers to its emphasis on
the spoken word—a quality that distinguishes documentary from fictional

genres. In chapter 3, "'Having a Voice': Toward an Autistic Counterdiscourse of Documentary," I examine how the challenges of autistic voicing complicate the documentary tropes of persuasive and legitimate speech and urge us to rethink the implicit logocentrism of the documentary politics of "having a voice." My inquiry centers on the trope of the first-person documentary voice-over. The authoritative immediacy of this trope, which lends alarm to the controversial advocacy videos of the humanitarian organization Autism Speaks, has also been appropriated in a number of recent films that depict autistic protagonists resisting humanitarian representation by "speaking for themselves." I isolate and analyze two of these films: Gerardine Wurzburg's CNN documentary, *Autism Is a World* (2004), and Mel Baggs's short video "In My Language" (2007). Whereas Wurzburg's conventional use of the first-person voice-over promises to liberate protagonist Sue Rubin's autistic interiority, Baggs's subversion of this convention shows how the documentary tropes of articulate speech pathologize autistic modes of communication. Her work evokes an autistic counterdiscourse of voicing that animates Foucault's ideas regarding a discourse of unreason on reason. I position the videos of Autism Speaks and the films of Wurzburg and Baggs as different approaches to the politics of documentary voicing (dominant, resistant, and autistic) that also map onto various representational tendencies in contemporary diagnostic debates around autism.

Baggs develops a yielding, tactile approach to the audiovisual medium that is informed by perceptual and environmental modes that are ordinarily regarded as nonrelational or even nonhuman—modes that I suggest are imperceptible to a humanitarian radar. I continue to investigate this theme through the rubric of "mimetic surrender" in chapter 4, "The Documentary Art of Surrender: Humane-itarian and Posthumanist Encounters with Animals." This chapter begins with a reading of a viral video of an elephant painting a self-portrait—an example of the increasingly popular humanitarian practice of rehabilitating endangered animals as artists. I argue that the anthropocentric discourse of exposing the selfhood of animals as evidence of their worth has an unexpected analogue in the posthumanist technique of "bringing to light" formerly imperceptible and invisible nonhuman modes of agency. Both approaches are challenged by the French social theorist Roger Caillois's writings, inspired by insect behavior, on mimesis as a radically passive comportment toward a media milieu. *Immediations* concludes with readings of experiments by a number of contemporary artists who surrender media such as video cameras and GPS devices within nonhuman milieus to invite animal collaborators to physically manipulate, inscribe, and repurpose them. In them, I find a suggestive and provocative model of how a mimetic ethic of surrender can transform our understanding of what can come before, and after, documentary.

Chapter 1

FERAL INNOCENCE

THE HUMANITARIAN AESTHETIC OF

DEMATERIALIZED CHILD LABOR

Taming the Wild Child

Few scenes capture the ascendency of the child as a humanitarian emblem, or the fantasies of domination and submission that animated this event, as dramatically as François Truffaut's rendition of the "rescue" of Victor of Aveyron in his film *The Wild Child* (*L'Enfant Sauvage*), released in 1970. Truffaut's film narrates the story of Western humanitarian intervention using a cast of characters from its prehistory—disabled, abandoned children and emissaries of the state medical apparatus—and the fables that orchestrated the encounter between them. The setting is Enlightenment-era France. The film, we are told, is based on a "true story" that "begins in a forest in France in 1798," where a mute, naked, androgynous, and seemingly feral young child (played by Jean-Pierre Cargol, a French Roma nonprofessional actor) is hunted down by a group of villagers with dogs and torches. The Wild Boy of Aveyron, as the child becomes known in the papers, is forcibly transported to Paris, amid a series of escape attempts and violent altercations with his captors, to be studied as a specimen of a "wild child."

The scene in question takes place at the National Institute for Deaf Mutes, where the boy is evaluated by the resident physician, Jean-Marc Gaspard Itard, played by Truffaut, and Philippe Pinel, a physician at the state asylum at Bicêtre and a significant figure in the history of modern psychiatric medicine. Pinel pronounces the boy an "inferior being, lower than an animal," no different from the "idiots in [his] charge at Bicêtre," citing that the boy appears indifferent to human voices and vocal sounds.[1] Itard, on the other hand, defends the humanity of the "wild boy." He argues that the boy's animallike sensory attunements (he responds to the sound of a nut being cracked behind him) may have developed in response to his abandonment and isolation, and could therefore offer insight into the condition of "an adolescent deprived since childhood of all education because he has lived apart from any individuals of his species." Itard offers to personally undertake the boy's education and care to prevent him from being consigned to Bicêtre in the manner of an animal.

Itard's invocation of "man in the state of nature" partakes of a frequent speculation among philosophers and scientists of the time, from Jean-Jacques Rousseau to Carl Linnaeus. Linnaeus itemizes ten instances of *Homo sapiens ferus*, or "feral man," in the thirteenth edition of *Systema naturae* published in 1788, the most extensive of which are documented cases of "wild children."[2] In this romantic mythography, cognitively and affectively impaired children such as Marie of Champagne, Peter of Hanover, and Victor of Aveyron (for whom the diagnosis of autism has been retrospectively proposed) were considered a species of wild children "raised by wolves," providing evidence of an anterior, innocent condition unsullied by human contact.[3] The next few scenes from Truffaut's film are remarkable as an illustration of how the figure of the child served as a screen for the interlocking scientific and moral sentiments that ignited the therapeutic interventions of the nascent humanitarian state. The wild child is taken to Itard's country estate, where he is inserted into a nuclear family structure, with Itard in the role of the authoritarian father and Itard's housekeeper, Madame Guérin, as an indulgent, kindhearted mother figure.[4] Here, Itard and Madame Guérin undertake a daily regimen of activities designed to civilize the wild boy. They bathe and clean him, straighten his posture and gait, accustom him to gender-appropriate clothing and shoes, teach him table manners, wear down his resistance to living indoors, develop drills to train his memory, and teach him how to read and speak—the biggest challenge of all, to which over thirty minutes of screen time are devoted. Itard trains the boy to respond to his directives using a system of incitements and punishments revolving around the boy's favorite treats, milk and water, so that they gradually become synonymous with Itard's affection for the boy, eliciting tears from the boy when either is withheld.

The brilliance of Truffaut's film lies in its way of amplifying the brutality of these perfectly ordinary scenes of childhood and family life. Itard's efforts to socialize and educate Victor have limited success. The language exercises that he forces Victor to relentlessly practice culminate in fits of frustration, startling acts of violence, and at least one attempted escape on Victor's part. Although the film does not cover this full period, we know from Itard's communiqués with the government that he would relinquish his experiment after five short years, admitting to the boy's "incurable dumbness"—Victor would die at the age of forty, while still in Madame Guérin's care.[5] Truffaut's nostalgic visual aesthetic clings to Itard's romantic vision of the child even as it unravels. The black-and-white photography, reminiscent of early cinema, is punctuated by soft irises, accompanied by harpsichord music, that come to a close on Victor's cherubic face, his eyes gazing out a window toward the distant forests in an expression of longing. But this sentimental portrait of innocence is difficult to reconcile with Victor's violent and unpredictable behavior—the romantic fantasy of the so-called state of nature is shattered in one of the earliest scenes of the film, which features Victor in his forest milieu ruthlessly breaking a hunting dog's jaw.

Itard nevertheless clings grimly to his convictions, determined to redeem Victor's lost idyll using the same technological forces that he blames for the wild child's "fall" into civilization. If Itard falters in his resolve, he never shows it, reserving his doubts for rueful entries in his medical diary that confess the futility of his endeavor—a perpetual internal dialogue that becomes the voice of the film's guilty conscience: "I condemned the sterile curiosity of the men who had wrenched him away from his innocent and happy life." The film concludes on an ambivalent note: Victor has returned home after a pathetic attempt at escape, realizing that he no longer possesses the physical endurance to survive in the wild. It is difficult to resist Madame Guérin's infectious maternal joy, or Itard's renewed resolve to resume Victor's lessons the next day. As Victor ascends the stairs to his bedroom one final time, his enigmatic look backward at Itard—and by extension, at us—catches the spectator red-handed in identifying with Itard's humanitarian mission.

I begin with this reading of The Wild Child because this film stages and confronts the central problematic of this chapter: the enduring humanitarian myth of childhood innocence. Truffaut shows that the fabled innocence of children—an essential, untouched kernel of "humanity" that is located in the shadowy borders between the animal and the human—is a fantasy whose dissolution imperils the very humanitarian morality that claims to protect it from peril. The interactions between Itard and Victor show how the sadomasochistic rituals of becoming a humanitarian subject play out in relation

FIGURE 1.1. Still from *The Wild Child* by François Truffaut (1970)

to this fantasy, in a spiral of incitement and punishment, sacrifice and reward. As a central myth of the humanitarian imagination, childhood innocence also inspires the aesthetic forms of participatory documentary. This
chapter historicizes the emergence of the child as a target of humanitarian
intervention and analyzes the ambivalent role of participatory documentary
in the drama of taming the wild child, as a technological supplement that
sullies and simultaneously redeems the child's innocent humanity. I examine
contemporary global humanitarian interventions that employ documentary
media as a means of empowering "at-risk" children, often in tandem with
neoliberal narratives of autonomy that reference the logic of human rights.
My principle object of analysis is the award-winning film *Born into Brothels*
(dir. Zana Briski and Ross Kauffman, 2004). This film documents an advocacy project carried out by codirector and photojournalist Zana Briski that
begins as photography lessons among the children of prostitutes in Calcutta,
India. Briski's lessons pave the way for a rescue mission: the sale of the children's photographs becomes instrumental in her plan to liberate the children
from the brothels and install them on a path to legality, higher education, and
social repute.

I contend that the documentary rhetoric of *Born into Brothels* is "pseudoparticipatory": Briski enlists the children as collaborators only to shore up her
own humanitarian vision of the brothels. I analyze the film's pseudoparticipatory rhetoric alongside the aesthetic strategies and itineraries of the children's
photographs, which continue to be sold under the auspices of Briski's non-

profit organization, Kids with Cameras. My goal is to understand what types of humanitarian documentary forms, ideological frameworks, and cultural institutions are sustained by the children's artistic production. I propose that the colonial, paternal dynamics between the characters of Itard and Victor (mirrored in Truffaut and his young Roma costar) are reborn in the neoliberal dynamic of the humanitarian West "empowering" the non-West to assume an agential role in its self-governance. Where Briski claims to have empowered the students, I show that their freedom is restricted to a choice between two closely related but seemingly distinct modes of governance, the humanitarian and the penal intervention, which, respectively, position the children as subjects who are at risk or as subjects who pose a risk.

My readings of Briski's participatory mode of narration and the children's photographs suggest that art and reform represent the two opposing poles of the humanitarian imaginary of the child. Documentary plays a special role in navigating the aesthetic, ideological, and economic space between art and reform. The contradictory impulses of celebrating children as a source of untamed creative inspiration while taming their savagery are reconciled in the photographic aesthetic of "feral innocence" that Briski cultivates among her young students. I develop the concept of feral innocence by bringing together two scholarly perspectives that are seldom discussed in tandem: critical childhood studies and theories of photography. Feral innocence is a potent example of a documentary strategy of "immediation": its quality of contained immediacy or spontaneity relies on our acceptance of the children's photographs as untutored and spontaneous rather than expressions of a thoroughly cultivated aesthetic. Briski's strategic use of this trope affirms the humanitarian fantasy of the child as a figure that exists outside mediation and political economy—a fantasy that explicitly excludes non-Western working children—even as she actively enlists the labor of Third World children in producing humanitarian media commodities.

The final two sections of this chapter focus on the economic, ideological, and technological shifts that represent the conditions of possibility for Briski's mode of humanitarian media intervention. *Born into Brothels* provides an occasion for reevaluating contemporary debates regarding child labor, and the relatively recent status of the child as a rights-bearing entity. Briski's intention to safeguard the children of prostitutes from an imminent future as sex workers by occupying them in playful creative work finds legitimation, I argue, in twentieth-century statutes that advocate the elimination of "harmful" forms of child labor in lieu of "benign" child work. This self-evidently progressive hierarchy of priorities—which implicitly guides much of the contemporary activism around children's rights, such as campaigns against the recruitment of child soldiers—is widely accepted as axiomatic. However, the humanitarian support for benign forms of child work takes on a less desirable cast when it is historicized as part of what Maurizio Lazzarato and other Marxist cultural critics have described as the neoliberal hegemony of affective, virtuosic, and creative modalities of labor that are not recognized or compensated as such. Whereas Briski's humanitarian media intervention purports to protect her students from exploitation, I use Lazzarato's work to show how it actively enlists them in an insidious form of child labor that is recast as self-actualization.

Briski's pseudoparticipatory mode of narration and the photographic aesthetic of feral innocence exemplify how the tropes of documentary immediacy cover over, obfuscate, or otherwise dematerialize the aesthetic and ideological labor of participatory media production. In an effort to resuscitate these material realities, I conclude with a reading of an experiment in participatory documentary conducted in 1966 that represents an early precursor of contemporary media empowerment initiatives. Sol Worth and John Adair's "bio-documentary" project, chronicled in their book *Through Navajo Eyes*, trained Navajo subjects who had never before encountered film to produce their own 16 mm films. Despite its influential role in shaping subsequent engagements of visual media in anthropology, this project has been summarily dismissed for its positivist investments in cultural difference as the determining factor in film form. I make a case for reconsidering this project, whose modernist, dialectical investment in "film children" (as Worth and Adair refer to the Navajo) defamiliarizes and complicates the instrumental view of the documentary image that became popular among proponents of participatory media with the emergence of video as an activist medium.[6] In addition to modeling a dialectical engagement with documentary images of immediacy, Worth and Adair's project also offers valuable insights into the ways in which the figure of the child has structured the technological imagination of the West. The limits of defamiliarization as a mode of formal reflexivity, as practiced by Worth and Adair, is a topic to which I return in chapter 4, with a less reassuring prognosis, but for the purposes of this chapter I focus on its enabling possibilities.

With these historical perspectives in mind, I propose that we can read the images in *Born into Brothels* not as fetishized fictions that deify the child outside of productive economies but as documents that evince a far more complex and compelling portrait of the humanity of children—one in which childhood uniquely encapsulates the condition of the neoliberal laboring subject.

Pseudoparticipatory Documentary

It's almost impossible to photograph in the Red Light district. Everyone is terrified of the camera. They're frightened of being found out. Everything's illegal. . . .
I knew I couldn't do it as a visitor—I wanted to stay with them, and understand their lives. And of course, as soon as I entered the brothels, I met the children. The brothels are filled with children, they're everywhere. And they were so curious; they didn't understand why this woman had come and what I was doing there. They were all over me, and I would play with them, and take their photographs, and they would take mine. They wanted to learn how to use the camera. That's when I thought it would be really great to teach them, and to see this world through their eyes.
—Excerpt from *Born into Brothels*

These words, voiced by Briski over photographs and video footage of the brothels, function both as the film's introduction and as its "mission statement." They explain Briski's fascination with, and presence in, the brothels of Sonagachi, and frame our spectatorial expectations of her role as facilitator, rather than observer or orchestrator, of the perspectives and desires of the eight children profiled in *Born into Brothels*. Briski justifies her missionary intervention into Calcutta's red light district as a selfless humanitarian act demanded by her future students. The rhetoric of participatory documentary plays a subtle but critical role in this transaction: it offers a visual idiom that seems to emanate directly from the "eyes" of the children, effacing Briski's mediation and her role in the education of their vision. Furthermore, it supplies a thrusting, driving temporality that naturalizes the film's race to save the children from their inevitable future in prostitution. Together with the photographic aesthetic of feral innocence (discussed in the following section), the visual codes and narrative logic of what I call the pseudoparticipatory documentary demonstrate the vexed role of immediations in the governance of humanitarian subjects.

As Briski openly confesses, the level of intimacy afforded by her position as the children's photography teacher was not readily available to her as a Cambridge-educated professional photojournalist who had already spent several years living among and photographing sex workers in the brothels of Rambagan and Sonagachi (by the time Briski began filming *Born into Brothels*, these photographs had already won her several international awards and fellowships).[7] Briski's monologue frames her transition into the role of photography teacher as a means of aesthetic inspiration—a way of seeing anew, prompted by her perceptive young students. However, the visual sequence that accompanies Briski's narration suggests that a more complicated transaction is under way. Bearing a bag full of consumer point-and-shoot cameras, contact sheets, and magnifying lenses, Briski is led by several children to a locked room, where one of the children unlocks the door to admit her. This interaction poetically captures the trade-off embedded in Briski's altruistic claim of setting aside her own artistic aspirations to foster those of her students—a claim that has been championed in reviews of the film and has become part of its mythology.[8] In exchange for lessons in photography, Briski's students afford her literal and representational access to a space that is, by her own admission, indecipherable and impenetrable to a visitor.

The result of this transaction is not quite a film that acknowledges "a sense of partialness, of *situated* presence and *local* knowledge that derives from the actual encounter of filmmaker and other," to quote from Bill Nichols's description of the participatory or interactive documentary mode.[9] The mark of a genuinely participatory documentary practice, as Nichols sees it at work in the widely ranging idioms of filmmakers such as Jean Rouch, Trinh T. Minh-ha, Errol Morris, and Ross McElwee, lies in how it brings in the conflicting voices of other social actors, thereby raising questions regarding the ethics of what is implicitly or explicitly argued by the filmmaker. In the 1980s and 1990s, these filmmakers explicitly challenged the totalizing character of expository or observational conventions by calling into question their spoken and unspoken tropes of objectivity (e.g., "voice-of-God" narration, the long take, the wide-angle shot). Their films experimented with dialogic and reflexive modes of exchange that would "unmask" the work of production (e.g., the conversation, a highly subjective voice-over, dialogue, and interview)—they aimed to implicate the viewer in the ethics and politics of the documentary encounter by turning the framing of the spoken word and the image into sites of dissent and debate.[10]

Born into Brothels illustrates a consensus-driven counterpart of this approach: the pseudoparticipatory documentary in the humanitarian mode. Briski develops a moral consensus regarding the children's status as innocent victims requiring urgent intervention through a formal approach that, rather than calling attention to the friction between her perspective and those of her subjects, tends to blur it. She does so through a mode of narration that attributes her own humanitarian views to the children, so that the appeal for rescue appears to emanate directly from the children's eyes and lips. The result is a documentary idiom that is thoroughly abstracted from the concrete, local realities of the children's lives, so that the figure of the innocent, vulnerable child emerges as a universal ethical ground that "dissolve[s] contradiction and dissent into pools of basic and also higher truth," to borrow a phrase from Lauren Berlant.[11] As I will show in the next section, the encapsulation of this abstract and universal humanity in the children's photographs is directly connected to the images' global mobility as international humanitarian art commodities. The pseudoparticipatory documentary thus plays a critical role in forging new aesthetic and economic routes between the crisis zone and the art gallery.

For now, I focus on articulating how the pseudoparticipatory devices of narration, cinematography, and editing operate at a technical level to achieve a slippage between Briski's views and those of the children. Although Briski's commentary is interspersed throughout the film in the form of voice-over, dialogue, and her own images of Sonagachi, the children are positioned as its frame narrators, that is, as the subjectivity that structures the film. The first spoken words in the film are uttered by ten-year-old Kochi, who observes that the men who frequent the tenement house where she lives, shouting and swearing, are "bad men," and speculates that it won't be long before she too is made to "join the line." Cast in the light of Kochi's despondent testimony, the immediately preceding opening montage of the film is retrospectively confirmed as a child's hunted impression of the immoral and threatening space of the red light district, rather than the perspective of Briski and Kauffman, who share credit as codirectors and cocinematographers of the film.[12]

The audiovisual design of the two-minute-long opening montage is stylized to convey a vision of the brothels as a dangerous, illicit space in which susceptible children are embroiled against their will. The lighting is predominantly red, and the footage slows down and speeds up in alternation. The unpredictable, jagged texture of the sequence, which is filmed with a handheld

camera, coupled with unusual perspectives from the tops of tenement build-
ings and from low angles through the legs of passing pedestrians, invokes the
chaotic point of view of a running child. The music, an ominous, plaintive
raga in a minor key, sets a somber tone as the camera captures various iconic,
intimate scenes of brothel street life—young girls in thin, shiny clothing and
bright lipstick waiting for customers at street corners, men approaching them
in groups and alone, women emerging half-clothed from barely shielded
doorways, liquor being poured into cheap glass tumblers, cigarettes being
smoked, drugs and money changing hands—and children of all ages running amuck in the midst of it all. Nothing stays on-screen for very long. The
camera, snaking from place to place, down narrow alleyways, up and down
staircases, and around corners, creates the impression of a child's elusive but
discerning point of view.

Any confusion regarding this fact is clarified by the editing of this sequence, which fades back and forth between these scenes of the brothels and
the faces of children framed in extreme close-up, their eyes soulfully lit in
chiaroscuro style. We later identify these faces as those of Puja, Shanti, Suchitra, Tapasi, Avijit, Gour, Kochi, and Manik, the eight children profiled in the
film. The music and the editing pick up in energy and pace as the sequence
builds to an urgent crescendo that dissolves kaleidoscopically into the film's
title, nestled amid an animated spread of photographic negatives. It is not
necessary to recognize these images as the photographs taken by the children to be persuaded that the disturbing, intimate perspective of brothel life
depicted in the sequence is that of the children, or to perceive their presence
there as a crisis in need of immediate resolution.

The realist techniques employed by Briski for attributing her own perspective to the children resemble those employed by recent fiction films that
have cast impoverished children as actors, such as *Salaam Bombay* (dir. Mira
Nair, 1988), *City of God* (dir. Fernando Meirelles, 2002), and *Slumdog Millionaire* (dir. Danny Boyle and Loveleen Tandon, 2008). Poonam Arora has
argued that Nair relies on the ethnographic authority of "real" street children
to authenticate her film as a form of indigenous ethnography by a diasporic
Indian studying her own culture. In practice, Arora demurs, Nair's stereo-
typical characters and generic plot repeatedly disengage from the complexities and specificity of the sociopolitical and economic conditions that she
claims to document, with the result that the film functions as a form of virtual
tourism that produces reified Third World subjectivities for effortless con-

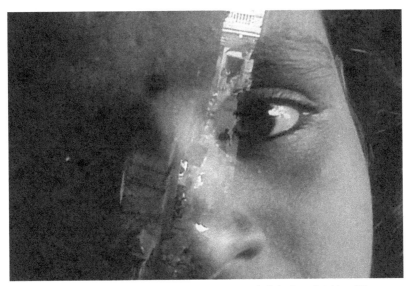

FIGURE 1.2 Still from opening sequence of *Born into Brothels* by Zana Briski and Ross Kauffman (2004)

sumption by the West.[13] Daniel O. Mosquera argues that contemporary Latin American films that feature documentary self-representations by street children rely on similar strategies. He argues that the "instantaneous, if often ahistorical, intimate language" of these documentary images of precarious lives cuts through the conventional forms that make these films palatable for Euro-American audiences (such as the "transformation" narrative of social uplift, which borrows heavily from reality television conventions).[14]

Born into Brothels partakes of both these strategies, but Briski's main contribution to the pseudoparticipatory lexicon is the technique of deliberate formal slippage. The childlike visual language of Briski's cinematography replicates the color palette, amateur quality, and point of view of the children's photographs, while her editorial decisions attribute her own footage to the children through perspectival and stylistic matches. Throughout the first half of the film, the framing and curation of the children's individual photo portfolios appear to be motivated by their own narration: Briski introduces the eight protagonists of the film by layering handheld video footage of each of them in the style of the opening montage with audio commentary by eleven-year-old Puja, who provides charming observations about her friends ("Avijit gets angry if you call him fat"; "Gour picks his teeth all the time"). These

FIGURE 1.3 Still from *Born into Brothels* by Zana Briski and Ross Kauffman (2004)

small details overwhelm Briski's footage in the manner of a *punctum*, or what Roland Barthes calls an "off-center detail" with "no preference for morality or good taste," capable of undermining the conventional cultural and stylistic codes of photography.[15] Puja's idiosyncratic and childlike interjections similarly divest Briski's footage of its moral compunctions and invest it with a sense of immediacy and serendipity.

Briski often employs a graphic match, or restages the mise-en-scène of the children's photographs as a way of blending her footage seamlessly with the content and framing of the photographs, such that both appear as spontaneous snapshots snatched from the stream of the children's daily experience. In one such instance, Briski re-creates the setting of a photograph taken by her student Avijit by capturing another student, Manik, in the midst of the same activity: flying a kite from the roof of a tenement house. The camera alternates between shots of Manik and his sister, Shanti, and finally cuts to a long shot of the blue kite in the distance. The image freezes to a still of this kite and fades into an image of a red kite in a similar framing, finally zooming out to reveal a still photograph of a shirtless boy on the same rooftop, flying a red kite. This still image introduces the segment that follows: "Photos by Manik."

Formal slippages of this kind cover over the more complex ideological substitutions in which Briski's perception of the children's victimhood is pre-

sented as a plea for help mouthed directly by them. Interviews with Briski's female students are key moments where this substitution takes place: fourteen-
year-old Suchitra, who is motherless, testifies that she sees "no alternative" to
her aunt's plans to send her to "work in the line" in Bombay, and the interviews with Kochi and eleven-year-old Tapasi are interspersed with sequences
in which the girls are shown squatting on the filthy floor of a communal bathroom, scrubbing dishes, and filling buckets with water for other tenants in
their building. As Tapasi begins hauling the buckets up several flights of stairs,
a woman, presumably another sex worker who is also her employer, heaps
verbal abuse on her: "You selfish fucking bitch, you can't even fetch water
properly!" Similar scenes play out later in the film, cementing Briski's portrayal of the children as victims: Tapasi's mother casually calls her "a little
bitch" and threatens to throw her out. Manik is caught in the crossfire of an
argument among several sex workers, possibly including his mother, one of
whom beats and curses him.

Wendy S. Hesford has argued that such scenes, which represent the children as victims of pathological mothers who are as morally bankrupt and
self-centered as "Zana Auntie" is selfless and empathetic, "reinforce the perception of the need for external intervention on behalf of the children."[16]
Briski makes no attempt to represent the perspective of the mothers, or the
structural challenges they face. The film does little to analyze the role of sex
work in supporting the children, or that of the children's labor in supporting
their families and providing a source of self-esteem — that both are sites of
extensive local activism never merits a mention. Such inattention to the complex interplay of discourses around sex work among local activist agents reinscribes the space of the brothels as a humanitarian crisis zone, with Briski
and the children cast in the ritualized roles of the paternalistic white savior
and infantilized brown victim with no intermediaries separating them.[17]

Briski's abstraction of the children from their familial, communal, and
national struggles "airlifts" them out of their local cultural context and turns
them into emblems of universal humanity. This tactic makes the children
available for a form of identification that Erica Burman has called "projective identification," a dynamic in which the notion that "'they are' (or should
be) 'like us'— [can] function to deny difference."[18] It also legitimizes Briski's
transformation from facilitator-teacher to protagonist-reformer at the half-
way point of the film. Briski muses, "These are my students. They have abso-
lutely no opportunity without education. . . . I'm not a social worker. I'm not

a teacher even . . . but without help, they're doomed." Briski's proclamation, notable for her use of the possessive form ("*my* students"), signals an uptick in her narrative agency in the second half of the film as she embarks on a project of "civilizing" the brothel children. She announces, "My goal now is to teach them but also to raise money for them using their own photography, selling their photographs to raise money for them. Amnesty International is going to use the kids' photos for their calendar, and the photos are being auctioned at Sotheby's. The whole point of this is to get the kids out of the brothels."

As Briski's photography lessons morph into a vehicle for extracting the children from the brothels, the film racks focus from the children to Briski's own psychic journey as she struggles to secure a morally and economically stable future for the children. She painstakingly navigates a series of bureaucratic hurdles associated with admitting the children to private boarding schools and shelters—such as applying for ration cards, conducting blood tests for HIV, and gathering medical certificates, school transcripts, and passport photographs—while raising money for their education. Briski's frustration and determination in overcoming these hurdles become a major point of identification in the film, seamlessly taking the place of her original mission of "seeing through the children's eyes"—the hardships borne by their families and the resistance of several of the children to her plan are represented less as dissonances than as obstacles to be overcome.

Kimberly Juanita Brown has described this process of affective transference, whereby liberal empathy is redirected from the predicament of humanitarian subjects to the pain of Western photojournalists, as a "fallacy of liberal intention."[19] Brown points to the example of Kevin Carter's award-winning photograph, taken in 1993, of a vulture watching a starving Sudanese girl-child: after Carter's suicide in 1994, his iconic image of the suffering caused by famine and civil war in Sudan posthumously became a signifier of the psychic trauma of photojournalists working in war zones. A more recent example of affective transference can be found in the humanitarian documentary *Invisible Children* (dir. Jason Russell, Bobby Bailey, and Laren Poole, 2006), which narrates the predicament of child soldiers in Uganda through the moving travails of their North American youth advocates. Brown's analysis aptly identifies the work of the subaltern image in the pseudoparticipatory documentary: it is a symbol, as she notes, with only the Western photojournalist as a referent.

The dual mechanisms of projective identification and affective transference allow us to understand how education becomes the gentler, humanitarian face of penal reform in Briski's film. Just as rescuing Victor from the insane asylum becomes Itard's primary preoccupation in Truffaut's film, the task of rescuing the children from the brothels becomes Briski's primary and incontrovertible ethical obligation. All other considerations—including the politics of the institutions in which she seeks admission for the children—become secondary. As Hesford notes, this explains the film's careless portrayal of Sanlaap—a nongovernmental organization devoted to the rehabilitation of sex workers and their female children to prevent second-generation prostitution—as an educational institution.[20]

The apotheosis of Briski's reform project can be seen in the construction plans for "Hope House," a planned residential school and safe house for the female children of sex workers from Calcutta's red light district that is funded in part by proceeds from sales of the children's photographs. The flagship project of Kids with Cameras and Kids with Destiny, the two nonprofit organizations that have evolved from the film *Born into Brothels*, Hope House is located one hour away from downtown Calcutta, "close enough that parents can still play an active role in their daughter's life, but safely distanced from the risks of their home neighborhood."[21] If municipal schools are examples of what Louis Althusser calls ideological state apparatuses, we might describe Hope House as an ideological *humanitarian* apparatus that seeks to reproduce the children of sex workers in its own antiseptic image.[22] Photographs of the construction site reveal a clean, modern structure with brightly lit classrooms built around an open courtyard. The architectural renderings of the finished structure depict a panoptic space of clarity and visibility where young girls participate in wholesome age-appropriate activities under the watchful eyes of an authority figure—in every way the inverse of the space of the brothels that Briski found so difficult to access.[23]

I now turn to an analysis of the children's photographs to understand how the discourse of art education becomes a conduit for humanitarian reform, repositioning the children as subjects whose humanity is at risk rather than subjects who pose a risk *to* (humanitarian visions of their) humanity. The photographic aesthetic of feral innocence that the children are taught to adopt exemplifies how documentary immediations are involved in universalizing—and sterilizing—the discourse of childhood innocence.

Feral Innocence: Child Photography between Crisis Zone and Gallery

In his landmark history of childhood, Philippe Ariès argues that the concept of childhood as a discrete, fragile stage of life in need of protection and safeguarding is uniquely modern. Far from being universal or transhistorical, Ariès argues that the discourse of childhood innocence derives from a specifically Christian, western European strain of moral pedagogy that evolved in concert with emerging biopolitical institutions such as the family, the social classes, medicine, and higher education. Before this biopolitical turn, which Ariès dates to approximately the seventeenth century, children were regarded with indifference. Childhood was a period of exceptional brevity whose transition to adulthood was not demarcated with any clarity (in the medieval era, it was as common for children as young as fourteen and eleven to be married or join the army as it was for the elderly to attend school). The modern concepts of education and the family as spaces of apprenticeship and protection, Ariès proposes, were coextensive with the emergence of age, class, and individuality as demographic sites of regulation.[24]

Other historians of childhood add that in the premodern Christian theological tradition, children were seen as savages, or "inheritors of original sin," who could be redeemed only through a rigorous program of discipline, labor, and punishment.[25] British novelist and mythographer Marina Warner argues that the association of the child with moral disarray and polymorphous perversity—that is, with an alien order set apart from the prescriptions and proscriptions of culture—haunts the romantic myth of originary innocence that replaced the mythology of originary sin in the Enlightenment era, enduring well into the present. She writes, "The child holds up an image of origin, but origins are compounded of good and evil together, battling it out."[26] "We call children 'little devils,' 'little monsters,' 'little beasts'—with the full ambiguous force of the terms, all the complications of love and longing, repulsion and fear."[27]

This tension is seldom apparent in the visual culture of contemporary humanitarianism. On the contrary, Liisa Malkki argues that childlike innocence serves as a way of forgetting this history—"a way of making recipients of humanitarian assistance a tabula rasa, innocent of politics and history."[28] The idiomatic distillation of non-Western suffering in the figure of the individual starving child evokes "a common humanity, able to appeal—across the boundaries of race, culture, and nation—to an underlying, essential humanity many of us (at certain times) believe we all share. [Children] are the 'principle of hope' set apart from the complications of history."[29] Malkki ventures that this is why children are often featured in contemporary humanitarian representations as the essence of an ideal, unsullied humanity: as ambassadors of peace, blameless sufferers, seers of truth, or beacons of futurity and hope. She argues that the humanitarian iconography of childhood suppresses non-Western and historical experiences of childhood that depart from this narrative and that are therefore incongruous with the generalized expectation of children's innocence: for instance, the realities of child soldiers in Africa—or child laborers in India, apropos of this chapter—are both depoliticized and pathologized when they are domesticated in the form of childhood innocence. While reflecting on the broader ramifications of her analysis, Malkki calls for further critical study of "how that domestication occurs, and with what consequences."[30]

The photographs taken by Briski's students offer exemplary insight into the dynamics of the humanitarian domestication of childhood in an era shaped by new forms of media access and global circulatory flows. These dynamics come to light in a striking way when we consider the "controversial" photographs that are relegated to the diegetic margins of *Born into Brothels* alongside those photographs that are singled out for attention in the film and that have subsequently achieved an iconic status in and beyond the film's diegesis. Whereas the former threaten to unsettle the humanitarian discourse of childhood innocence in their stark acknowledgment of the children's exposure to squalor, sex, and labor, the photographs celebrated by Briski exoticize and romanticize the realities of brothel life by turning them into a fetish. I use the term *feral innocence* to describe the aesthetic appeal of these photographs. Feral innocence disavows the romantic heritage of Briski's photographic pedagogy by drawing on two mutually affirming myths: the myth of the child's untutored genius and the myth of photographic spontaneity.

Several of the photographs taken by Briski's students indicate a complex, troubling subjectivity at odds with the film's characterization of the children's guileless innocence. One such photograph is Manik's *Puja*. Eleven-year-old Puja, another of Briski's students, leans against a parked car. The expression on her face, turned to the right, is inscrutable. Her arms are splayed open in sensuous abandon against the car's darkened windows, and her hair is shaken loose from its hairband, which hangs loose around her neck, suggesting an eroticism that is difficult to reconcile with her white dress and the sweater

FIGURE 1.4 *Puja* by Manik; still from *Born into Brothels* by Zana Briski and Ross Kauffman (2004)

knotted around her waist, which visibly announce her youth. With its black-and-white palette, this image is easily confused with one of Briski's still photographs, which are distinguished from the children's bright color photos by their somber monotone and sexual content, often capturing men and women in the act of embracing. In the symbolic equivalent of averting its gaze, the film allows this confusion to linger: this image is left out of the slide show of Manik's images and appears out of place elsewhere in the film, although it is attributed to Manik on the Kids with Cameras website.

Tapasi's *Dressing*, an image of a woman, presumably her mother, in the act of pulling on her underclothes, also mutely acknowledges the children's quotidian exposure to adult sexual acts, often conducted mere feet away from them in single-room homes. The image recalls a snippet from an interview with Shanti, in which she reveals, "In our room there is a rod, and from there we close the curtain, that way we don't see anything that's going on." The shock value of Tapasi's image, however, owes less to the intimacy of the woman's act than to the realization that the filthy pillow, stained wall, and paltry mattress in the immediate background are the same as those we see in two other photographs by Tapasi that separately depict her younger sister and baby brother—who is naked from the waist down, save for his purple

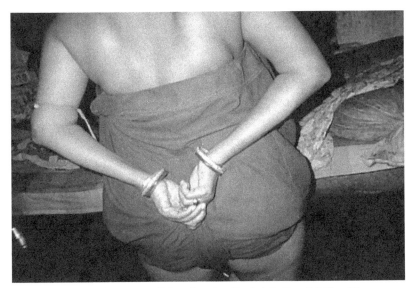

FIGURE 1.5 *Dressing* by Tapasi; still from *Born into Brothels* by Zana Briski and Ross Kauffman (2004)

socks, and with his arms above his head, in a pose of utter vulnerability—asleep in the same bed. In other photographs too, the irreconcilable meanings conveyed by the mise-en-scène of their homes as places of habitation, play, worship, and sex work become a rich metaphor for the many conflicting roles and desires of the children. For example, the backdrop to Manik's *Self Portrait* reveals a television set, a wall clock, garlanded images of deities, mattresses, and a woman's discarded clothing, all crammed into a few square feet of living space. The empathy invited by such images is also complex—it makes it possible to appreciate why, for instance, Tapasi maintains that she loves her mother despite Briski's efforts to paint her as abusive.

These images allow us to glimpse what art historian Anne Higonnet refers to as the "Knowing Child," or so-called abnormal children whose taboo awareness of penury, violence, and passion threatens to unravel the romantic myth of childhood plenitude and innocence.[31] Their pensive quality sets them apart from the overwhelming exuberance and playfulness characteristic of the majority of the children's photographs showcased in *Born into Brothels*. Many of the photographs selected for inclusion in the film, as well as for sale on the Kids with Cameras website, "arrest" their young subjects in the midst of various affective gestures or iconic childhood activities. Climbing,

FIGURE 1.6 *Hand* by Manik; still from *Born into Brothels* by Zana Briski and Ross Kauffman (2004)

laughing, playing, and jumping are frequent subjects. Other images, which capture horses and sheep, and policemen and mendicants in mid-movement in streets and alleyways, invoke the disarming speed and alacrity of the young photographers. A few of these images are isolated as "teachable moments" during Briski's photography workshops. These images, discussed below, point toward the specific brand of childlike spontaneity and alterity that Briski seeks to cultivate.

Manik's *Hand* has become more iconically associated with the *Born into Brothels* project than any other image produced by the children. It is often used as the cover image in sets of the children's photographs available for sale, and it enjoys a special visibility in the film. *Hand* is prominently displayed in the invitation used to publicize the first local exhibition of the children's photographs in a Calcutta bookstore, as well as in a front-page article on the *Brothels* project in one of India's most widely read newspapers that is circulated during one of Briski's workshops. When asked to describe the process of producing this image, Manik explains that his sister, Shanti, put her hand in front of the camera as he was pressing the shutter, producing the unusual effect of a blown-up silhouette of a hand against a backdrop of festive lights in the distance. Even though the film hints at the contentious rivalry between the two siblings, there is no discussion of the social context of this photograph, for instance, whether Shanti's gesture may have been an intentional attempt to foil her brother's efforts or to arrest the intrusion of his camera. Instead, Briski praises the photograph for its spontaneity: an instance in which breaking all of the objective rules of photographic composition and exposure proves to be aesthetically generative. At the bookstore exhibition, Shanti repeatedly mimics her "instinctive" gesture, to the amusement of many delighted members of the Calcutta literati, reinforcing the impression of her naive artistic genius.

Briski also reserves high praise for photographic portraits that hint at the flavor of the children's environment without adding undue specificity to the attribute that encapsulates their essential humanity: their faces. A self-portrait by her star pupil, Avijit, who is often singled out for his "unique" artistic talent, serves as an object lesson in achieving this goal. Avijit's *Self Portrait* frames his face against the background of a Sonagachi street. The background is crisply clear: we see a dirty tenement building behind the boy, the walls spattered with mud and dirt, betel stains, graffiti, and posters. A woman stands behind Avijit in a doorway, and, several stories above them both, we see clothes hung up to dry outside windows. But it is on Avijit's face, eyebrows knit in concentration as he extends his arm to take the shot, that the lines of the image converge, notwithstanding the blurriness of his face. Briski displays Avijit's self-portrait during a critique session as an example of a "good photograph," noting approvingly that "we can see the street, the environment in which he lives." While the background abounds with signifying elements that suggest Avijit's socioeconomic and cultural identity, his face demands the universal regard accorded to what has now become well known as the genre of the selfie.

Suchitra's portrait of a female friend, *Girl on a Roof*, chosen as the cover image of Amnesty International's calendar for 2003, similarly turns the visible evidence of the cramped living quarters of the brothels into signs of local color that function as compositional elements framing a picture of demure South Asian femininity. The girl is framed in medium close-up against a vibrant blue wall, while small slivers of geographic context, visible only in the far-right quarter of the frame—a corrugated roof, sacks of clothing, and brightly colored saris and dresses drying in the wind—exist less to situate the image in time and place than to provide pleasing contrasting color blocks of saturated pink. The blue of the girl's modest kurta top and the pale green of

FIGURE 1.7 *Self-Portrait* by Avijit; still from *Born into Brothels* by Zana Briski and Ross Kauffman (2004)

FIGURE 1.8 *Girl on a Roof* by Suchitra; still from *Born into Brothels* by Zana Briski and Ross Kauffman (2004)

her scarf, which covers her head and neck, blend seamlessly into the blue of the background wall, setting her luminous face in relief as she meets our gaze head-on with a bashful smile.

Briski and fellow photojournalist Robert Pledge, who have together brought international attention to the children's photographs, repeatedly praise these three photographs as examples of the children's innate "artistic genius." The discourse of latent genius has been crucial in boosting the exhibition value of the children's photographs, which have been displayed and sold in a number of national and international art galleries, auction houses, and online platforms—including on the Kids with Cameras website—in the form of individual prints, postcards, and a companion coffee-table book authored by Briski.[32] The introduction to this book includes the following quote from Diane Weyerman (the erstwhile director of the Sundance Documentary Film Program), which appears frequently in reviews and publicity for the film: "Briski, a professional photographer, gives [the children] lessons and cameras, igniting sparks of artistic genius that reside in these children who live in the most sordid and seemingly hopeless world. . . . *Their photographs are prisms into their souls*, rather than anthropological curiosities or primitive imagery. . . . [T]hey reflect . . . art as an immensely liberating and empowering force."[33]

As so-called virgin photographers, the child artists of *Born into Brothels* command a peculiar fascination that has been reserved in modernist discourse for the naive genius of children.[34] The "innocent" or "untutored" eye of the child, regarded as both innocent of visual convention and preternaturally intuitive, has since the romantic period been praised as a model for the artist. In the romantic tradition, Jonathan Fineberg elaborates, "art comes as a gift of revelation and the child represents—in inverse proportion to its acquisition of the conventions of civilized culture—both a more direct path to such inspiration and an ability to see the 'truth' of what it is."[35] Weyerman's description of the children's photographs as "prisms into their souls" turns the romantic discourse of the child's untutored eye into a means of disavowing the cultural and technical aspects of photographic mediation. In a throwback to the proto-photographic discourse of devising "a means by which nature . . . could be made to represent itself automatically," to quote Geoffrey Batchen, the child's eye behind the lens guarantees the documentary status, or truth-value, of the photographic image.[36]

The documentary guarantee of the child's "untutored eye" has a special currency in discourses surrounding humanitarian photojournalism. When it comes to photographing the real, especially under conditions of crisis or atrocity, unpolished, amateur images are often thought to possess a certain authenticity that elevates them above professional images. In such a context, as Susan Sontag has noted, properly lit and composed images are regarded with suspicion, and their artistry as a sign of insincerity. She explains, "Photography is the only major art in which professional training and years of experience do not confer an insuperable advantage over the untrained and inexperienced—this for many reasons, among them the large role that chance (or luck) plays in the taking of pictures, and the bias toward the spontaneous, the rough, the imperfect."[37] More recently, Adam Broomberg and Oliver Chanarin have argued, citing the dilemmas of judging the World Press Photo photojournalism contest, that the preference for the amateur and the spontaneous over the professional and the composed has left the genre of photojournalism in crisis. They speculate that professional photojournalists might profit from embracing the aesthetic of failure and discomposed spontaneity characteristic of amateur eyewitness photography. They point to a photograph taken during the assassination of Benazir Bhutto in 2007 as a standard to strive toward, writing, "It is not really a photograph at all, but a blur, a piece of smudged evidence that testifies to the fact that our journalist was there."[38] Broomberg and Chanarin's recommendations echo Briski's rationale for turning to her students as a means of aesthetic inspiration: the value of the untutored eye in this discourse has less to do with proficiency or genius than with the documentary guarantee of its "spontaneity."

The photojournalistic discourse of spontaneity and the artistic discourse of the child's untutored genius have the combined effect of disavowing the romantic aesthetic tradition in which Briski's photographic pedagogy is steeped. Far from being innate, the talent of Briski's students is closely related to their success in reproducing what Higonnet has described as the tropes of "Romantic childhood"—a nostalgic iconography that became popular among portrait painters of the seventeenth century as a visual reflection of the emerging discourse of childhood innocence. Higonnet argues that the iconography of romantic childhood remains strong in contemporary photography, encompassing a variety of genres: images of children in special costumes; depictions of children with or as cuddly animals; the representation of children as angels, fairies, or winged Cupids; the mother-and-child portrait (a continuation of the Madonna convention); and the portrayal of children humorously failing at being adults in sanctioned roles (such as "playing house"). These tropes, Higonnet argues, have the effect of decorporealizing children's bodies by effacing any jarring traces of culture, such as class, gender, ethnicity, sexuality, or historical and cultural context.[39] Paradoxically, even as this imaging convention suspends children in a domain of innocence set apart from the worldly realms of history and the economy—a timeless utopia that Johannes Fabian might call an "allochronism"—it has tremendous commercial appeal.[40] As Higonnet notes, images of children not only circulate in the form of photographs, postcards, and the like (the success of contemporary photographers like Betsy Cameron and Anne Geddes is a case in point) but are used to market a host of domestic commodities.[41]

The photographs made famous by *Born into Brothels* exemplify the commercial viability of a thriving genre of romantic humanitarian photography whose main aesthetic strategy is "feral innocence." Feral innocence both exploits and disavows the frisson of "barbaric" subaltern childhoods: the economic and moral "atrocities" of the children's lives are spectacularized even as their threat to Western notions of civilization is sterilized by the romantic tropes of childhood innocence. In images like *Hand, Self Portrait*, and *Girl on a Roof*, the quotidian sensuality and violence of the children's daily lives are rendered in soft focus as a series of pleasing colors, textures, and shapes, so that the concrete realities of brothel life are turned into a horizon for a surface encounter with an otherness that is both abstract and anodyne. These are photographs that Barthes would describe as "unary," in that their composition discourages contemplation of the complex social context that subtends the photographic frame—the "blind field" that other photographs, like *Puja* and *Dressing*, threaten to activate.[42] The thoroughly contrived aesthetic of feral innocence appears, moreover, to emanate spontaneously from the child's untutored eye, from a space beyond culture. Its hallmark is its contained immediacy, which holds the child's "wildness" at a safe distance to prevent it from taking over the scene.

Feral innocence operates as a fetish in both the Freudian and Marxian senses—that is, as a sexual fetish as well as a commodity fetish. Freud's notion of the fetish refers, as is well known, to the displacement of unconscious and taboo sexual desires into socially acceptable forms. A version of this displacement is at work in the carefully chosen photographs featured in the film and compiled in Briski's book, which permit audiences abroad to enjoy the sexuality of impoverished children in the sanctioned guise of benevolent, ethnographic curiosity. Any discomfort that comes from getting too close to the real in some of the more erotic images is dissipated by others, which reposition the children in the innocent and playful realm of the imaginary. In Higonnet's words, "we are being offered visual pleasure, but only on the condition that we perceive children's bodies in terms of their utter difference from adult bodies, or even that we perceive them as beings who hardly inhabit the present physical world at all."[43] The children's photographs are also fetishized commodities in that they encapsulate the actual social conditions of their production in a seductive surface that is both deceptive and distracting. The exchange value of these photographs is directly related to the childlike status of their authors at the moment of taking the picture—a playfully sensuous capacity that is threatened with extinction as the children grow into young adults. It is telling in this regard that Briski's nonprofit organization, Kids with Cameras, does not advertise the sale of more recent photographs by the now-young adult stars of *Born into Brothels*.

When we trace the routes of images like *Hand*, *Self Portrait*, and *Girl on a Roof* between the humanitarian crisis zone and the global art circuit, we witness a disconcerting wager being brokered between the domains of art and humanitarian governance in which Third World children are transformed from penal subjects into humanitarian subjects. The journey of Briski's favorite student, Avijit, from troubled youth to star photographer is instructive in this regard. The future success of Avijit, now a filmmaker and a graduate of New York University's Tisch School of the Arts, is prefigured in the film's narrative arc, which pivots on his story. Avijit is singled out by Briski and Pledge as exceptionally gifted, but his artistic promise is threatened by a number of personal tragedies: his mother is the victim of what Briski strongly suggests is a dowry-related murder, and his father is portrayed as a self-destructive alcoholic. After his mother's death, Avijit becomes reclusive and diffident, and his interest in producing photographs dwindles rapidly. Avijit's lapse into nonproductiveness leads Briski to speculate that he may become a "bad kid" and get in trouble with the law. This convinces her of the urgency of getting the children "out of the brothels."

Avijit subsequently becomes the focal point of Briski's rehabilitative efforts, as she works tirelessly to secure his admission to a corrective educational facility and to acquire a passport to enable Avijit to travel to Amsterdam as a child delegate at the awards show of the World Press Photo photojournalism contest. The role of the art gallery as an emerging humanitarian domain, and, reciprocally, the role of aesthetic education in the governance of humanitarian subjects, can be glimpsed during the finale of the film, when Avijit obligingly models his photographic training during a children's tour of the photo contest in Amsterdam. Smartly outfitted in Western clothing, Avijit expounds to a rapt audience of children gathered over a photograph, "This is a good picture. We get a good sense of how these people live. And though there is sadness in it, and though it's hard to face, we must look at it because it is *truth*." In this moment, Avijit is acting both as a brand ambassador for the *Brothels* project and as a poster child for humanitarian reform—the scene is an uncanny return of the wild boy Victor performing his lessons for Itard's approval in *The Wild Child*.

In the following section, I suggest that the economic and ideological valences of Briski's humanitarian media intervention can be seen in a new and discomfiting light if we situate the children's artistic production, as well as their subjective transformation, in the context of contemporary debates regarding child labor.

Child Media Empowerment as Dematerialized Child Labor

Since the establishment of Briski's Kids with Cameras initiative in 2002, several other child media empowerment initiatives have duplicated its rhetoric and aims. To name just a few: in 2006 ZoomUganda, a project funded by the Harambee Center, an Oregon-based nonprofit, equipped twelve orphaned Ugandan girls with 35 mm consumer SLR cameras to enable them to "tell their own stories through their own lenses." Ninos de la Amazonia, founded in 2009 by schoolteacher Amy Coplan, sold photographs taken by six indigenous children from the Peruvian Amazon "who had never seen a camera prior to the project" to fund scholarships for the child-photographers and other children from the same village. Through Our Own Eyes, initiated in 2010 by Plan International, a Europe- and Canada-based nonprofit organization, trained fourteen street children in Dhaka, Bangladesh, to document their lives using photography and video so as to "speak out and promote their own rights."[44] Photographs and films produced by disadvantaged children in art workshops or after-school programs have also become a frequent feature in urban art galleries, community spaces, and film festivals: examples include after-school projects focused on inner-city children, like Charleston Kids with Cameras, founded in 2003; traveling gallery exhibits such as the show Eyes of New California in 2005, which showcased photographs taken by immigrant and refugee teens; and online initiatives such as the Girl Project, founded by Kate Engelbrecht in 2007, which featured a curated selection of photographs taken by young girls who were supplied with cameras.[45]

Although humanitarian art initiatives among marginalized children have been ongoing since the 1960s, the recent proliferation of media empowerment initiatives emphasizing the "child's voice" can be traced to a number of epistemic shifts in the 1980s and 1990s having to do with the postmodernization of technology and subjectivity.[46] These shifts include (1) the innovation of cheap, portable consumer photographic and video technologies beginning in the 1980s; (2) the turn toward embodied, personal, and autobiographical knowledge in documentary since the mid-1990s, in which, to quote Michael Renov, "subjectivity is no longer construed as 'something shameful'; it is the filter through which the real enters discourse"; and (3) the legal recognition of the child as a rights-bearing entity in 1989, and the subsequent introduction of conventions regarding child labor standards.[47]

I am concerned primarily with the third of these shifts, and with the legitimacy it confers on the discourse of child media empowerment. Recent child labor conventions, as I elaborate below, distinguish between "harmful" child labor and "benign" creative work. These conventions render self-evident the emphasis of initiatives like Kids with Cameras on media production as an empowering, creative substitute for physically or morally harmful forms of child labor. I will suggest, however, that the distinction between labor and creative work driving contemporary child labor standards is far from self-evident. The humanitarian ethic that undergirds these standards simultaneously pathologizes non-Western working children and incentivizes neoliberal, affective modalities of child labor—and does so, moreover, through an appeal to human rights. I return to the children's photographs in Born into Brothels with these insights in mind. I propose that the photographic aesthetic of feral innocence dematerializes the ideological stakes of the labor that Briski's students undertake in the name of their universal human rights.

In contemporary debates regarding child labor, the near-universal ratification of the United Nations Convention on the Rights of the Child in 1989 is widely regarded as a watershed event that inaugurated the emergence of the child as a rights-bearing agent with relative autonomy.[48] Before this convention, International Labour Organization (ILO) conventions aimed to abolish *all* child labor by treating it as an issue of labor regulation to be resolved by establishing laws stipulating minimum ages for employment. The introduction of the concept of children's rights means that international standards drafted since 1989 do not view *all* child labor as violative of human rights. These recent conventions uphold "child welfare," which concerns necessary goods and capabilities for well-being, as a primary humanitarian principle over and against "child agency," which concerns chosen and therefore secondary goods and capabilities.

One of the key conceptual interventions of the ILO Convention Concerning the Prohibition and Immediate Elimination of the Worst Forms of Child Labour (ILO C182) in 1999 lies in differentiating "child labor" (harmful for child welfare, hence impermissible) from "child work" (benign and having to do with child agency, hence permissible). This convention includes special protocols for prioritizing and eliminating forms of child labor that are deemed "truly abusive or exploitative." Apropos of *Born into Brothels*, the involvement of children in prostitution is seen as one of the four "worst forms" of child labor: it is ranked second after child slavery and is followed by the recruitment of children in drug trafficking and work harmful to the health, safety, and morals of children.[49]

The assumptions underpinning ILO C182 and its implications for working children in non-Western contexts have been the topic of heated discussion and critique among contemporary children's rights scholars. The main thrust of these debates has been to challenge the conception of the innocent, victimized child that informs ILO C182's single-minded humanitarian focus on protecting children from harmful forms of labor. As Olga Nieuwenhuys notes in her field-shaping essay, "The Paradox of Anthropology and Child Labor," twentieth-century child labor standards rely on a fundamentally modern Western moral conception of childhood as a domain that should be dissociated from the production of value. As a result, conventions such as ILO C182 end up pathologizing cultures with a more fluid understanding of the spectrum between childhood and adulthood without acknowledging that labor is often the only avenue through which many marginalized children can fashion self-esteem and identity.

A number of scholars have turned to rights-based discourse for a more nuanced understanding of the relationship between labor and agency in non-Western contexts. Some have proffered the concept of the "working child" as a way of emphasizing the agency of children as social actors who are actively involved in shaping their social world.[50] Although "agency" remains a topic of conflict, with others pointing out that structural forces like need, poverty, caste, and class impinge on children's supposed "active participation" in "child work," there remains a resounding emphasis on the rights and privileges of children as active agents engaged in voluntarily chosen activities.[51] Rights-based discourse has made undeniable strides in displacing the monolithically Western notion of childhood innocence that informs the humanitarian, pro-tectionist tenor of contemporary child labor standards. At the same time, its countervailing endorsement of the agency of children also tacitly endorses "benign" and "voluntarily chosen" child work as the best possible substitute for truly abusive and coercive forms of labor without adequately interrogat-ing the historical valences and implications of such "benign" work.

The embrace of agency as a central philosophy of the working child be-comes more problematic when "benign" child work is historicized as an in-stance of emerging forms of labor that are not necessarily recognizable or measurable as labor. Marxist scholars working in the autonomist tradition, including Maurizio Lazzarato and Paolo Virno, have argued that the forms of labor that contemporary child labor standards seek to eliminate can no longer be regarded as the dominant global modality of alienated labor. Tra-ditional forms of capitalist labor—including the eighteenth-century model of Western factory-based labor that arguably informs recent child labor conventions—are typically associated with physicality and coercion, as well as the alienation of the worker's labor power in the form of a tangible com-modity.[52] However, under neoliberalism, these scholars insist, increasing numbers of workers are exhorted to perform creative, intellectual, and com-municative tasks that blur the lines between leisure and labor, and that are correspondingly routinely un- or undercompensated. The end result of such labor, Lazzarato argues, is not always, or only, materially tangible. Instead, alienation takes place at an affective level, producing a subtle and evanescent transformation in the subjectivity of the worker, who is willingly enlisted in their own exploitation. Lazzarato has suggested the label of "immaterial labor" for this new regime.[53]

The term *immaterial labor* has proved controversial for its suggestion that these emerging modes of labor have no material basis.[54] I would counter, however, that Lazzarato is pointing out the ways in which the material basis of such labor is *dematerialized* and subject to erasure as a function of its per-formative, affective, or "virtuosic" characteristics, to borrow a term from

Virno. As Virno notes, actors, teachers, performance artists, and musicians represent, in many regards, the prototype for postmodern workers like call-center executives, software programmers, and entrepreneurs.[55] Perhaps most significantly, for our present purposes, Lazzarato and Virno insist that the most effective and insidious forms of exploitative labor under neoliberalism operate not through coercion but through appeals to agency, choice, and creativity—in other words, the very attributes praised by advocates of children's rights. We might even go so far as to say that the humanitarian fantasy of the innocent child, with its invocations of leisure, recreation, and play, represents the ultimate inspiration for contemporary forms of dematerialized labor.[56]

The humanitarian ethical imperative of recent ILO child labor conventions casts benign or voluntarily chosen child work as a necessarily empowering alternative to harmful or coercive child labor. The problem with this binary opposition is that it fails to interrogate, as Lazzarato and Virno would urge, whether such voluntarily chosen work might be all the more effective as a mode of child labor because it does not *feel* alienating, harmful, or coercive. Humanitarian media interventions that mobilize this opposition interpellate the spectator within what Lee Edelman has described as the "ideological Möbius strip" of contemporary children's rights rhetoric.[57] *Born into Brothels* is a case in point: it is impossible to disagree with the film's advocacy of art as a benign alternative to sex work without being against children, and therefore against the future that they so potently symbolize. The concept of dematerialized child labor undoes this binary, revealing art and labor to be two sides of the same problematic or ideological Möbius strip.

When we reexamine the children's photographic efforts through the lens of this concept, we can see how the children are not simply engaged in producing tangible humanitarian commodities for which they receive a basic charitable compensation. They are also engaged in producing something far more intangible: a humanitarian aesthetic that circulates independently of them, with unquantifiable effects. The photographic aesthetic of feral innocence dematerializes the children's labor by representing it as play and simultaneously effaces their subjective transformation as neoliberal laboring subjects. Meanwhile, the legitimating discursive framework of artistic genius and photographic spontaneity allows Briski to position the children's "aptitude for art" as a dormant creative instinct rather than a repository of untapped economic potential, or labor power, in Marxian terms. The moral obligation of saving the children from the brothels—and therefore from what is legally regarded as one of the "worst forms" of child labor—provides an alibi for liberating this potential from the limits of a local economy that is deemed economically unproductive. If the children were initially born into brothels, as the film claims, then Briski's humanitarian intervention arguably facilitates their rebirth into the global flows of capital.

Prehistories and Futures

The central problematic of child media empowerment can be described as a tension between the materiality of the documentary image and the humanitarian discourse of immediacy. The photographs produced by Briski's students materialize the concrete conditions of their production, but the rhetorical and aesthetic frames of her film insist that the urgent task of humanitarian intervention takes precedence over the task of reading these images. In this concluding section, I turn to the prehistory of participatory documentary to locate a productively dialectical solution to this impasse. Sol Worth and John Adair's Navajo Film Themselves Project, conducted in 1966, was an early experiment in participatory film production that has been criticized by its successors for overemphasizing form at the expense of social purpose. I propose that the dismissal of this project should be seen as a symptom of a humanitarian turn in participatory documentary in the 1980s and 1990s that coincided with the adoption of video as an activist technology. As a consequence of this turn toward the discourse of humanitarian intervention, some of the most compelling aspects of Worth and Adair's project have been ignored, including their dialectical investment in the concept of "film children" as a means of disrupting the habituated conventions of documentary immediacy. I propose that resuscitating this investment is an important starting point for a critique of the humanitarian impulse in documentary.

In the summer of 1966, the anthropologists Worth and Adair arrived at a Navajo reservation in Pine Springs, Arizona, with nonsync 16 mm film cameras, tripods, and editing equipment and initiated the Navajo Film Themselves Project, now widely acknowledged as one of the earliest attempts to "put the camera directly into native hands."[58] Their book-length chronicle of the project, *Through Navajo Eyes*, is a fascinating artifact of a time when positivist, ethnographic approaches to documentary were being challenged by poststructuralist and postcolonialist ways of thinking. Worth and Adair describe their approach as "bio-documentary," or a study of "how a group of people structure their view of the world—their reality—through film."[59]

They write, "A Bio-Documentary is a film made by a person to show how he feels about himself and his world. It is a subjective way of showing what the objective world that a person sees is 'really' like. In part, this kind of film bears the same relation to documentary film that a self-portrait has to a portrait or a [biography to an] autobiography. In addition, because of the specific way that this kind of film is made, it often captures feelings and reveals values, attitudes, and concerns that lie beyond conscious control of the maker."[60] To demonstrate their hypothesis, Worth and Adair identified seven Navajo students, six of whom had never before encountered a film or camera. The anthropologists then "neutrally" introduced camera and editing equipment to these students as mere machinery, without suggesting the cultural purpose of cinema or predetermining the content, form, or execution of the films produced by the Navajo. Their premise was that the visual coding, narrative syntax, style, and textual organization of the films produced by their students—whom they call "film children," to indicate their unfamiliarity with film—would evidence a "uniquely Navajo" film grammar.[61]

Worth and Adair's interest in bio-documentary was prescient in many ways. At a time when many anthropologists employed film as a transparent recording device, Worth and Adair intended to show how the seemingly objective aspects of cinematic language were bearers of culturally and subjectively coded meanings. Their visionary application of linguistic analysis to cinema prefigured the embrace of semiotic approaches in film theory, and their participatory approach to documentary practice is widely regarded as a precursor of the work of video activists working in collaboration with indigenous communities in subsequent decades. The anthropologists' emphasis on a subjective approach to documentary arguably precipitated the turn toward reflexive, autobiographical methods that would come to dominate ethnographic and documentary practices in the mid-1980s and onward. The Navajo Film Themselves Project played an important role in legitimizing film as an object of anthropological study and in laying the foundations for the academic discipline of visual anthropology.

Despite its many groundbreaking contributions, *Through Navajo Eyes* has been chronicled mainly in the form of critique, much of which focuses on Worth and Adair's naive and patronizing view of autochthonous identity.[62] These critiques are well warranted: Worth and Adair's choice of students indicates their static, inflexible view of identitarian categories: "an artist" or "acculturated Navajo," "a girl," "a craftsman or woman," "a person with political ambitions," and "a Navajo who had no craft, artistic, political, or personal interest or aptitude in filmmaking."[63] Their view of film is similarly rigid and does not account for the premediation of cinematic literacy by other audio-visual and literary forms—the anthropologists are said to have chosen an "acculturated" Navajo as one of their students for the express purpose of studying the effect of acculturation on "Navajo visual grammar," which is otherwise argued to be "unique" and untouched by Western conventions.[64] Thus, rather than regarding film language and cultural context as mutually structuring, Worth and Adair treat their students' physical handling of filmmaking equipment as evidence that their visual production is distinctly and authentically "Navajo."[65]

Worth and Adair routinely resort to essentializing stereotypes and outmoded anthropological explanations of Navajo language and culture when interpreting the formal innovations of their students' films. For instance, they hypothesize that the Navajo's reticence regarding facial close-ups and photographing of strangers may be a result of "cultural, perceptual, and cognitive" taboos on owning the property of others.[66] The repeated motifs of walking in several of the films are interpreted, as Leighton C. Peterson notes, as references to "Navajo creation stories, which often include journeys."[67] Worth and Adair interpret such shots as a way of giving mythologically significant events a "proper place in the scheme of things," while the Navajo's emphasis on following motion smoothly and precisely is treated as an expression of their group's "constant motion . . . in balance and harmony with their environment."[68] The anthropologists' residual commitment to structuralist and determinist approaches to language leads them to read their students' cinematic language as scientific evidence of the Navajo's mythic thought processes, which they view as an unchanging, isolable essence rather than an evolving, hybridized result of cross-cultural encounters.

The most vocal critics of the Navajo Film Themselves Project have been scholars and practitioners who subsequently adapted Worth and Adair's model of participatory documentary in video-based collaborations with indigenous and aboriginal groups. Their main criticism of the Navajo project, to quote Faye Ginsburg, is that it "focused overmuch on the filmic rather than the social frame."[69] As evidence, Ginsburg points to an infamous exchange between Worth and Adair and Sam Yazzie, a medicine man and elder on the Pine Springs reservation. When Worth and Adair explained their intentions to Yazzie, he is reported to have asked a question that perplexed the anthropologists: "Will making movies do the sheep any good?" When Worth admitted that it was unlikely, Yazzie rejoined, "Then why make movies?" Ginsburg interprets Worth and Adair's failure to respond to Yazzie's question as a symptom of their larger failure to account for "potential cultural differences in the social relations around image-making and viewing."[70] Monica Feitosa similarly distinguishes between *Through Navajo Eyes* and her own participatory video work among the Kayapo people in Brazil in the mid-1980s. Feitosa argues that *Through Navajo Eyes* was focused more on the scientific interests of the researchers than on the interests of the makers, whereas her project sought to use video to address the immediate political needs of the Kayapo in their negotiations with the Brazilian government.[71]

Ginsburg and Feitosa argue that the medium specificity of video technology—its affordability, portability, and ease of operation and distribution—was especially well suited for the articulation of indigenous social concerns. These scholars were less concerned with the formal sensibilities of indigenously produced video than with the support that video technology offered for indigenous modes of social organization and communication at a time when hegemonically controlled mass media were threatening to permanently erode traditional cultures and lifeways. As a case in point, Ginsburg cites researcher Eric Michaels's pioneering work in introducing video production and broadcast to a Warlpiri community in Australia, writing, "The ways in which tapes are made, shown, and used reflect Warlpiri understandings of kinship and group responsibilities for display and access to traditional knowledge."[72] The discourse surrounding indigenous video is centrally concerned with "issues of power regarding who controls the production and distribution of imagery," to quote Ginsburg, which can be seen in the warlike metaphors used as descriptions of indigenous uses of video: "defiant" appropriation, "taking aim," and "shooting back."[73]

These military metaphors offer striking evidence of the emergence of the rhetoric of humanitarian intervention in discourses of participatory media. Whereas the contemplation of formal mediation was one of the key elements of the Navajo Film Themselves Project, indigenous video practitioners view formal concerns as secondary to the immediate task of handing over the camera to the other. In the process, they reinstate the positivist approach to the documentary image that Worth and Adair were attempting to displace. The activist embrace of video as a solution to the problems of ethnographic representation has taken place, as Rachel Moore writes, at the cost of investigating how "indigenous video inherits the theoretical burdens of [ethnographic] representation."[74] The de facto authenticity associated with indigenous video makers has meant that their documentary images have been treated as self-evident expressions of the "native voice." This brackets the question of how the articulation of such a voice replicates or complicates the problems involved in the formal tropes and narrative conventions of ethnographic documentary, or what role such articulations play in deepening the hierarchical power structures that exist within the indigenous societies in question.

Despite its problematic premises and conclusions, *Through Navajo Eyes*, in its concept of "film children," contains a potentially valuable antidote to the discourse of immediation that characterizes the interventionist turn in participatory documentary. Worth and Adair's comparison of their students to children is, on one hand, proof of their patronizing and primitivizing attitudes toward the Navajo.[75] At the same time, the anthropologists' attempt to inhabit the embodied experience of so-called film primitives is enabling as a result of, and not despite, their problematic premises: Worth and Adair may have failed in their quest for a uniquely Navajo film grammar, but they were successful in thoroughly defamiliarizing their own habitualized relationship to the prevailing cinematographic and narrative conventions of documentary filmmaking. They write, "It became clear to us that our rules were being broken. It wasn't until we noted that the Navajo were doing it 'wrong' that we realized the prescriptive strength of some of our rules of syntactic organization."[76]

When we examine Worth and Adair's reflections on the "clear examples of 'wrong' filmmaking" in the Navajo-made films, we find that the cinematic conventions defamiliarized in their analysis include the received tropes of documentary immediacy, such as the facial close-up, the long take, the wide-angle landscape shot, minimal editing, handheld camera work, and the filming of nonprofessional actors. These are the very tropes that Trinh has criticized as the authenticating visual lexicon of ethnographic documentary realism.[77] As my previous analysis of *Born into Brothels* illustrates, these tropes have endured and become a salient feature of contemporary humanitarian documentaries in the pseudoparticipatory mode.

At one point, Worth and Adair compare the formally disorienting cinematic idiom of their students with the work of avant-garde filmmakers and painters who have been inspired by "primitive" art forms, with the important distinction that the Navajo were not deliberately breaking any prescribed rules. They cite the example of one of their students, Maxine Tsosie:

It might be thought that these "rule breakings" are evidence of lack of skill on the part of the Navajo, or lack of a conceptual ability at that stage in their filmmaking. That is, that when they "got better" they would "naturally" follow the rule. But remember the description of Maxine's first editing effort with the seesaw described in Chapter 6. She deliberately and with great skill *chose* to connect her pieces of film so that the motion of the seesaw was uninterrupted. . . . It will become clear that when the Navajo didn't make smooth transitions, or used jump cuts, they weren't breaking our rules at all. They just didn't accept the rule that a jump cut was strange or unnatural.[78]

In turning to "primitive" cultures to rejuvenate their own cinematic practice and imbue it with a new vigor and vitality, Worth and Adair mobilize the "dialectic between formal innovation and primitivism" that Rey Chow has described as one of the basic maneuvers of modernist critique.[79] What remains noteworthy and valuable about *Through Navajo Eyes* is Worth and Adair's emphasis on friction, dissent, and contradiction as a source of dialectical rejuvenation in their participatory endeavor, as well as their framing of the documentary image as a crucial site of this contradiction.

A pernicious and undialectical version of this maneuver is at work in the contemporary pseudoparticipatory documentary, as exemplified by *Born into Brothels*. The "primitive" figure of the child remains a source of creative inspiration for humanitarian representation, but its contradictions and complications are flattened into a fetish. The prehistory of participatory documentary offers us one possible model for recouping the dialectical potential of the figure of the child. Like Worth and Adair, we can pay attention to the formal contours of those rule-breaking utterances that interrupt and defamiliarize the conventional documentary logic of humanitarian claims. Tapasi's *Dressing* and Manik's *Hand* interrupt the humanitarian photographic discourse of childhood innocence. They demonstrate that seeing "through children's eyes," as the film claims, paradoxically requires us to develop a critical distance from the humanitarian frames of documentary immediacy. At stake is an altogether more complex, contradictory, and confounding image of the humanity of children than these frames make visible.

Chapter 2

BARE LIVENESS

THE EYEWITNESS TO CATASTROPHE IN THE
AGE OF HUMANITARIAN EMERGENCY

Tele Geto: "Live from Haiti"

In the months following the earthquake in Haiti in January 2010, a humanitarian organization named Global Nomads Group broadcast a series of YouTube videos that exemplified their practice of connecting students around the world using participatory and social media. Filmed by North American students in their Students Rebuild program, these videos showcase a Port-au-Prince–based youth collective named Tele Geto ("Ghetto TV"). In each video, a teenage boy is shown holding a video camera while another plays the role of reporter, handling the microphone and conducting interviews with Haitian locals about various topics pertaining to the postearthquake political, economic, and cultural landscape in Haiti.[1]

The high seriousness of these videos is rendered somewhat surreal by the realization that the camera and microphone brandished by Tele Geto's "cameramen" are obviously fake props fashioned from scrap materials. A plastic bottle is painted black, with red and purple foam knobs, to resemble a digital video camera. The neck of the bottle points forward to serve as a lens; its side is cut and splayed open in a crude semblance of an LCD screen. A pair of broken headphones and a "microphone" consisting of steel wire duct-taped roughly to a stump of wood complete the ensemble. Remarkably, the men and women approached by the boys still direct their responses to Tele Geto's "reporter" and his makeshift apparatus, rather than at the real video camera presumably borne by the Global Nomads youth delegates, who remain off-screen, positioned at a remove from the Tele Geto crew.

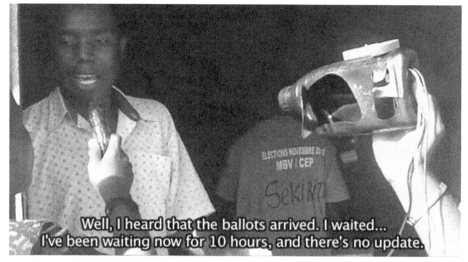

Well, I heard that the ballots arrived. I waited...
I've been waiting now for 10 hours, and there's no update.

FIGURE 2.1 Still from "Teleghetto—Election Part 2" YouTube video (2010)

In another Global Nomads video, the Tele Geto "crew" explain that they conceived their project as a performance art piece during the inaugural Ghetto Biennale, an art event initiated in November 2009 by Atis Rezistans (Artists of Resistance), a resident collective of sculptors from the impoverished Ghetto Leanne area of Port-au-Prince.[2] Originally trained as artisanal wood-carvers producing tourist souvenirs, the founders of Atis Rezistans have evolved a unique, Vodou-inspired style of bricolage by repurposing unclaimed human skulls and bones and found industrial materials discarded from the scrap-metal dealers and junkyards that border their Grand Rue workspace. The towering sculptural figures that crowd Atis Rezistans's studio and courtyard feature massive phallic appendages—a reference to the hyper-masculine Vodou spirit and trickster Gede, who is a ubiquitous presence in their artworks. These overtly eroticized figures simultaneously protest the position of impotence to which Haitian art is relegated in Euro-American contexts, and shamelessly parade the frisson for which it is sought.[3]

According to one attendee, the Tele Geto performance was prompted by the international attendees and domestic and foreign journalists at the inaugural Ghetto Biennale, each of whom carried personal and professional camera equipment. Sensing an opportunity to showcase their art practice, some of Atis Rezistans's youth apprentices (between six and eighteen years old) constructed an improvised camera unit with found materials and set about imitating the reporters and photographers, much to the latter's delight.[4] Tele Geto's teasing play on the sober self-importance of legitimate journalism captures the tongue-in-cheek attitude of the Rezistans artists toward the elite art world. It also ironizes the gaze from abroad that inevitably mediates the production, exhibition, and circulation of Haitian art, echoing the mixed sentiments of the Ghetto Biennale.[5]

When introducing their project to the Global Nomads students, the Tele Geto crew shrewdly repackage their performance art project as a human rights appeal for their new audience of young humanitarian aid workers. Whereas the Ghetto Biennale performance originated as a response to the structural inequities between Haitian artists and their foreign counterparts, the boys now reframe Tele Geto as a form of art therapy for Haitian earthquake victims neglected by the international news media, explaining, "The objective of Tele Ghetto is to pick up all of Haiti. We started with a fake camera and it was therapeutic for the people. . . . When we asked them questions, it made them feel better."[6] The viewer is inspired to join Global Nomads in cheering on these intrepid street artists, whose wishful role play of television reporter and interviewee conjures a worldly public existence beyond their reach. The story of empowerment through media is a compelling one, but the winking presence of the fake Tele Geto camera ironizes this narrative of progress, pointing instead to the paltry page views for each video (numbering in the hundreds or low thousands at the time of writing in 2016).

Remarkably, through a series of timely humanitarian interventions, also catalyzed by media, Tele Geto has been transformed from a satirical performance commenting on the documentary gaze of the West into a sober instantiation of "live" eyewitness media, with its founders taking seriously the framing narrative of media empowerment at which they previously looked askance. On January 12, 2010, the Haitian photographer Daniel Morel was in the midst of photographing the junior Rezistans artists in their studio when the earthquake hit, compelling Morel to abandon his assignment in favor of the more urgent role of eyewitness reporter. Morel's photographs of injured and bewildered Ghetto Leanne pedestrians buried under rubble by the very first tremors were broadcast throughout the international press in the days following the event and quickly became icons of the Haitian earthquake, winning Morel two World Press Photo awards in 2011.[7] In the reflected light of Morel's award-winning reportage, Tele Geto has emerged at the center of numerous news stories, online videos, and gallery shows devoted to the Haitian recovery effort.[8] The teenagers' improvised props and inventive mimicry of their mentors' salvage aesthetic have led many to herald their youthful potential as a hopeful allegory of Haiti's regeneration, hailing them as "visionaries [emerging from] ruin."[9] After their homes and studio were destroyed in the earthquake, London-based artist, scholar, and Ghetto Biennale supporter John Cussans presented the youths with an actual video camera and microphone to enable them to emulate Morel by documenting postdisaster life in the ghettos of Port-au-Prince.[10]

The six videos produced by Tele Geto in their new role as eyewitness documentarians offer evidence of their lives in the aftermath of the disaster, but not merely of the variety sought by Cussans.[11] They also offer striking evidence of the testimonial tropes of documentary immediacy that the youths must deploy to be recognizable to their humanitarian audiences as young "visionaries" engaged in "vibrant" "citizen media activity."[12] The Tele Geto crew offer frequent assurances regarding the unmediated documentary quality of their reporting: "we're not editing," "we show it to you like it is," "the real thing," "making you experience the reality." But as they walk through the destroyed streets and tent cities of Port-au-Prince, they find the locals suspicious about being interviewed on camera. Unperturbed, they keep up a nonstop commentary: they describe what the camera sees ("as you see, many streets are destroyed, many schools are destroyed"), offer analysis of the disaster, and repeatedly index their own eyewitness status ("we're *here* as Tele Geto journalists"). The image leaps in and out of focus as the boys clamber through rubble-laden streets, destroyed homes, and temporary settlements, the audio lurching between deafening and inaudible with each unexpected jolt. These blemished sounds and images invest Tele Geto's documentary footage with an aura of immediacy, relative to the skillfully edited and well-produced Global Nomads videos. The reality effect of these videos is enhanced rather than reduced by their amateurish or "fuzzy" quality, to quote André Bazin; indeed, this quality seems to realize Bazin's fantasy of encountering the world in its "virginal purity" through photography.[13]

The fake Tele Geto camera is notably absent in these videos. The teenagers repeatedly clarify to their audience that "this is not a joke" and "it is not a toy." The implicit message is that the seriousness and urgency of disaster requires setting aside childish fun and games. Documentary is called for, not theater. Given the profusion of constative speech acts in these videos, it is easy to forget that the youths are still engaged in a performance, this time playing the

And because of the earthquake here, we're going to take some images that may interest you once again in Haiti, some you will have seen before and some you won't.

FIGURE 2.2 Still from "Tele Geto 1" YouTube video (2010)

role of an eyewitness television crew in a disaster zone. But without the ironic framing device of the prop camera, Tele Geto's performance assumes an air of unmediated truth. Cussans even extolls the "honest and direct" quality of their video documents. His commentary contains echoes of the romantic discourse regarding the untutored eye of the child, discussed in the previous chapter: "the respondents are totally unguarded, because the kids are young people—and they're Haitian, they aren't white, they're not from the UN, they're not intimidating, so the locals tell them what they think."[14]

This chapter asks what happens when "liveness," a set of theatrical behaviors associated with the professional television reporter, is recast as a sober documentary idiom of humanitarian testimony. I begin my analysis by using Tele Geto to examine an ongoing debate regarding the discursive blurring of humanitarianism and human rights in the governance of catastrophe. Some critics argue that the humanitarian emphasis on saving lives as a first-order principle extends the logic of sovereign power by distinguishing between "bare" lives and politically valuable lives. Others view the replacement of civil rights with human rights as a potential political opening that displaces the citizen, humanitarian agent, or sovereign subject as the ground or standpoint from which rights can be claimed. Tele Geto affirms the latter perspective by demonstrating how representatives of "bare life"—that is, individuals whose political status has been suspended—nonetheless assert their political agency and claim their human rights. For critics of humanitarianism, speech acts like these affirm the radicalizing impact of human rights discourse on the seemingly neutral, punctual, and apolitical practice of humanitarian intervention.

Less attention has been paid to how the concrete testimonial codes of the humanitarian emergency mediate human rights speech acts. I argue that Tele Geto represents a troubling new mode of human rights claim that is shaped by the humanitarian emergency as a "live" media event. The humanitarian live media event brings together two optics: (1) the humanitarian emergency, whose suspension of politics brings what has been called "bare life" into the purview of governance; and (2) the televisual discourse of catastrophe, which promises a suspension of the conventional forms of televisual mediation in favor of documentary contact with the real. The outcome of these merging optics can be seen in the transformation of the "live eyewitness" from a theatrical convention of televisual catastrophe into the prescribed testimonial code through which the subjects of humanitarian emergencies become legible to humanitarian audiences. The theater of liveness consists of conveying that the professional reporter faces the same physical risks as the disaster victims whom they have been sent to cover—risks that are nonetheless held in abeyance by the privileges of the reporter's celebrity. The humanitarian discourse of participatory documentary effectively transforms the trope of the eyewitness from a coded performance of referentiality into documentary evidence of the bare lives of disaster victims—evidence that is, moreover, agentially and entrepreneurially performed by them as a human rights claim.

I examine the implications of the live eyewitness as a testimonial idiom through readings of two documentary texts produced during and in the aftermath of Hurricane Katrina: Anderson Cooper's award-winning coverage of Hurricane Katrina for CNN, and *Trouble the Water* (dir. Tia Lessin and Carl Deal, 2008), a film that has been critically acclaimed in part for its inclusion of several minutes of eyewitness footage shot by Katrina survivor Kimberly Rivers Roberts. I use these texts to demonstrate the changing poetics of liveness in the context of the humanitarian emergency, as the deadliest and most urgent of catastrophes. Cooper's highly physical and visceral coverage of Katrina, I argue, exemplifies the growing appeal of the eyewitness body as an index of imperiled life that pierces through the exhausted televisual tropes of catastrophe.

In *Trouble the Water*, the actual vulnerability of disaster victims guarantees the unmediated contact with the real that the live television reporter performs but fails to deliver. As a humanitarian platform for Roberts's testimonial footage, *Trouble the Water* "gives voice" to her and other survivors of the hurricane. But the voices of these disenfranchised subjects simultaneously authenticate the documentary status of Lessin and Deal's film, which leverages Roberts's "real" eyewitness footage against the "fakery" of mainstream live television coverage of Katrina. I propose that the film's inclusive rhetoric of participatory media effectively extends the predatory cultural logic of disaster capitalism: by interpellating disaster victims as eyewitness journalists, it calls on the most vulnerable social subjects to actively absorb professional risks as personal liabilities. Thus, this chapter extends the argument of chapter 1 regarding the ways in which humanitarian media economies are fueled by the labors of "media empowerment." Whereas the previous chapter argued that the humanitarian fantasy of the innocent, creative child inspires aesthetic techniques that dematerialize child labor, I now examine how the actual situation of disaster victims inspires the documentary strategies of depicting catastrophe as a live spectacle.

The larger question driving this chapter concerns the stakes of the contemporary critical investment in dispossessed states, or states of emergency, as sites of political potential. Critics of state racism, or what Michel Foucault calls biopower, have located Michael Hardt and Antonio Negri's account of "communicative biopolitics"—a discourse that emphasizes the communicative potential of the dispossessed—as an empowering alternative to Giorgio Agamben's "thanatopolitics," which sees no political recourse for bare life. I discuss one such critic, Henry Giroux, and his mobilization of Hardt and Negri in an argument about the importance of participatory media after Hurricane Katrina, at some length. Hardt and Negri's work resonates with the humanitarian discourse of participatory documentary in that they locate struggles for human rights as the quintessential biopolitical struggle, and therefore view the dispossessed as paradigmatic figures of resistance. Like critics of humanitarianism, these scholars locate states of emergency as sites of political potential that can catalyze an unexpected encounter with the new, the minor, or the emergent in the form of human rights speech acts. I argue that such thinking is both seductive and dangerous because it subscribes to a rhetoric of immediacy—it is unable to account for the actual testimonial forms that mediate the communicative potential of the dispossessed. *Trouble the Water* illustrates the consequences of such thinking in action: the film is so invested in the documentary immediacy of Roberts's speech act that it fails to notice how she spectacularizes — and ultimately further imperils — her bare life in accordance with the testimonial codes of liveness.

Humanitarianism and Human Rights in the Governance of Emergency

Tele Geto earned the positive regard of their humanitarian advocates by imitating them — that is, by imitating the behavior and formal conventions of the professional media volunteer bearing witness to disaster. The nature of Tele Geto's appeal, as well as the praise they have received for their agential attitude in the face of calamity, tells us much about the merger currently taking place between the discourses of humanitarian intervention and those of human rights advocacy in the governance of states of emergency. Some scholars regard this merger as a "crisis of contemporary humanitarianism" that paves the way for a permanent state of political exception. Others view human rights as the radical underside of the seemingly apolitical humanitarian view of life under emergency conditions: human rights claims demonstrate, they argue, that the right to speak as a political agent can be claimed not just by those who have political standing (for example, humanitarian aid workers) but by anyone, including those bare lives that are thought to lack political value. I turn now to these debates, with the proposal that we must critique the representational codes of the humanitarian emergency in order to fully understand the implications and limitations of human rights claims emerging from sites of emergency.

When surveying the damage done by Hurricane Tomas in October 2010 to the flimsy plastic-tented refugee shelters across Port-au-Prince, the members of Tele Geto direct their appeal not to the Haitian government but to an imagined, sympathetic audience of Western relief providers. The nature of the assistance they seek and the form of their appeal are indexes of the diffuse forms of action that are presently grouped under the banner of "humanitarian intervention." The youths beseech the "whites" not only to hold local officials accountable for their corruption in dispensing medical relief supplies but also to send them durable materials capable of withstanding the Haitian weather, and to continue recognizing and supporting the efforts of Tele Geto. The hazy invocation to "whites" as bearers of political authority, dispensers of charity, and promoters of democracy calls to mind the heterogeneous types of humanitarian organizations that were present in Haiti at the time of this appeal. These included United Nations peacekeeping forces and the U.S. military, who together assumed emergency control of numerous civil functions in Haiti, including transportation and law and order; the major global emergency relief organizations, such as the International Federation of the Red Cross and Médecins Sans Frontières (Doctors without Borders), both of which were among the first nongovernmental medical responders after the January earthquake; and a variety of smaller nonprofit organizations like Global Nomads Group, providing a combination of emergency relief and political advocacy.[15]

We witness here the capaciousness of humanitarian intervention as a discourse that is theoretically distinct from the modes of political governance and human rights advocacy but that is nonetheless exercised as a complex amalgam of these modes in the discursive space of the humanitarian emergency. This blurring of political modes has occasioned a profusion of debate across the humanities and social sciences in the past decade regarding what is called the "crisis of contemporary humanitarianism." The discourse of human rights emerges within these debates as the saving grace of humanitarian discourse in times when humanitarian intervention is most alarmingly complicit with the *zoëpolitics* of emergency.

Didier Fassin and Mariella Pandolfi observe that "humanitarian intervention" is a concept of relatively recent invention, dating to the emergence, in the late twentieth century, of "saving human lives" as a moral justification for the suspension of the rule of law.[16] Humanitarian intervention is based on two founding principles: the principle of political neutrality or impartiality and, relatedly, the moral obligation to save lives on the basis of their common humanity in instances when lives are placed in jeopardy for political reasons, for instance, owing to a failure or breach of proper governance. Humanitarianism is philosophically opposed to politics in its investment in the preservation of life as a first-order principle, separate from the social forms that give political meaning to the "mere" fact of living, such as nationality, race, gender, class, religion, and culture. The temporality of humanitarian action is defined by emergency, understood as a "sudden, unpredictable event emerging against a background of ostensible normalcy, causing suffering or danger and demanding urgent response."[17] The brief, punctual duration of humanitarian action is therefore opposed to the temporality of political work—whether governance, advocacy, or analysis—which is seen as the norm against which humanitarianism's own exceptional, condensed, urgent time frame is defined.

Recently, a number of commentators have spoken out against the dangers of maintaining an uncritical investment in the founding principles of humanitarian action, pointing out not only that they are untenable in practice but also that their underlying binaries—apolitical versus political, timely versus prolonged, exception versus norm—are riddled with internal contradictions.[18] It has been shown, for instance, that humanitarian and military powers routinely collude in designating states of emergency, in which the moral obligation to save lives provides an alibi for extralegal and often life-threatening military interventions, while humanitarian volunteers benefit from military protections and extraterritorial privileges. Humanitarian actors are inevitably involved in the governance of emergency at various levels, such as the management of refugee camps and negotiations with military representatives and human rights advocates to regulate the use of violence. Even though political work targeting the causes of social upheaval falls beyond the humanitarian purview, the humanitarian emergency occasions the presence of a variety of para-, inter-, and nongovernmental organizations in emergency zones, devoted to projects such as human rights advocacy, democracy promotion, peace building, reconstruction, and development.[19] Indeed, the familiar scenario in which civil functions are gradually replaced by various forms of long-term humanitarian governance has led many critics to comment on the ways in which the discourse of humanitarianism can pave the way for states of emergency to become permanent, with the exception becoming the norm.[20]

Some of the most scathing contemporary critiques of humanitarian intervention focus on its politics of life and the reduced, limited form of humanity to which it is committed. There is now a growing consensus that the ostensibly "apolitical" humanitarian view of life is inherently and insidiously political: Agamben argues that the humanitarian gaze at humanity in the abstract, outside of its political forms and contexts, reinforces the false distinction between bare life (*zoë*) and the realm of politics (*bios*) that is the originary basis of sovereign power, thereby confirming the complicity of humanitarianism with the very form of political power to which it is theoretically opposed.[21] Fassin adds that the practice of humanitarian intervention reinscribes the distinction between the valuable lives of humanitarian agents and the dispensable lives of the populations among whom they intervene at multiple levels: (1) the discourse of risk assessment surrounding intervention implicitly distinguishes between political lives that may be risked (humanitarian agents) and abject lives that may be sacrificed (humanitarian victims); (2) expatriate humanitarian workers are systematically privileged over local employees in terms of decision making, medical coverage, remuneration, political protection, and institutional immunity (a schism that is confirmed by the convention of referring to expatriate workers as "volunteers," while local workers are regarded as mere paid employees; the suggestion is that expatriate workers willingly risk their lives in disaster zones, while local workers don't have this choice); and (3) as spokespersons for the local population, humanitarian agents represent their testimony to the broader public—this practice of "bearing witness" effectively turns humanitarian victims into objects who are spoken about in the third person, and removes them from the intersubjective dialogue between humanitarian agents and audiences.[22]

Fassin believes that the humanitarian practice of bearing witness reinforces the depoliticized view of humanity that drives humanitarian intervention: he points out that oppressed populations often shape their testimony to conform with the reductive humanitarian vision of their victimhood as a way of securing the sympathies of their humanitarian advocates.[23] Others, like Thomas Keenan, take a different view of such testimonial acts. Keenan argues that, far from evidencing the foreclosure of politics occasioned by the collusion of humanitarian and sovereign power, these speech acts indicate the possible political openings enabled by the simultaneous merger taking place between humanitarianism and human rights. Keenan views testimony of the kind described by Fassin as human rights claims, or speculative speech acts in which the dispossessed urgently mimic, repeat, or quote the testimonial codes of hegemonic speech acts with the aim of gaining political recognition. Even if the forms of political access gained from these acts are limited in practice, Keenan argues that they demonstrate a radical principle: that politics can begin only with the withdrawal of foundations such as identity, citizenship, or subjectivity. Human rights speech acts demonstrate that the right to define humanity does not belong to any one sovereign agency; rather, it can be claimed or declared by anyone, including those "mere" human beings who are thought to be devoid of political standing. Thus, human rights assert that the "human," as a placeholder for the aporia of politics, does not preexist the act of being called into being or claimed.[24]

Tele Geto, I would argue, has been celebrated as such a human rights speech act—one that confirms the radical political potential of states of emergency. By imitating the behavior of the humanitarian volunteer bearing witness to disaster, rather than playing the part of the victim, these youths would seem to performatively call forth precisely the political agency to which they are denied access under the conditions of the humanitarian emergency, asserting in the process that the right to this agency can be claimed by anyone. However, a more complex and disturbing picture begins to emerge when we pay attention to the mediatized forms of speech that Tele Geto mobilize as a human rights claim. In a discursive context in which the hegemonic grammar of human rights claims is often subtended by catastrophic events, the risks and benefits of Tele Geto's mimicry of humanitarian agents need to be assessed in relation to the formal codes of testimony of the humanitarian emergency, as the most urgent and deadly of catastrophes.

The Live Eyewitness as Performance and Index

Of the testimonial codes of emergency, none is more relevant to Tele Geto's mimicry than that of the live eyewitness. I now examine the changing role of the eyewitness in a medial context where the vulnerable body represents one of the last refuges of authenticity or referentiality for live media. Using Mary Ann Doane's analysis of NBC's coverage of the *Challenger* explosion in 1986 as a counterexample, I look at Anderson Cooper's live reporting for CNN during Hurricane Katrina as an illustration of how the humanitarian optic of bare life has inspired and renewed the televisual discourse of catastrophe. The changing function of the eyewitness as a testimonial code of liveness is emblematic of these shifts: traditionally a signifier of television's presence at the scene of disaster, and hence its capacity to "cover" and contain the threat, the live eyewitness has a new significance in the context of the humanitarian emergency as an index of bare, exposed life whose agential performance of presence disavows the political incapacitation of being exposed to death. I pay particular attention to the interplay between these referential and performative elements in Cooper's eyewitness reports. I argue that Cooper's decision to "weather the storm" along with hurricane victims, coupled with CNN's call to Katrina survivors to emulate Cooper as "citizen journalists," provided a way to exploit the spectacle of bare life while disavowing the differing levels of risk faced by disaster victims and professional media personalities, who, like humanitarian agents, "volunteer" to risk their lives in disaster zones.

Liveness—the technical capacity to capture and broadcast distant events as they unfold in real time—has been famously described by Jane Feuer as television's defining claim and ideological problematic.[25] The allure of liveness has to do with the possibility of spontaneity and contingency. Even though live telecasts are inevitably editorialized and narrativized (through conventions like the instant replay, analytical editing, the introduction of canned elements, etc., all of which are made possible through a brief tape delay), the promise of the unfolding present inheres in the suggestion that we might encounter what lies beyond the control of mediation. As a discourse regarding unmediatedness, liveness is frequently signified through supplementary mediation (for instance, the icon "LIVE" in television news). The realism of liveness is of a documentary order: it relies on the spectator's faith in the credibility of what is told rather than what is shown. To restate these insights somewhat differently, we might say that the televisual discourse of liveness partakes of the documentary logic of immediation, in that the promised contact with the real time of the present can nevertheless be achieved only through mediation.

Catastrophe, Doane argues, is implicated in the political economy of television at a fundamental level; as the "ultimate drama of the instantaneous," catastrophe offers a unique opportunity to authenticate television's claim to liveness, that is, its discourse of immediation.[26] Doane analyzes NBC's coverage of the *Challenger* explosion in 1986, which was broadcast live by CNN, as an example of how the "catastrophic" nature of the event was conveyed through the suspension or negation of the conventional forms of televisual mediation. Even though the scale of the disaster did not match those of recent wars, in terms of body count, it was nonetheless coded as catastrophic by the suspension of television's regularly scheduled commercial programming and, just as important, by the interruption in the ordinarily controlled, scripted, and poised speech of the news anchor, Tom Brokaw. Doane elaborates, "The 'liveness,' the 'real time' of the catastrophe is that of the television anchor's discourse—its nonstop quality a part of a fascination which is linked to the spectator's knowledge that Brokaw faces him/her without a complete script, underlining the alleged authenticity of his discourse."[27] The television anchor's discourse routinely invokes a *sensation* of liveness even when the news is not technically live: as Margaret Morse notes, the anchor's direct address to the audience, and the use of shifters relating to the present instance of discourse (*I, you, here, now*), borrows from the conventions of face-to-face communication to produce an impression of shared space and time.[28] The heightened liveness of catastrophe is additionally signified, as Doane notes above, by the unanchoring of the anchor's conventional modes of discourse: as a case in point, the disruptive impacts of the *Challenger* explosion were indexed by the improvisational, emotional, and stumbling address of the usually unruffled Brokaw, as he attempted to make sense of the space shuttle's destruction for his traumatized audience.

The fascination of catastrophe, Doane argues, and the reason it remains profitable for television and compelling for its audiences, lies in the interplay of referential and dramatic elements, implied in the etymology of the word *catastrophe*. Traceable to the Greek *kata* (over) and *strephein* (turn), that is, "to overturn," *catastrophe* not only implies sudden and tragic misfortune or death but also has its roots in the Greek tragic tradition, referring to the final event in a drama.[29] The televisual discourse of catastrophe alternates between traumatic immediations that authenticate the medium's claim to liveness, and compensatory forms of mediation that stave off the abstract threat posed by catastrophe to the discourse of technological control and, more locally, to television's commodified scheduling of time. Doane identifies three such compensatory mediations in NBC's coverage of the *Challenger* explosion: (1) the anchor's role in locating the event, however traumatic, in a reassuring master narrative of progress and national unity; (2) fetishistic displays of the latest technology in the form of video replays, maps, diagrams, forecasts, and animated simulations that attempt to master the traumatic event; and (3) eyewitness accounts that attest to television's presence at the scene of disaster and thus its ability to cover the event.[30]

Cooper's on-location coverage of Hurricane Katrina for CNN in 2005, which has been widely hailed as the advent of a new era of "unanchored" or "raw" catastrophe reporting, offers compelling insights into the changing poetics of liveness twenty years after the events analyzed by Doane. Cooper's frequent breaches of journalistic decorum, Jonathan Van Meter argues, marked "a fork in the road for the future of broadcast journalism": while the stolid affect of NBC's Brian Williams channeled an older era of anchors like Brokaw and Dan Rather, whose reassuring air of authority soothed previous generations of catastrophe spectators, Cooper's "raw emotion [and] honest humanity . . . removed the filter."[31] Steve Classen cites Cooper's success as an example of how "some of the most emotional, confrontational and 'out of control' journalists effectively advanced their careers via their 'wild' and provocative performances in the early hours of Katrina coverage."[32] Cooper's impassioned outbursts of rage against government officials during live transmissions from affected areas of the Gulf Coast earned him a reputation as America's favorite "emo-anchor," and his highly physical mode of crisis reporting was described by the then president of CNN, Jonathan Klein, as being "about visceral experience" rather than "cerebral analysis."[33]

Cooper's early coverage of Katrina for CNN demonstrates how the exhausted televisual discourse of catastrophe finds renewed inspiration in the humanitarian emergency. Cooper's "out-of-control" reporting is symptomatic, I argue, of the representational challenges of an era in which the suspension of television's medial conventions—once a reliable signifier of immediacy or liveness—has itself become a canned convention that is routinely exploited to suffuse other television genres (the local news, the weather, etc.) with the charge of referentiality that was once reserved for catastrophe. If catastrophe is, at a metaphorical level, always about a confrontation with death, then the humanitarian emergency makes this confrontation literal, by capturing life at the brink of its obliteration, often at a large and graphic scale. The live telecast from the Gulf Coast as Katrina made landfall exemplifies how the humanitarian emergency, as the most deadly of catastrophes, gives rise to a new language of liveness inspired by bare life—that is, life exposed to destruction.

I focus below on the August 29, 2005, edition of CNN's *American Morning*, which featured a live feed of Cooper reporting from Baton Rouge. This broadcast is remarkable not for the informational content provided by the on-location correspondents or their high-tech machinery—in fact, the "information" consists mainly of illegible images and inaudible words—but for the way the anchor turns the shortcomings of the live feed into documentary evidence of lives at risk. Here, the anchor's discourse, the high-tech visualization, and the eyewitness body function as indices of bare life. Whereas these compensatory mediations once signified television's capacity to cover the scene of the catastrophe, and thereby contain its threat, they are used here as direct proof of the deadly impact of the storm. I pay particular attention to Cooper's highly physical performance of the role of live eyewitness. The vulnerable-but-still-alive eyewitness body, I propose, is a troubling testimonial code of the humanitarian emergency as a live media event—one that channels the actual vulnerability of disaster victims as a way of penetrating through the exhausted, canned tropes of catastrophe. This is an example of what Barbie Zelizer calls the "about-to-die" image, one whose piercing of the visual frame offsets the predictability and lack of surprise associated with images of death, and permits a renewed confrontation with the threat associated with catastrophe.[34]

The August 29, 2005, edition of *American Morning* consists of reports from Cooper and numerous other correspondents and affiliates stationed along the Gulf Coast (including John Zarrella, Gary Tuchman, and Jeanne Meserve), woven into an ongoing consultation between CNN anchor Daryn Kagan and meteorologist Chad Myers. The stated purpose, in Kagan's words, was to provide residents and evacuees "in harm's way" with up-to-date information about the hurricane's path and conditions on the ground.[35] Myers and Kagan, who are stationed at a remove from the site of the hurricane, trade off in extolling the advanced sophistication of CNN's satellite and on-site weather-tracking technologies relative to its peer networks. Myers cites CNN's use of the cutting-edge VIPIR imaging system to provide three-dimensional digital simulations and forecasts of the storm's predicted trajectory, while Kagan explains the sophisticated file-transfer protocols employed in CNN's mobile live-casting unit, "Hurricane One."[36]

However, even as Kagan insists that Hurricane One's "amazing technology" enables CNN to retrieve "pictures and images even from places where we can't get a satellite truck in," the live video footage broadcast from Baton Rouge, downtown New Orleans, and Gulfport offers little support for her claims.[37] All three feeds feature barely discernible cityscapes behind a cloudy barricade of falling rain, with an audio track similarly consisting of a wall of static through which the local correspondents struggle to be heard. Attempts at obtaining synced audio and video footage of CNN's on-location correspondents are similarly frustrated: Zarrella is only able to join in by telephone, and Kagan initially fails to establish a connection with Meserve, who later appears only from within the relatively safe confines of the Superdome.

Undeterred, Kagan hastens to add that the paucity of eyewitness visuals available to complement Myers's VIPIR maps and forecasts is not evidence of technological failure but rather of the fact that, in Myers's words, "there's literally nothing to see."[38] Thus, in CNN's own discourse, liveness resides not in the technological capacity to overcome the poor visibility on the ground but in the vulnerability of the machinery, which indexes the unmediated "power of mother nature."[39] These impoverished images and sounds do not exist to provide any actual informational content—their value lies instead in their role as second-order signs that signify "exposure to death." The blindness of the visual signifies the seriousness of the storm, which reduces everyone and everything to the status of bare life devoid of speech, vision, or protection. Along with Kagan's frequent references to the challenges faced by CNN's

FIGURE 2.3 Still from CNN's *American Morning* (August 29, 2005)

heroic reporters owing to communications failures all along the Gulf Coast, these obscure images become a testimonial to the network's commitment to live coverage at any cost.

The vulnerable body of the live eyewitness reporter is the most potent of these signs. Nowhere is this more apparent than when Kagan finally brings in "the man himself, Anderson [Cooper]," anxiously adding, "Take it away, but don't go away . . . or blow away."[40] Perched precariously on the edge of a pier in Baton Rouge, and facing directly into 120 mile-per-hour winds (described in graphic detail by Myers immediately before Cooper's appearance), Cooper's body functions as a barometer of some of the severest weather conditions documented live during Katrina. Apologizing for his uncharacteristic disarray, with a reddened face and blinking eyes that are barely protected from the torrential weather by his thin orange CNN Windbreaker, Cooper explains, "It's very hard to look in this direction. The wind—the rain—is just coming horizontally, and it's like pinpricks in your face as you try to turn north and look into the wind."[41] The content of Cooper's testimony contains little information of actual import regarding the conditions on the ground in Baton Rouge. His words are a banal and repetitive description of what little he can see: discarded ice chests bobbing in the water, an unanchored barge moving dangerously fast toward the shore, a broken crane colliding repeatedly with the pier. He repeatedly emphasizes how little he can see, given the poor visibility at the scene.

The real impact of the scene comes from Cooper's barely audible words, the palpable panic in his speech, and, most of all, his embodied and verbal demonstrations of physical discomfort. Another scene later in the same broadcast features correspondent Kareen Wynter being batted about by the wind for over two minutes. Wynter falls more than once and assures the camera, "Yes, I'm fine," each time she is dragged to her feet by her crew. The exaggerated drama of this live spectacle invokes the staged amateur reality show, in which the disaster is set up from the start. The anchor steps in here to keep it from teetering over the edge from reality into comedy, reminding the audience of the appropriate response: when we cut back to Kagan in the studio, she glowingly reports, "That is our Kareen Wynter. A strong, dedicated reporter, a great young woman. And you didn't hear one bit of whining out of her. And thanks to her crew for holding on to her so that she didn't blow away."[42]

What lingers in public memory is not the physical comedy but the personal sacrifice of these brave patriots. Cooper's live report from Baton Rouge has pride of place in his memoir of Katrina, the bulk of which is devoted to graphic descriptions of the physical strains of weathering the storm. He writes:

At the height of Katrina, I'm holding on to the railing of a pier, surrounded by a whirling wall of white. . . . The storm is a phantom, rearing, retreating, charging. It spins and slaps, pirouettes and punishes. I'm submerged in water, corseted by the air. . . . I've felt the tug. A few more steps and I'd be gone. Crushed by the wall of water and wind. It's that close. I can feel it. . . . By noon the worst of it is over. . . . Face scrubbed raw, whipped for hours by the elements, eyes itching, I long for sleep.[43]

Cooper's devotion to the motions of reporting from the scene despite being all but incapacitated indicates that the testimonial efficacy of the eyewitness to the humanitarian emergency combines the performance of presence with the duration of real time. The vulnerable eyewitness body fleshes out our sense of liveness: it is the close-up that tethers the technically live but abstract establishing shot of the satellite or radar image in the real. This is why the trope of the "reporter in the rain" has become such a standard accompaniment to high-tech satellite visuals in contemporary weather reports: the algorithmic claim to indexicality needs confirmation from a documentary image whose palpable authenticity strips away every appearance of mediation. As Marita Sturken puts it in her recent analysis of the Weather Channel: "In the increasingly technologized story of the weather, the weather reporter remains a crucial human element. The physical body of the on-site weather news reporter must by convention be subject in uncomfortable ways to the weather. Hence, while the 'real' information about the weather and its impact may be coming from satellite images and helicopter news footage, the signification of the real seems to demand a surrogate body that can feel and speak the weather corporeally."[44]

At the same time, even as the limits of Cooper's endurance ground the abstract horror of the humanitarian emergency in a concrete body, they also represent the limit of the live feed that guarantees CNN's competitive edge. Physical risk to Cooper implies a potential financial loss for the television network, and the loss of an icon for audiences in the United States and beyond. This became eminently clear in February 2011, after attacks on Cooper and his crew by supporters of the soon-to-be-deposed Egyptian president Hosni Mubarak resulted in Cooper being relieved of his assignment in Cairo. As talk show host Jon Stewart pointed out in his ironic commentary on the event ("All right, Hosni, now you've gone too far! Hands off Anderson Cooper! There is not to be a silvery wisp out of place on that man's glorious head!"), Cooper's eyewitness reportage is made possible by powerful legal, economic, and geopolitical apparatuses that also ensure his privileged social position.[45] Stewart's satire teases out the theatrical dimensions of live reportage that are inevitably obscured by its documentary aura of high seriousness.

These anecdotes make clear that the impression of "raw" documentary immediacy associated with the humanitarian live media event is in fact a highly artificial effect produced by placing the reporter in the middle of the storm, wherein television produces the real situation of disaster victims as a coded drama. Cooper's decision to "weather the storm" aligns him with Gulf Coast residents who did not evacuate, but this identification effaces his relative invulnerability in comparison with those for whom evacuation represented a luxury out of reach, and not a choice. The emphatically visible physical threat to Cooper and other correspondents during their on-location reports conveyed a shared sense of vulnerability, allowing an inclusive nationalist message to prevail: "We are all in this together." Meanwhile, the civic imperatives

FIGURE 2.4 Still from CNN's *American Morning* (August 29, 2005)

of this spirit of commonality were extended outward to the (predominantly poor and black) hurricane victims watching CNN's telecast who did not evacuate, with Kagan periodically issuing the following missive: "If you live in an area impacted by Hurricane Katrina, we're encouraging you, if you're able to, to e-mail us your photos and video and become one of CNN's citizen journalists. You can do that by logging on to cnn.com/stories. Please include your name, location, phone number. Your safety, of course, is of utmost importance. So, please, don't put yourself in harm's way"[46]

The television network's unremitting appetite for live material was disguised here as an appeal to the patriotic sentiments of its most marginalized viewers. This sentimental call to participate directly in what Daniel Dayan and Elihu Katz call the "nationalistic mass ceremony" of the live media event glosses over the fact that exposure to environmental risk is thoroughly striated by race, class, and other categories of structural marginalization.[47] The exploitative nature of this appeal was set in relief, however, at other moments during the broadcast, where CNN reporters repeatedly referred to residents seeking shelter from the storm locally as "refugees," or citizens denied the political protections of citizenship.[48]

The hailing of hurricane victims as active agents bearing witness to their own predicament rather than as passive victims indicates how the humanitarian live media event blends the temporal modes of catastrophe and crisis. Whereas catastrophe is a "subject-less," abstract discourse of instantaneous and punctual timing, Doane describes crisis as "an event of some duration which is startling and momentous precisely because it demands resolution within a limited period of time. Etymologically, crisis stems from the Greek *krisis*, or decision, and hence always seems to suggest the necessity of human agency."[49] That the agency in question was attributed by CNN to hurricane victims as documentary producers and users of *digital* media, and not just television viewers, recalls Wendy Hui Kyong Chun's argument that moments of crisis provide opportunities to distinguish the liveness of new media technologies in relation to older media such as television. If televisual catastrophe promises reference, or a possibility of touching the real, then, Chun argues, the allure of new media is that of intervening in the real as an "empowered user" rather than passively "watching" events take place. She elaborates, "Crises—moments that demand real time response—make new media valuable and empowering by tying certain information to a decision, personal or political (in this sense, new media also personalizes crises)."[50] "Crisis promises to take us out of normal time, not by referencing the real but rather by indexing real time, by touching a time that touches a real, different time: a time of real decision, a time of our lives."[51]

The real time of the humanitarian emergency, which is shot through with the literal significance of human lives hanging in the balance, provides an opportunity like none other to affirm the participatory, interventionist capacity of new "personal" media technologies. What is crucial to note about the narrative of crisis, as it played out in CNN's coverage of Hurricane Katrina, is the way in which the discourse of participatory documentary was used to hail hurricane victims as humanitarian volunteers ("citizen journalists") intervening in their own fate. In the following section, I examine the implications of this narrative through a reading of the film *Trouble the Water* (2008), directed by a pair of Caucasian filmmakers from New York whose fame derives from the film's incorporation of several minutes of live camcorder footage of the storm obtained at considerable risk by Kimberly Rivers Roberts, an African American Katrina survivor from the economically depressed Lower Ninth Ward of New Orleans.

I am particularly interested in how Lessin and Deal's treatment of Roberts's eyewitness footage affirms the critical and empowering role of participatory media during crises. I argue that Lessin and Deal's insistence on the immediacy of Roberts's "live and direct" missives from the disaster zone in relation to mainstream television coverage of Katrina fails to recognize her ambivalent performance of the role of live eyewitness reporter. Robert's performance of "bare liveness" can be understood, I propose, as a cynical spectacularization of her own vulnerability in conjunction with the testimonial codes of the humanitarian emergency, in a desperate bid for survival. Lessin and Deal's misrecognition of Roberts's performance of agency as actual agency effaces the compromising testimonial forms that mediate humanitarian recognition and ends up exploiting rather than remedying Roberts's vulnerable position.

Bare Liveness

Trouble the Water stages a critique of the U.S. government's abandonment of the poor black citizens of New Orleans during and after Hurricane Katrina, many of whom were, as Lessin and Deal point out, relegated to the position of refugees in the absence of effective governmental and nongovernmental assistance—without homes or papers, and therefore without evidence of their "right to return," to cite the film's oft-repeated message. Whereas a film like Spike Lee's *When the Levees Broke* (2006) develops a scalar argument connecting the large-scale displacement of low-income residents across the Gulf Coast following Katrina with the patterns of neoliberal disaster management and privatization, Lessin and Deal's film individualizes this narrative through the story of its protagonist, Kimberly Roberts, and her husband, Scott, tracing their displacement to relatives' homes in Memphis, Tennessee, and Houston, Texas, and their struggle to return home to New Orleans amid a variety of bureaucratic obstacles. Within the narrative logic of *Trouble the Water*, Roberts's camcorder footage of the storm functions in an evidentiary capacity: in the face of her dispossession, Roberts's agential decision to "weather the storm" as an eyewitness reporter becomes proof of and justification for her right to return.

Lessin and Deal operate as humanitarian agents bearing witness to Roberts's testimony: they leverage Roberts's eyewitness video—the film within their film—as a convincing human rights claim by bringing it to a sympathetic audience and framing it in a manner that amplifies its credibility. They do so, I argue, by contrasting the unmediated or bare liveness of Roberts's footage with the televisual performance of liveness, which only promises the brush with death that Roberts's footage actually delivers. *Trouble the Water* positions Roberts as an "un-anchor" of sorts, whose credibility as a survivor of the storm authorizes her to narrate the true story of Katrina. The film thereby draws on televisual strategies of immediation to distinguish its own truth-value relative to the mainstream news. My analysis focuses on how Roberts cynically performs the role of eyewitness reporter as a means of enhancing the exchange value of her eyewitness footage, as well as her own credibility as a local media personality. I argue that Lessin and Deal's well-meaning framing of Roberts's footage as a raw, unfiltered document covers over Roberts's subtle critique of the compromising testimonial codes of the humanitarian emergency that she must perform to earn the support of her humanitarian advocates.

If there is a central immediation on which *Trouble the Water* is founded, it has to do with the expurgation from the diegetic frame of the film of the mutually beneficial transaction between the Roberts and the filmmakers. This collaboration has yielded returns for both parties: *Trouble the Water* has won multiple major documentary awards, including Grand Jury Awards in 2008 at both the Sundance Film Festival and the Full Frame Documentary Film Festival, as well as Oscar and Emmy nominations, while Kimberly and Scott Roberts have successfully used the film as a platform for establishing a record label, Born Hustler Records, which has in turn launched Kimberly's career as a rap artist.[52] In addition to Kimberly's music, the website for Born Hustler Records also advertises a clothing line designed by her, as well as her work as a filmmaker. In press releases and interviews, Scott and Kimberly report that they premeditatedly approached Lessin and Deal and their crew when they converged at a Red Cross shelter in Alexandria, Louisiana, two weeks after the storm. Scott explains that he and Kimberly recognized in the film crew, who happened to be passing through after a failed attempt to make a film on the return of Louisiana's National Guard from Iraq, an opportunity to "get that story out."[53] Scott's backstory makes it possible to see the introductory sequence of the film in which we first encounter the protagonists—an impromptu scene shot at the Red Cross shelter—as a complex transaction in which Kimberly appeals simultaneously to the humanitarian and entrepreneurial sentiments of the documentary filmmakers by offering them a chance to bear witness to a unique testimonial commodity. Facing the documentarians' camera, Kimberly differentiates herself and her husband from the scores of other survivors assembled at the shelter by emphasizing the uniqueness of the footage that she shot during the storm on her $20 store-bought Hi8 camcorder, exclaiming, "All the footage I seen on TV, nobody ain't got what I got. I've got right there *in* the hurricane. . . . But I ain't gonna give it to nobody local, y'know, for them to mess around with. This needs to be worldwide!"[54] It is clear, from the very start of the film, that its protagonists are well versed in the logic of disposability that drives television catastrophe coverage, and presumably skeptical of the exploitative call for citizen journalists that was periodically issued by CNN and other news networks. Kimberly is fully aware of the commodity value of her camcorder eyewitness footage, and her reluctance to turn this footage over to the local news suggests her wariness of compounding her existing economic disadvantage by being transformed into a stock supplier of generic information.

In exchange for the public platform of their film, Kimberly stands in for Lessin and Deal, the film's invisible narrators, as the enunciator of the film's discourse. Her enunciative presence in the film has been described by Janet Walker as an "autobiographical" form of "situated testimony"—a geographically grounded mode of bearing witness that "realizes the materiality of testimony in the power of place."[55] I would argue that Kimberly can alternately be seen as a "news anchor" whose grounding in the local lends credibility to the film's discourse. Morse writes that television news derives its credibility in large part from the coded sincerity, stability, and trustworthiness of the news anchor. Traditionally male and white, network news anchors must emanate "patriarchal authority and middle-aged accessibility"; anchors of other genders, races, and sexuality either aspire to this conservative norm or are relegated to the morning and nightly news.[56]

For Lessin and Deal, Kimberly's credibility derives from her *departure* from this norm as a black, female Katrina survivor from a particularly impoverished neighborhood of New Orleans. Just as the television news anchor reserves the authority to speak directly to the audience, and authorizes others to do so through a shift of their gaze, Kimberly's is the gaze that mediates our look at *Trouble the Water*'s representations of Katrina. As we continually return to Kimberly, her discursive and corporeal presence mediates and coheres together the disparate elements of the film, which moves between recorded television broadcasts of the storm, Kimberly's eyewitness footage, and "walking testimonials" in which Kimberly and Scott are shown returning to

FIGURE 2.5 Still from opening sequence of *Trouble the Water* by Tia Lessin and Carl Deal (2008)

their devastated neighborhood after the storm, as well as retracing their eventual path of self-evacuation.

In the opening credit sequence of the film, Lessin and Deal take pains to distinguish the credibility of Kimberly's perspective as a survivor of the storm in comparison with the "outsider" perspective of mainstream news outlets. In this opening montage, the filmmakers stitch together their own flow of silent vignettes from the documentary, set to cacophonous audio samples drawn from television and radio coverage of the storm and its immediate aftermath. The slow-motion footage of these silent black faces (those of the film's protagonists, as well as those of their neighbors and other survivors) gains a certain austere sincerity in the midst of the audible confusion; the pensive background music claims for the film a position of calm at the heart of the storm, which is also the discursive storm of the humanitarian live media event. This sequence is notable because Lessin and Deal mirror Kimberly's own strategy of drawing on television's centrality to the spectator's experience of catastrophe in order to distinguish the sobriety and immediacy of their film—as Deal emphasizes in interviews, conveying the "immediate" nature of Kimberly's eyewitness testimony was a priority that led their filmmaking.[57]

This obviously produced and, indeed, highly televisual effect of immediacy serves, as the film proceeds, to emphasize the constative or indexical quality of Kimberly's eyewitness footage in contrast to the empty performatives of televisual speech. The difficulty with this strategy, however, is that the credibility, and hence the value, of this footage rests on Kimberly's capacity to perform the testimonial codes of liveness, which, as I have previously argued, combine the performance of presence with the endurance of the real time of the event. When we first cut to Kimberly's approximately fifteen minutes' worth of documentary video of the day before and the morning of the hurricane, her enterprising stance regarding the televisual sources of credibility of this testimony is unmistakable, as she vernacularizes the behavior of the eyewitness reporter in order to mark her vulnerability—and therefore her credibility—as someone who was unable to evacuate.

Training the camera on the television in her living room, which is tuned to the Weather Channel, Kimberly pans away to focus on herself and her home, pets, and neighborhood. She imitates the stance of a television reporter, stating the date ("August 28, 2005"), location, and purpose of her "report," if only to distinguish her own intimate, handheld vérité-style coverage as the "real deal" compared to "what you see on TV," assuring, "You know me, it's still me, Kimberly Rivers, breaking it down for the '05 documentary, how it *really* is, starting right now." As she continues her commentary, she turns her own inability to evacuate (as she explains to her neighbors, "If I had wheels, I'd be leaving too") into a source of journalistic authority, announcing, "I ain't going nowhere, I'm gonna be right here to give y'all this live and direct footage of this thing when it go down." At the same time, when she jokes with friends down the block that "if I get some exciting shit, maybe I can sell it to the white folks," she unabashedly acknowledges that the situated, live quality of her testimony is authenticated by the racial and class difference visibly marked on her body and those of her Ninth Ward neighbors, as well as in her accented vocal delivery.

When the hurricane finally makes its landfall, Kimberly finds it less easy to distance herself from the threat of imminent death by assuming the avatar of the eyewitness reporter. She strains under the pressure of performing her eyewitness status, or what Doane describes as the televisual demand for "presence in space."[58] As the storm gains in intensity, driving Kimberly, Scott, and a few neighbors seeking shelter to the upper levels and finally into the attic of their home, her authorial voice becomes melancholy, panicked, and fatalistically calm by turns. Her commentary shifts from ironic critique to affirmations of spiritual faith as she realizes there is nowhere left to escape to.[59]

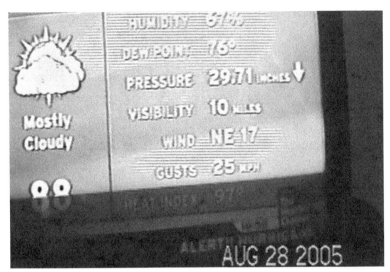

FIGURE 2.6 Still from Kimberly Roberts's video footage in *Trouble the Water* by Tia Lessin and Carl Deal (2008)

FIGURE 2.7 Still from Kimberly Roberts's video footage in *Trouble the Water* by Tia Lessin and Carl Deal (2008)

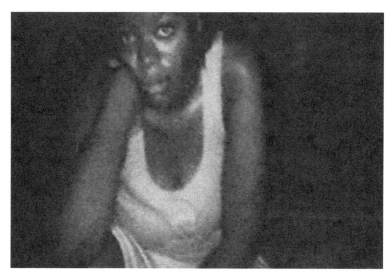

FIGURE 2.8 Still from Kimberly Roberts's video footage in *Trouble the Water* by Tia Lessin and Carl Deal (2008)

FIGURE 2.9 Still from Kimberly Roberts's video footage in *Trouble the Water* by Tia Lessin and Carl Deal (2008)

Still, Kimberly keeps up the show of describing the scene for the camera, seemingly as much to elevate the spirits of her small group—a confirmation that they are alive—as to maintain the perpetual stream of vocal commentary expected of the television reporter. She is also cognizant of the need to provide visual proof of her endurance over time, in order to back up her claim and status as an authentic eyewitness. Over the course of the seven-minute-long attic sequence, she repeatedly alternates between close-ups of her fellow survivors' distraught faces and a stop sign on the deluged street outside, framed by the sole attic window. This stop sign appears in three different shots, as an index of the rising water (as well as the only point of view available to Kimberly from her place of refuge) but, perhaps more important, as a sign of rising urgency—a marker of time slipping away.

Lessin and Deal cross-cut between Kimberly's footage and excerpts from television coverage of the storm—from Mayor Ray Nagin's announcement of mandatory evacuation, to footage of the Superdome, where evacuees were told to gather, to aerial images of the levees breaking—and an interview with Michael D. Brown, the director of the Federal Emergency Management Agency (FEMA). In addition to establishing a timeline for Kimberly's footage, this editorial tactic also has the effect of emphasizing the unmediated reality—the bare liveness—of her eyewitness video in comparison with the performative excesses of the televisual tropes of liveness. Intercut between George Bush's live presidential address to the nation from a resort in Arizona and broadcast footage of an unnamed television news correspondent theatrically throwing various objects (including his own body) to the gale to illustrate the strength of the hurricane-force winds, before being rescued by his waiting crew, the tense final moments of Kimberly's footage in the attic function in relation to the former images in a manner analogous to the body of the weather reporter in relation to satellite images of the weather: her unmediated exposure to death, that is, her bare life, guarantees the referentiality of the vulnerable-but-still-alive body that the professional media volunteer only performs as a coded spectacle of liveness.

When Kimberly worries out loud toward the end of her recorded footage that she's "running out of juice" for her camera, she correctly identifies the direct connection between her ability to provide a document of enduring the storm and her ability to endure the aftermath of the storm. In this moment, before technology fails her—mere minutes before a friend fortuitously arrives with an inflated punching bag to rescue the group in a dramatic ending

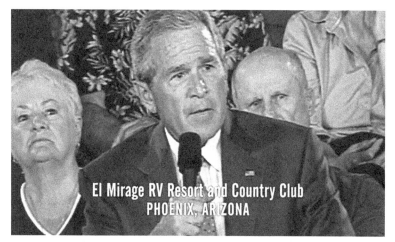

FIGURE 2.10 Still from *Trouble the Water* by Tia Lessin and Carl Deal (2008)

FIGURE 2.11 Still from *Trouble the Water* by Tia Lessin and Carl Deal (2008)

that is only partially captured on tape—we realize the profoundly postmodern conundrum facing Kimberly. For someone in her precarious position, the failure of a link to the discursive reality that is the media, the cutting off of the medium of the live humanitarian appeal, can be the real disaster. By locating the value of such a troubling document in its unmediatedness, Lessin and Deal well-meaningly enact what is perhaps the most dangerous mediation of all: far from challenging the testimonial codes of the humanitarian emergency, they intensify their insistence on referentiality, reinforcing a racialized discourse of catastrophe in which black bodies at risk represent the ultimate live spectacle. Kimberly's subtle and ambivalent performance of the role of live eyewitness is rendered by Lessin and Deal as a drama of "real" versus "fake," so that her footage functions as a device to puncture the falsehoods of the mainstream media and the governmental apparatus that the latter is shown to prop up.

In a way, it would seem as though Lessin and Deal have bought into Kimberly's performance of liveness: they interpret her decision to film the storm as proof of the capacity of participatory media to "empower" dispossessed individuals to insist on their rights and to intervene on their own behalf. This is also the overt message of Kimberly's musical track "Amazing," which is featured in the film as an impromptu performance by Kimberly as her rap avatar, Kold Madina. This sequence captures her improvising an impassioned rendition of her song, an autobiographical journey through the impossible odds she has faced and survived throughout her life (Kimberly sings that she started life as "a little girl caught up in the storm"), culminating in Katrina. This bravura performance contains the "money shot" of Lessin and Deal's film. Kimberly reveals in the song that as a teenager, she made the papers for slashing a man's face with a knife—a man she later fell in love with and married. The filmmakers cut to Scott's scarred face before returning to Kimberly's performance. This incident is never mentioned again because the subtle editing says what is needed: love conquers all.

The words of Kimberly's song are organized around the refrain "I don't need you to tell me that I'm amazing." Kimberly explains that she wrote "Amazing" when she was depressed, and she performs the song now to lift her spirits after the funeral of her beloved grandmother, who helped her to survive a childhood of poverty, crime, and drug addiction. The mise-en-scène of the performance, a dingy room with peeling paint in Kimberly's uncle's home in Houston in which she, Scott, and their friend Brian (another recovering addict) are huddled, and its sobering context—her grandmother has died during Katrina, and the family has struggled for weeks to retrieve her body and to arrange for Kimberly's brother to be released from prison to attend the funeral—confess to the anguish beneath Kimberly's bravado. Kimberly needs to perform what Lauren Berlant calls "cruel optimism" in order to motivate herself to survive, even as she recognizes that her attachment to self-reliance is killing her slowly.[60] It is this song's cruel optimism, not the desperation it barely conceals, that is mirrored in the narrative arc of *Trouble the Water*, which concludes with the Roberts' return home to New Orleans after a Sisyphean battle with a failed bureaucracy: both insist on the resilience of individuals who have been abandoned by the state, as well as their capacity to speak for and rescue themselves despite being neglected by the mainstream media.

We may say that *Trouble the Water* is founded on a basic misrecognition. Lessin and Deal recognize Kimberly's footage as a sign of agency, and thus of her political subjectivity, precisely because it is articulated in the recognizable grammar of humanitarian media volunteers who willingly and agentially risk their lives as a means of intervening in crises. They conclude on this basis that the Roberts have a right to return—a right to be recognized as citizens rather than as refugees—and that they deserve the advocacy platform of the film. The misrecognition lies in Lessin and Deal's inability to recognize how the testimonial codes of the humanitarian emergency mediate the speech acts of the dispossessed: in this case, Kimberly can assert her agency only by performing the role of live eyewitness to disaster—a role that involves voluntarily risking her life for the sake of demonstrating her vulnerability, without any of the protections granted to the professional volunteer. While the film appears to celebrate a narrative of media empowerment, it invites the most vulnerable individuals to voluntarily and even heroically assume personal risk as a means of intervening in their own fate, which illustrates with startling clarity the precise opposite: the coercive, biopolitical logic that constitutes the racist division of society into "us" and "them."

In the concluding section of this chapter, I examine how this narrative finds unexpected support in a prevalent mode of argumentation in cultural theory that positions participatory media as the catalyst of a biopolitical struggle against the increasingly common social condition of dispossession. While these debates may not at first seem related to the problematic of documentary immediacy, I will show that their investment in the political potential of exceptional political states is thoroughly bound up with the concerns that I have laid out regarding emergency, human rights, and liveness.

The Mediation of Biopolitical Emergence

Over the past two decades, a number of cultural critics have turned to the vocabulary of "biopolitics" to assess the political options available to the subjects of humanitarian emergencies. The concept of biopolitics, initially elaborated by Foucault, refers to a transformation in the strategies and techniques of power, coincident with the series of epistemic shifts that we now refer to as modernity, characterized by the entrance of "life" into the field of politics. Foucault notes the myriad ways in which private, biological functions, most prominently those related to health and sexuality, were turned into objects of administration through a series of normalizing, regulatory processes that aimed to enhance life and stave off death. He contrasts the affirmative logic of biopower, which "makes live and lets die," with sovereign power, which "makes die and lets live," but notes that racism functions as the primary rationalizing technique of biopower, introducing a caesura into the social field at those crucial moments in which decisions must be made regarding who lives and who dies.[61]

Although Foucault's account of biopolitical racism provides an astute theoretical assessment of the politics of humanitarian intervention and governance, as analyzed by Fassin as well as other scholars (Miriam Ticktin, Peter Redfield), the competing biopolitical theories of Foucault's interlocutors, Agamben and Hardt and Negri, have compelled cultural critics writing about the mediatization of contemporary humanitarian emergencies.[62] In this final section, I examine Henry Giroux's analysis of the Hurricane Katrina media event as an emblematic instance of the turn to Hardt and Negri's model of communicative biopower, a model that Giroux sees as a solution to Agamben's pessimistic view of the excommunication of depoliticized life under emergency circumstances.[63] Where Agamben envisions the humanitarian emergency as a catastrophic state that divests individuals of their political subjectivity and exposes bare life directly to sovereign power, Hardt and Negri see states of emergency as an opportunity for the emergence of a new social subject whose strength lies precisely in "the unmediated relationship between power and subjectivities."[64]

I am interested in how Hardt and Negri's emphasis on the communicative immediacy of the dispossessed—one that is articulated in relation to human rights—authorizes Giroux's advocacy of an oppositional media program aimed at the exposure of invisible black suffering. I propose that Hardt and Negri represent another version of the same problem as Agamben when it comes to Giroux's proposal to liberate black bodies from invisibility: both approaches fail to account for Foucault's argument that biopolitical racism operates through discursive liberation rather than repression. (I return to this topic in chapter 4, where I examine a similar argument regarding the emancipation of animals in captivity.) The discourse of bare liveness mobilized by Kimberly Roberts is an example of this blind spot—one that requires us to address the counterintuitive articulation of racism in relation to the testimonial codes that mediate the communicative potential of the dispossessed.

Among scholars writing about the post-Katrina media landscape, Agamben's Holocaust-based model of biopolitics, or "thanatopolitics," has provided a potent set of visual metaphors for theorizing the exclusionary racial politics of the governance of catastrophe. In a much-cited essay, Giroux coins the term *biopolitics of disposability* to describe how the merger between a racist state and the mainstream media apparatus resulted in a form of racialized neglect that operated through excommunication. During Katrina, these institutions operated in collusion, he argues, to condemn the victims of disaster, especially the poor and people of color, to the discursive "black holes" of prisons, ghettos, and media invisibility. His elaboration of this argument is worth quoting at length:

> Something more systematic and deep-rooted [than incompetence or failed national leadership] was revealed in the wake of Katrina—namely that the state no longer provided a safety net for the poor, sick, elderly, and homeless. Instead, it had been transformed into a punishing institution intent on dismantling the welfare state and treating the homeless, unemployed, illiterate and disabled as dispensable populations to be managed, criminalized, and made to disappear into prisons, ghettos, and the black hole of despair. . . . This is what I call the *new biopolitics of disposability*: the poor, especially people of color, not only have to fend for themselves in the face of life's tragedies but are also supposed to do it without being seen by the dominant society. Excommunicated from the sphere of human concern, they have been rendered invisible, utterly disposable.[65]

A few pages later, Giroux continues: "Biopower in its current shape has produced a new form of biopolitics marked by a cleansed visual and social landscape in which the poor, the elderly, the infirm, and criminalized populations all share a common fate of disappearing from public view."[66] Giroux argues here that state racism, which Foucault identifies as the main technique of bio-power, operates through "excommunication," that is, by actively cutting off certain populations from public view, as well as from the discursive reality of media. His argument directly invokes Agamben's theory of sovereign power, which Agamben describes as a form of power that renders certain lives bare by stripping away the mediating forms that give them meaning, context, and value, so that such lives can be eliminated without consequence. The rhetorical force of Giroux's critique of the "biopolitics of disposability" derives from Agamben's example of the concentration camp. The camp haunts the figurative "black hole" of the disaster zone as a visual metaphor for racial outcasting in an age of media ubiquity—a dark dungeon in which society's others may be condemned to unspeakable injustices, unrelieved by the light of public exposure.

Giroux positions the exposure of black suffering as an urgent corrective to the racist collusion of the state and mainstream media apparatus. He finds support for his remedial views in Hardt and Negri's competing analysis of communicative biopolitics. Whereas Agamben's devastating reading of bare life cut off from its media milieu offers no recourse for a humanitarian media intervention "from below," Hardt and Negri provide an appealing theoretical model that positions new media networks as the milieu and catalyst of biopolitical resistance. Inspired by Hardt and Negri's proposal to "move matters of culture, especially those aimed at 'the production of information, communication, [and] social relations[,] . . . to the center of politics itself,'" Giroux insists on the pedagogical capacity of "new media technologies [to] construct subjects differently with multiple forms of literacy that engage a range of intellectual capacities," designating these literacies as "symbolic forms and processes conducive to democratization."[67] Having thus identified the communications media as a biopolitical battlefield, Giroux celebrates the flood of media documentations of Hurricane Katrina that "broke through the visual blackout of poverty," suggesting that this revelation of the catastrophic scale of racist biopower was a means of reclaiming *bios*, or cultural and political meaning, for *zoë*, or those lives that were neglected to the point of being divested of their citizenship rights.[68]

Giroux likens these images of dead and suffering black bodies to the unedited photo of Emmett Till's mutilated body that launched the civil rights movement, insisting on their capacity to "shock and shame" the U.S. government and the international community.[69] In an extension of the racialized metaphors of light and dark in the lengthy passage quoted earlier, Giroux equates releasing black bodies from the black hole of media invisibility with a measure of social inclusion. The self-evident visibility of race marking the black bodies of the dead confirms for Giroux that the remedy lies in liberating the destitute (represented here by the darkest bodies) into the light in order to reveal the everyday marginalization of the country's poor. He accordingly proposes that the Internet, camcorders, and cell phones should be used as documentary tools of the oppressed against the "sanitized" corporate media landscape, labeling such autoethnographic uses of media as an "oppositional biopolitics" oriented toward democracy and social empowerment.[70]

Giroux's faith in the power of images to compensate for the failures of democracy is fully consistent with what Keenan calls the logic of "mobilizing shame." The discourse of "exposing dirty deeds" to the "light" of public reason is, Keenan writes, "the predominant practice of human rights organizations, and the dominant metaphor through which human rights NGOs understand their own work."[71] The shortcomings of this logic have been enumerated at length by scholars working at the intersections of public sphere theory, trauma studies, and visual culture: for instance, Keenan notes that the deployment of public embarrassment to enforce the absent conscience of malevolent states and corporations maintains an anachronistic faith in the Enlightenment power of reason and in the integrity of the conditions for public action under postmodern conditions. J. M. Bernstein has argued, furthermore, that the benefits of public exposure cannot be taken for granted in a media environment in which such exposure can further disadvantage those stripped of their human rights by eviscerating their privacy or, worse, aestheticizing its lack.[72] As a case in point, Joy Fuqua describes how the violent exposure and desecration of private spaces during Katrina was experienced by many as "inside-outing"—a form of public humiliation that became a "shaming ritual" for citizens.[73]

Giroux's argument regarding the virtues of enlightenment as a corrective for state racism also raises other complications. I need to take a detour to situate how these complications are motivated by Giroux's turn to Hardt and Negri. As previously mentioned, Hardt and Negri appeal to Giroux because, unlike Agamben, they view media and communication as the milieu and catalyst of biopolitical resistance, as opposed to a medium of excommunication.

Hardt and Negri also envision the dispossessed as the paradigmatic subject of biopolitical struggle, and, despite their immanentist philosophical leanings, many of their concrete proposals for change are articulated in the language of human rights. The purpose of my detour is to show how Hardt and Negri's inattention to the concrete testimonial codes that mediate the communicative potential of the dispossessed leads Giroux, just like Agamben, to a repressive interpretation of biopolitical racism. As a result, Giroux is unable to account for the counterintuitive, affirmative ways in which racism's mediation of the emergence of biopolitical subjects contradicts the visual hermeneutics of racialized excommunication.

The key difference of Hardt and Negri's theory of biopolitics is also the key to understanding their appeal in the context of Giroux's argument: Hardt and Negri argue that the entrance of life into the domain of politics takes place in conjunction with the emergence of media forms that exhort their users to participate, often without compensation, in new modes of communicative labor that harness and permeate bodies at the presubjective level of affects and cognition, to the point of "treating and organizing them in the totality of their activities."[74] They view "immaterial" communicative labor, which spans the production of "ideas, images, knowledges, communication, cooperation, and affective relations," as the hegemonic form of postmodern cultural production: one that is exploitative in the same degree as it is potentially revolutionary.[75] On one hand, Hardt and Negri argue that the blurring of the entrenched distinctions between private and public, leisure and work, and domination and subjection involves a thoroughgoing expropriation of productive capacities across the social field. By the same token, they argue, the new forms of knowledge, collaboration, and communication that result from immaterial production liberate the productive synergies of laboring bodies from the standardizing forces of the classical commodity cycle *and* from the traditional mediating categories of social life, such as race, class, and gender, thus potentially transforming the nature of subjectivity and the subjective conditions of relationality.

It follows, Hardt and Negri propose, that the generalized existential predicament of dispossession that marks the hegemony of immaterial labor would also enable new modes of commonality with the poor and the dispossessed, who then logically stand for universality. Throughout their work, Hardt and Negri turn to figures of dispossessed existence such as the subaltern, the migrant, the refugee, and the poor—in short, figures that Agamben might regard as emblematic of bare life, or who Giroux argues were marked as disposable during Katrina — as paradigmatic figures of the "multitude," namely, the revolutionary subjectless subjectivity that is both exploited and activated by the new communicative milieu.[76] Hardt and Negri's staging of the radically disenfranchised at the heart of biopolitical struggle, together with their focus on communication as a universal human capacity, begins to suggest why their optimistic theory of biopolitics lends itself so comfortably to readings like Giroux's, which view communicative acts by the dispossessed, that is, human rights speech acts, as a radical insurrection against the depoliticizing logic of the humanitarian emergency.

As Slavoj Žižek has noted, many of Hardt and Negri's concrete proposals for change are articulated in the discourse of human rights — a discourse that accords with their opposition to private ownership, repressive nation-states, and a priori articulations of community. For instance, at the end of *Empire*, they advocate the institution of universal citizenship, a minimum income, and the reappropriation of communications media.[77] Human rights appeal to Hardt and Negri because they do not belong to any particular subject. As Jacques Rancière notes, human rights do not belong to either the citizen (a tautology, since citizens are those who already have rights) or the refugee (a paradox, since refugees are those with no rights at all) — these are the rights that belong to no one in particular but apply to everyone in common.[78] Human rights appear at the heart of the project of the common in Hardt and Negri's most recent collaboration, *Commonwealth*. This book rearticulates biopolitics as a struggle to actualize the common human potential for intellectual and affective communication, locating this potential, and not membership within any identitarian formation, as the necessary foundation for a truly democratic community.

Human rights discourse, as Keenan reminds us, following Rancière, holds out the promise of democracy in its most counterintuitive sense, as that which begins only when those who are excluded are included — indeed, are permitted to stand for universality.[79] The radicality of this discourse lies precisely in the fact that such universality cannot be taken for granted: the hegemonic grammar of rights speech is perpetually appropriated and transformed by concrete, particular speech acts; therefore, understanding the transformations of the universal depends on a constant process of translation. The dilemma of translating the communiqués of those who are usually invisible until insurgent, and who possess no rights or legal redress, has perhaps been articulated most poignantly by interlocutors of subaltern studies. Bishnupriya Ghosh sums up this dilemma: she argues, paraphrasing Ranajit Guha, that sighting subaltern insurgency—that is, sighting the pressure exerted by the subaltern on "semiotic codes that maintain established political and moral hierarchies"—requires a "semiotic leap of faith" on the part of the theorist. The task, she writes, lies in decoding this semiotic confusion without totally compromising the subversive potential of the subaltern to transform the social. She warns that such recodification is inevitable especially when popular cultural forms, which often trade in and play with hegemonic semiotic codes, apprehend the subaltern.[80]

One might logically conclude, from Hardt and Negri's emphasis on the terminology and problems of human rights, that the key to regaining the common lies in translating the speculative communicative acts of the disenfranchised in this manner—a task that I have attempted in reading Roberts's footage with and against the popularizing grain of Lessin and Deal's film, on one hand, and that of televised catastrophe, on the other. However, what is both seductive and troublesome about Hardt and Negri's theory of communicative biopolitics is that it fundamentally lacks a theory of mediation or translation. Hardt and Negri see such translation of the poor's specific modes of communication to be unnecessary: linguistic potential for them represents immediate mutual understanding rather than the inevitable perpetuity of translation. Because they assume that the conditions for universality have already been met under the hegemony of immaterial labor, in that "'the poor' is excluded from wealth and yet included in its circuits of social production," Hardt and Negri are able to conclude that the conditions for democracy are already immanent within the existing social field of biopolitical production in the form of the communicative potential of the poor.[81] The "communications media," elsewhere described in equally undifferentiated terms as "the network," are imagined to function as a connective tissue that unlocks this potential by paradoxically rendering "the set of all the exploited and subjugated, [as] a multitude that is directly opposed to Empire, with *no mediation between them.*"[82]

To sum up, if Agamben sees all of society by way of the nightmare of the concentration camp, Hardt and Negri, in contrast, see all of society as bathing in the light of communication. These competing accounts of biopolitics represent two sides of an ideology of immediacy, neither of which is attuned to the concrete testimonial codes that mediate the speech of the dispossessed when it is articulated in the form of human rights claims. The consequences of such thinking come to light in a particularly compelling way when we consider *Trouble the Water* as a symptomatic instance of the desire to read the communicative acts of the dispossessed immediately, at their face value. In their haste to "recognize" Roberts's footage as a sign of political agency, Lessin and Deal end up buying into the surface politics of her resourceful mobilization of race, interpreting the simple fact of the visibility of her black body as a sign of her empowerment through media. Indeed, the indexical appeal of race as a mark of self-evidence has the same structure of immediacy as documentary realism: both signal "truth and nothing but the truth."[83] The film's framing of Roberts's eyewitness footage as the sober truth fails to recognize that its subversive potential lies in Roberts's ironic performance of the compulsory and coercive visibility of the vulnerable body as a code of testimonial presence—a visibility that only exacerbated the vulnerability of those who were already marked by a racist state as disposable.[84]

With each self-affirming refrain ("I don't need you to tell me that I'm amazing") it becomes more apparent that Roberts needs Lessin and Deal as much as they need her, and also more difficult to disavow the fact that there is no "outside" awaiting the Roberts after their escape from Giroux's "black hole of despair," because the logic of capital works here, as always, by converting the vernacular into a universal and giving it a general equivalence by commodifying it. The subaltern, speaking in this manner, can be seen and heard only as an index. Returning to the anecdote with which I began this chapter, we can see how a similar recodification is at work in the humanitarian impulse to interpret and reward Tele Geto's ironic mimicry of television reporters as a form of sober documentary testimony. The hidden cost of Tele Geto's abandonment of their satirical, locally bound aesthetic practice in favor of a globally mobile documentary discourse of immediacy is embedded in the universalizing meaning that their images convey to their humanitarian advocates, signifying a flat truthfulness rather than a complex layered cultural performance.

Roberts's critique of the testimonial codes of the humanitarian emergency begins to suggest how *Trouble the Water* combines Giroux's emphasis on the exposure of black suffering with Hardt and Negri's utopian belief in the oppositional communicative potential of the dispossessed to create a perfect storm, the brunt of which is borne precisely by those dispossessed individuals who are the beneficiaries of the film's universalizing immediations. Indeed, Roberts's desperate performance of bare liveness allows us to apprehend Foucault's most crucial intervention into biopolitics as it relates to media: that within the architectonics of surveillance society, it is through the medium of light, not darkness, that control is enforced—as Foucault famously writes in *Discipline and Punish*, "visibility is a trap."[85]

A similar reversal is at work in Foucault's thinking about biopolitics and race when he writes that racist biopower does not operate by exclusion and dispossession, in the manner of previous regimes of power, but rather by inclusion and affirmation.[86] The important point to grasp here is that Foucault refers to racism as a rationale whereby the life of a dominant group can be improved by neglecting those of marginal groups, rather than in the narrow sense, as a technology of discrimination oriented around race as a biological and discursive category. Giroux's conviction regarding the virtues of media visibility as a remedy for racial discrimination and excommunication misses this distinction. From a Foucauldian standpoint, Giroux's impulse to emancipate the racially disenfranchised victims of disaster by encouraging them to use visual media to represent their most visibly destitute moments reinforces the racist biopolitical rationale that fuels the spectacle of the humanitarian emergency. The analysis of bare liveness that I have laid out in this chapter makes this distinction clear: it allows us to see how the humanitarian appeal to the dispossessed to affirm the political value of their lives—to make themselves live—can operate, during moments of crisis, as a racist technique of letting them die.

Chapter 3

"HAVING A VOICE"

TOWARD AN AUTISTIC COUNTERDISCOURSE
OF DOCUMENTARY

"I Am Autism"

In September 2009 Autism Speaks, the world's largest autism research foundation, released a fund-raising video that drew vocal protests from the autistic community, forcing the organization to remove the link to the video from
its website.[1] Directed by the award-winning director Alfonso Cuarón, himself the parent of an autistic child, the four-minute-long video, titled "I Am
Autism," was met with "horror" by representatives of the Autistic Self Advocacy Network, who organized a series of protests denouncing the "fear-
mongering" tactics of Autism Speaks.[2] The first half of this video fuses a characteristic trope of the horror film with the documentary realism of the home
movie to insist on the urgency of finding a cure for autism. In a succession of
slowed-down home video–like scenes, a number of silent, anonymous, solitary children are revealed to be the unsuspecting victims of the protagonist,
autism, whose acousmatic voice emanates menacingly from off-screen. The
cool objectivity of this male voice, set off by the metallic hiss of the sparse
audioscape, heightens the horror of the words it utters in the first person:
"I am autism. I'm visible in your children, but if I can help it, I am invisible
to you until it's too late. I know where you live. And guess what? I live there
too. I hover around all of you. I know no color barrier, no religion, no morality, no currency. I speak your language fluently. And with every voice I take
away, I acquire yet another language. I work very quickly. I work faster than
pediatric AIDS, cancer, and diabetes combined. . . . You ignored me. That was
a mistake."[3] The video unfolds with autism promising to divest the families

FIGURE 3.1 Still from "I Am Autism" YouTube video (2009)

of autistic children of their marital bliss, money, sleep, and hope. With each threat, the wholesome landscapes of childhood seen in the brief vignettes — playground, baseball pen, backyard, beach, aquarium, school yard — assume the form of potential disease vectors, while the innocent gestures of the children as they strum their hands across a table or stare into space begin to resemble the symptoms of an epidemic that renders them mute and alien.

In the second half of the video, the crisis is abruptly averted. The scenes are played over but as family portraits: a new cast of characters — siblings, parents, extended families, and friends — emerges from off-screen to envelop the children in a communal embrace. The video speeds up, and the frozen faces of the children break into smiles, as an uplifting guitar theme and the sounds of youthful laughter announce their release into sociality. Paralleling these reversals, a chorus of predominantly female voices takes over the vocal commentary on behalf of the parents, families, siblings, friends, doctors, and therapeutic staff of autistics from "all climates" and "all faiths" the world over. This "community of warriors," we are told, are united across their differences by their common quest for a cure for autism — to "knock down" the "wall" imprisoning their children by any means necessary, be it "technology," "prayers," "voodoo," or "genetic studies." In unison they speak back to autism: "We have a voice!"

The most striking objections to this video have come from autistic individuals who resent Autism Speaks's attempts to ventriloquize their concerns. "Autism Speaks," these critics argue, "does not represent Autistic people or

FIGURE 3.2 Still from "I Am Autism" YouTube video (2009)

speak for us."[4] Furthermore, its attempts to do so actively "silence the voices of autistic people" and make it difficult for them and their families to be heard.[5] One activist group produced T-shirts emblazoned with the text, "Autism Speaks can go away. I have Autism. I can speak for myself."[6] These criticisms activate some of the most persistent and fraught questions of cross-cultural representation, such as: Who has a voice? What does it mean to be someone or something's mouthpiece? Does speaking necessarily equate to agency, or are there circumstances in which it does not pay to speak? When it comes to "speaking out," what kind of interiority is presupposed by a voice, and what kind of outside can be said to await the autistic speaking for themselves?

The problems of autistic voicing hone in on one of the most familiar and paradigmatic metaphors of humanitarian recognition and inclusion: giving a voice to the voiceless. The metaphor of "having a voice" that drives discourses of social justice turns on the importance of speech for participating in any political process. "Speaking out" is commonly understood as a liberatory act of giving expression to an interior idea, thought, opinion, or wish that inaugurates the subject's entrance into the political sphere and, indeed, into humanity. As Lisa Cartwright notes, "'coming to voice' is a figure of speech in a range of political movements connoting the achievement of agency, usually belatedly or through a political struggle before which the individual or collective subject who speaks is understood to have been 'silent' or 'invisible.'"[7] "Having a voice" presents concrete challenges for autistics, since autism manifests in a range of nonnormative verbal competencies and inclinations: some autistics are highly talkative and articulate, while others are nonverbal or minimally verbal and communicate through voice-to-text and other assistive technologies, including facilitated communication (FC), a technique in which a facilitator guides one's hand to letters or icons on a keyboard, reading the words and sentences aloud. Many autistics develop language on a nonnormative timeline, and some have been known to lose their verbal faculties later in life. In addition, autistics frequently exhibit echolalia, or the repetition of certain words or phrases in socially inappropriate or irrelevant circumstances, often detached from their conventional meanings.

From a humanitarian standpoint, the absence of articulate speech is regarded as a sign of underdevelopment. This stance, which is explicit in Autism Speaks's video, also implicitly guides the therapeutic treatment of autism spectrum disorders.[8] The acquisition of speech and language, like self-recognition, is considered a necessary step toward becoming human; this is why autistics, like children, animals, and other "primitives," are believed to require a vocal delegate speaking on their behalf until they can speak for themselves. In stark contrast, many autistics regard their range of verbal capacities as a spectrum of neurological diversity that they wish to preserve, and they assert the value of atypical neurological development as a normal human variation. They protest that autism is an integral part of their identity, not an imposition from without, as Autism Speaks's ominous rendition of the voice of autism suggests. While proponents of neurodiversity do not deny the real challenges of everyday life for autistics and their caregivers, they also acknowledge the desirable aspects of living with autism that would be eliminated by a cure. The assumption that autistics are in need of "saving" or a "cure," they argue, is profoundly "neurotypical": it misrecognizes neurological difference as a disease in need of rectification or, worse, elimination—an idea that many autistics strongly oppose.[9] Disability studies scholars have echoed this viewpoint, pointing out the contradictory investments of social justice discourses in "ableist" metaphors of bodily ability (such as speech and mobility) as benchmarks of political subjectivity.[10]

The predicament of autistics confronted by humanitarian agents speaking on their behalf also provides fresh insight into the positivist documentary tradition of presenting a subjective perspective about the world as an objective statement of fact. This tactic has historically been used, according to Johannes Fabian, in traditional ethnographies that purport to objectively depict non-Western cultures. Just as the ethnographic native is said to be "born with rhythm" by the anthropologist who did not see him grow up, learn, or practice (per Fabian), the autistic is seen and heard by humanitarian organizations like Autism Speaks as a primitive, lacking the capacity for mental reasoning that "proper" speech is thought to transmit.[11] Fabian argues that positivist approaches to ethnography deny the coevalness or contemporaneity of other cultures by placing them in a temporal frame outside the discursive present of the ethnographer and their audience.[12] Film scholar Fatimah Tobing Rony describes the ethnographic tendency to represent non-Western cultures as primitive or outside modern history as a form of cinematic taxidermy or mummification: a practice that seeks to artificially salvage a dying way of life by freezing it in time.[13] Autism Speaks's video enacts a similar temporal manipulation. The ejection of autistics from the intersubjective dialogue between the voice of autism and the parents and families of autistics—that is, the various humanitarian agents speaking on behalf of autistics—positions autistic modes of communication and relationality in a private self-referential world outside time.

When we reframe the question of speaking and being spoken for in this way, we can see how the rhetorical immediacy and persuasiveness of the voice-over in Autism Speaks's video turns on the temporal distancing of autistic modes of communication. This insight provides a point of departure for this chapter, in which I examine what happens when the documentary tropes of persuasive speech are used to "give a voice" to autistics. My inquiry centers on the first-person documentary voice-over. The authoritative immediacy of this trope, employed in Autism Speaks's video for the voice of autism, has in recent years been borrowed by a number of documentary films that respond to the problematic representational politics of Autism Speaks's video by depicting autistic protagonists speaking for themselves in the form of the first-person voice-over. Whereas this trope is synonymous in the humanitarian context with having a voice, and thus with being human, I argue that from an autistic perspective it can be seen as a documentary immediation—one whose effects of unmediated presence and proximity are achieved by denying the coevalness of autistic modes of language, communication, and relationality.

I begin with a survey of recent documentary films that depict autistic individuals as protagonists, filmmakers, and scriptwriters. I isolate and perform close readings of two of these films: *Autism Is a World* (dir. Gerardine Wurzburg, 2004), a television documentary produced for CNN, and "In My Language" (dir. Mel Baggs, aka Amanda Baggs, 2007), a short self-made video posted on YouTube by Baggs. In addition to participating in and producing very different conversations around autism, these two films also illustrate contradictory stances regarding the first-person voice-over as an index of autistic subjectivity. In Wurzburg's film, protagonist Sue Rubin's autobiographical commentary, voiced by a female surrogate, speaks "over" scenes featuring Rubin's laborious use of FC, promising intimate and authoritative access to the interior world of autism. Meanwhile, Baggs draws on experimental video techniques to position the first-person voice-over as a poor translation of hir "native language," one whose promise of interiority and personhood comes at the cost of being in a "constant conversation with every aspect of [hir] environment."[14]

Wurzburg's film belongs within a humanitarian tradition that reinforces a logocentric equation of voice with "inner speech," or *logos*, while Baggs's subversion of the first-person voice-over evokes an autistic counterdiscourse of voicing—one that lurks in the shadows of articulate or legitimate speech. I propose that Baggs and other autistic writers, like Tito Rajarshi Mukhopadhyay, Dawn Prince, and Temple Grandin, extend the work of scholars like Mladen Dolar and Roland Barthes in producing a critical counterdiscourse of the voice. Like Dolar and Barthes, autistic accounts of language and communication locate the voice in a space between the body and language that opens onto paralinguistic, embodied modes of meaning making and relationality. These autistic accounts of voicing stage a compelling critique of humanitarian notions of having and giving a voice. Rather than capitulating to the humanitarian call to "speak out" or "come to voice," they redefine voice as something that is not oriented exclusively toward the human, as it is understood in the logocentric tradition. They show, paradoxically, that the mode of voicing cultivated in contemporary therapeutic interventions around autism bears all of the characteristics commonly attributed to autistic communication.

I argue that this autistic counterdiscourse of the voice demands a critical reassessment of the role of the speaking voice in documentary. "Voice" is of both literal and metaphorical significance to the documentary film genre: documentary has historically distinguished itself from fiction films through an emphasis on the spoken word, in the form of vocal conventions such as the voice-over, the interview, and the observed conversation. Bill Nichols plays on this emphasis when he employs voice as a metaphor for a documentary's social point of view, charting the genre's evolution from objective, Griersonian exposition to more reflexive modes of narration as an indicator of its gradual departure from its realist, rhetorical origins. Other documentary scholars have corroborated Nichols's narrative, locating films featuring a highly reflexive first-person voice-over as an enlightened alternative to documentary realism. The concept of the autistic voice critiques the enduring role of the speaking voice in documentary's reality effects and, in so doing, joins the efforts of feminist documentary critics and filmmakers who have challenged the equation of speaking out and progress. This critique also points to the limitations of the way reflexivity is understood in documentary—a theme that chapter 4 takes up in greater detail.

In the final section of the chapter, I use Michel Foucault's landmark study, *Madness and Civilization*, as a guide to the humanitarian discursive history of autism. Foucault's method in this foundational book, which aimed to make unreason speak without destroying it, allows me to situate my three media examples— "I Am Autism," *Autism Is a World*, and "In My Language"—as different points along the representational spectrum of documentary voicing. These voices, which I dub *dominant*, *resistant*, and *autistic*, also map onto the major representational tendencies in contemporary diagnostic debates around autism and productively illuminate the contradictions of producing a "discourse of unreason on reason." I approach these debates by bringing together perspectives from science and technology studies, disability studies, and critical theory. This analysis of who speaks for autism also sheds light on the different voices speaking for the child and for the disaster victim in the previous two chapters.

Who Speaks for Autism? An Analysis of Three Voice-Overs

In the weeks following the release of Autism Speaks's controversial video, autistic self-advocates responded with number of parodies that foregrounded the epistemological sleight of hand involved in the original video's first-person voice-over commentary. The anonymous blogger Socrates's video "I Am Autism Speaks" makes a conservative but ingenious change to the text of the original commentary to reveal that the "I" in the video that purports to be the voice of autism itself is in fact the voice of the organization Autism Speaks. Much of the image track is left intact, while the delivery of the commentary in a monotonous electronic voice casts Autism Speaks as a soulless and shamelessly profit-driven corporation.[15] Another popular parody, "I'm Autistic: I Can Speak," reclaims the first-person voice for the autistic. The plain red background of this video focuses attention on the voice, which sings an altered commentary, describing itself as "different, not weak," "smart," "sensitive," and "equal in humanity."[16] Thus, each of these parodies shows how Autism Speaks camouflages its own perspective—the perspective of medical discourse—by introducing itself as the voice of autism ("I") speaking to an audience ("you") on behalf of its victims ("autistics who cannot speak for themselves").

Strikingly, the first-person voice-over has become the idiom of choice not only among parodists of the "I Am Autism" video but also in several recent documentaries seeking to authenticate the perspectives of autistic people. A number of documentary shorts released over the last two decades deploy the first-person voice-over to enable autistic individuals to speak authoritatively and directly about their experiences with autism. These include *Jam Jar* (dir. Simon Everson, 1995), *Autism Is a World* (dir. Gerardine Wurzburg, 2004), *My Classic Life as an Artist: A Portrait of Larry Bissonnette* (dir. Douglas Biklen, 2004), and "In My Language" (dir. Amanda Baggs, 2007). With the exception of "In My Language," which was written, directed, and published on YouTube by Baggs, the remaining films were produced by allies and advocates in collaboration with autistic subjects—respectively Donna Williams, Larry Bissonnette, and Sue Rubin.

Before I turn to these reappropriations of the first-person voice-over, I unpack how "I Am Autism" uses one of the oldest rhetorical tropes of documentary immediacy—voice-of-God narration—to authoritatively convey that autism is a humanitarian emergency requiring urgent intervention. I then examine the uses and subversions of this trope in Wurzburg's *Autism Is a World* and Baggs's "In My Language" in order to understand what is gained and what is lost when the first-person voice-over is deployed to give a voice to autistics.

The authoritative, incontrovertible message of Autism Speaks's video regarding the pathology of autism is the combined effect of several classic conventions of Griersonian narration. Many documentaries of the Griersonian school, inspired by the iconic series *The March of Time*, featured didactic expository commentary delivered in a stentorian male voice speaking in the third person from off-screen. The hierarchical location of this acousmatic voice "above" the diegetic sounds and images, its emanation from an unknowable off-screen space, and its economical and detached delivery worked in concert with its social and rhetorical coding to reinforce its meta-physical status and objectivity. Such a voice forcefully drew attention away from its own source, materiality, and embodiment toward its message, earning the informal moniker of "voice-of-God narration." John Grierson openly viewed documentary as a form of propaganda: the point of this form of vocal commentary was to strive for denotational clarity as much as possible, by anchoring or fixing the meanings of images as well as minimizing the grain that would open them up to interpretative play.[17]

The voice of autism in "I Am Autism" bears the trace of voice-of-God narration, with all of its connotations of omniscience, omnipotence, and omnipresence. The commanding presence of this disembodied voice has much to do with its emanation from an "other" space beyond the diegesis, its location "above" everything we see and hear, and the fact that its source remains unseen. According to Michel Chion, an acousmatic voice (a voice that is heard but whose source is not seen) evokes archaic and dramatic psychic vulnerabilities for the spectating subject, including those associated with the mother's unseen voice. The audiovisual architecture of cinema has the distinct capacity, he writes, to imbue the off-screen voice with a more-than-real presence that relies on the uncertain absence of an actual body that is liable to appear in the visual field at any moment.[18] The voice of autism makes overt the implied menace of its acousmatic presence when it states, "I am invisible to you until it's too late." It is unclear whether autism speaks from *within* the hapless, voiceless children seen in the images, or whether it hovers around them, threatening to possess them at any moment.

The urgent, forceful temporality of this video is also an effect of the expository voice-over's coded sonic logic of subtraction. Although the voice-over is "added" in the manner of a supplement, it works, as Rey Chow has noted, by "hollowing-out," or subtracting information from the image.[19] The removal of autistics from the intersubjective ("I-you") exchange between the speaking voice and the spectator can be regarded as a function of this hollowing out of the image by the voice-over: the autistic children represented in the video appear devoid of subjectivity because they are effectively reduced to visual evidence shoring up the video's message that autism is a deficit or impairment. In an essay on vocal narration in classical documentary, Charles Wolfe describes this dynamic as follows: "Those who speak in voice-over may know, comment on, or drown out sounds from the world a film depicts, but the relationship is asymmetrical: voices from that register have no reciprocal power to introduce or comment on the voices that overlay this world. We might want to say, then, that voice-over covers the world of the 'diegesis.'"[20]

This drowning out takes place at multiple textual levels in the "I Am Autism" video. Formally, as Wolfe describes, the voice-over flattens the meanings that lie beneath it in the audiovisual hierarchy. Furthermore, the narrative capacity of the voice-over to compress story time condenses the complex discursive history of autism into a tense, timely event. Rhetorically, it speaks directly to the audience, unlike the more distant third-person voice, eliding layers of mediation in an implied reference to face-to-face conversation. What this form of voicing loses in complexity, it gains in denotational clarity and authority—it is an especially compact, sharply defined, and impactful form of speech.[21] The rhetorical urgency of didactic expository narration explains why this convention—which, according to Wolfe, fell out of favor precisely because it took itself too seriously—continues to be used in humanitarian media: here, it unequivocally renders the so-called autism epidemic as an emergency requiring action, not contemplation.[22] The representation of autistics as victims requiring immediate therapeutic assistance is exacerbated by the conflation of autistics with children. This is a routine strategy in contemporary mainstream autism advocacy: even though autism is a lifelong spectrum condition, and not all autistics are nonverbal, the coded vulnerability of nonverbal autistic children makes them a universal target for projective identification, and thus for humanitarian intervention.[23]

Given the strategic advantages offered by a didactic expository voice-over, it is unsurprising that voice-over commentary has been employed in recent documentary films such as *Jam Jar*, *Autism Is a World*, and *My Classic Life as an Artist* as a way of foregrounding the perspectives of their autistic protagonists over and above those of doctors, medical experts, and other "foreign observers." To quote Donna Williams, the protagonist of *Jam Jar*, these films aim to take an "inside-out approach to making a documentary" from an autistic perspective.[24] To this end, all three films employ a first-person voice-over as their rhetorical spine, through which all other perspectives are mediated. In addition to providing an "inner perspective" on autism, this technique is also effective in enabling disabled subjects to exert as much authorial control as possible over the message of the film, short of producing the films themselves. The first-person voice-over is also chosen for its suitability in translating the autobiographical writings of the protagonists into an audiovisual idiom. In each of these films, the vocal commentary is compiled from the protagonists' writings: Williams reads her own writings aloud and alternates between serving as a frame narrator and directly addressing the camera, while in the cases of Rubin and Bissonnette, who are mostly nonverbal and communicate through FC, the commentary is read aloud by surrogate voice artists.

These films employ a mode of first-person voice-over narration that combines didactic exposition and an emotive, embodied, and expressive mode of address. They straddle the line between what Nichols calls the expository and performative modes of documentary and borrow elements from each: whereas the expository mode has a rhetorical and polemical agenda that is accomplished through an appeal to objectivity, the performative mode is more concerned with exploring a personal, autobiographical, and highly subjective perspective on the world, often that of an underrepresented or misrepresented social group.[25] The merger between expository and performative modes of voicing in these films evidences the operation of a pervasive idiom of humanitarian representation that I will call the *interventionist* first-person voice-over. This form of narration "pirates documentary's legendary authority for personal use," to borrow from Alisa Lebow's description of personal documentary.[26] The seemingly countervailing impulses of objectivity and subjectivity in this type of voice-over have the combined effect of establishing the unequivocal authority of the autistic protagonist's personal, subjective perspective on the world.

When subjectivity is mobilized for humanitarian purposes, as it is in the aforementioned films about autism, it assumes a referential and rhetorical function, far from being rendered in a complex, uncertain, or hybridized light (the latter are traits that Nichols attributes to the performative mode of first-person voicing). The interventionist first-person voice-over convinces us forcefully of the validity, authenticity, and legitimacy of the speaker's interior existence. This subjugated interiority serves, in turn, as a factual ground from which to counter and correct medical views of autism that would position it as an impairment. At such moments, autobiography becomes an evidentiary practice that has the effect of tethering or grounding the subjectivity of the autistic in the identitarian domain of their disability. The protagonist becomes a native informant of sorts, expounding directly and authoritatively on the subjective experience, practical challenges, and perceptual world of living with autism. The forceful authority of the interventionist first-person voice-over derives from the expository techniques of hollowing out, subtracting, or drowning out commonly seen in the Griersonian mode of voice-over narration.

The question then arises in relation to an aesthetics of immediation: Are the subtractions involved in first-person expository voice-over commentary also temporal? How do they impact the protracted time and mediated quality of autistic communication? I will answer this question through a close reading of Wurzburg's film *Autism Is a World*. Although several of my comments are equally pertinent to *My Classic Life as an Artist* and *Jam Jar*, Wurzburg's Oscar-nominated television documentary allows us to see the exclusions and subtractions of the interventionist first-person voice-over as a documentary immediation—as well as the larger medial and ideological frameworks that are held in place by these exclusions—in a particularly crystalline form.

As with the aforementioned films about Williams and Bissonnette, Rubin's personal struggles with autism, and especially her difficulties with communication, define the narrative arc of *Autism Is a World*. A twenty-six-year-old college history major at the time of the film's release, Rubin attributes to FC her transformation from a "nonperson" to a successful student living in an assisted-living facility, an involved participant in decisions regarding her life, and a frequent speaker at conferences for and about those on the autistic spectrum. The film chronicles Rubin's transformation upon being introduced to FC at the age of thirteen, before which she had been believed to be mentally retarded. With practice, Rubin explains, this communication system helped her to recognize voices and words in the sounds that floated over her. Her "mind began to wake up," even though she continues to struggle with echolalia and uncontrollable sounds and movements.[27] In her conference presentations, some of which are featured in the film, Rubin often offers motivational affirmation and aims to "enlighten [autistic] individuals as to the potential of their own voices."

In addition to serving as its thematic preoccupation, Rubin's difficulties with verbal communication also set up the formal problematic of Wurzburg's film when it comes to the discursive conventions of documentary. Rubin is mostly nonverbal. Although she communicates verbally with her support staff and family through a few words and phrases, her utterances are not comprehensible to most people. For all other conversations—in classes, at conferences, with professors and doctors, and so on—she relies on FC, picking out letters individually on a keyboard that are then read aloud by a support-staff member who sits by her side, or preprogramming questions

FIGURE 3.3 Still from *Autism Is a World* by Gerardine Wurzburg (2004)

into a speech-generating device that can be replayed electronically. But even as Rubin acknowledges how language and facilitated speech have allowed her to participate in social and intellectual life, she also confesses to feeling exhausted by the effort required to stay focused during conversations and in her college lectures. There are times when she needs to "zone out," retreat into solitude, and let the "autistic part of [her] brain take over." She does this by watching water run through a faucet, or drizzling water over the spoons that she carries about with her as an unexplainable source of comfort.

Scenes depicting FC are necessary and valuable subject matter for the film, in that they demonstrate the technological and interpersonal negotiations involved in everyday conversation for nonverbal autistic people. At the same time, this prolonged and visibly mediated form of communication also presents an obstacle when it comes to soliciting Rubin's version of events through interviews. As a mode of address, FC is antagonistic to the discursive immediacy of the documentary interview and the observed conversation, in that Rubin's comments and responses are never delivered spontaneously in her own voice. Instead, a facilitator, who reads off letters and words one by one, occasionally stopping to predict the text, voices them. The facilitator often provides her own interjections, prompting Rubin with facial expressions and interpretive remarks, and occasionally responds to others on Rubin's behalf. This laborious process is sometimes interrupted by episodes of echolalia that cause Rubin to stumble over spelling and grammar that she then goes back to correct, prompted by her support staff.

To accord with the time constraints of the broadcast documentary genre, these long scenes are presented in a truncated and heavily edited form that captures the gist of Rubin's communiqués and edits out the mediations of her facilitator. Much of the lag time is cut out so that we hear the facilitator name a couple of letters, followed by the complete phrase or sentence. These elisions are especially noticeable in scenes where Rubin is shown interviewing doctors about her condition—a technique used by the film to center her perspective—in that her utterances are subject to visible mediation while those of her interviewees are not. Although *Autism Is a World* is framed and marketed as a film narrated by an autistic voice, the unavoidable display of editorial interference at moments like these attests not to Rubin's voice but to Wurzburg's, as well as to the determining power of CNN, her cable network sponsor and coproducer of the film.

Wurzburg's truncation of scenes depicting FC in order to center Rubin's voice disavows the resolutely intersubjective nature of this mode of communication, as well as the complexly interconstitutive form of subjectivity that it facilitates. Cartwright notes that since its introduction in the United States, the legitimacy of FC in bringing autistics to voice has been questioned owing to widespread anxiety that the voices of autistics are manipulated by their facilitators.[28] The singular subjectivity implied by the first-person voice-over, to which Wurzburg turns to resolve the dilemmas of allowing Rubin to "speak for herself," wards off this anxiety. The film is cohered together by autobiographical commentary composed by Rubin (credited as the film's writer), voiced by the actress Julianna Margulies. As the film opens on Rubin's face framed in the doorway of her home, we hear Margulies's voice say, "My name is Sue Rubin. I am twenty-six years old. I've written these thoughts about my life because I don't really talk. This is not my voice, but these are my words." With this announcement of the centrality of Rubin's message rather than its vocal medium, her commentary is established from the start as the film's narrative voice and organizing principle. Subsequently, the remainder of the film is represented as a linguistic event of Rubin's speech, even though Margulies's delivery, which has been praised as "sensitive" and "dramatic," does much to set the emotional and subjective tone of the film.[29] Rubin's commentary is an intermittent presence throughout the film that supplies much of the

FIGURE 3.4 Still from opening sequence of *Autism Is a World* by Gerardine Wurzburg (2004)

film's story content and momentum: introducing characters, providing context, connecting past to present, and providing transitions between scenes. The association of Margulies's voice with Rubin's face in close-up in the film's opening scene, coupled with the voice's emanation from off-screen, accompanied by soft, contemplative music, also signals that we are in the presence of Rubin's inner voice, a choice evocative of the performative documentary mode. The voice-over often plays over scenes where Rubin is engaged in conversation with her facilitator or with a third party, offering intimate reflections on Rubin's relationships with her support staff. In more than one instance, including the only scene in which Rubin is shown being interviewed by Wurzburg, the voice-over fills in the response time during which Rubin painstakingly types out her answer, to tell us what she is "really" feeling. Margulies's voice also retrospectively makes sense of Rubin's own autistic behaviors, offering such explanations as: "When I watch water, I am zoning out and letting the autistic part of my brain take over. My mind goes blank, and I stop thinking." Strikingly, it is precisely at the moments when the voice-over offers up Rubin's most intimate and personal insights that it also operates in a didactic capacity, effectively mirroring the translation involved in FC in its way of explaining and making sense of Rubin's otherwise opaque feelings and behaviors.

What is more, the superior location of Margulies's voice-over in the audio-visual hierarchy naturalizes its status as the telos of Rubin's communicative efforts—one that reflects Rubin's own desire to be seen as a thinking, feeling person—rather than one mode of expression among others. Thus, even though Margulies's voice-over seems like an innocuous, natural, and empathetic choice for Rubin's inner voice, its operations are quite complex. The consequence of representing this voice-over commentary as the ideal, successful realization of Rubin's communicative potential is that the coevalness of all of the other, autistic forms of communication in which she is shown engaging, including FC, is effectively denied. In the formal hierarchy of the film, these halting, nonverbal utterances are cast as the primitive precursors of the "proper" speech evidenced in the voice-over.

The precise operation through which the film achieves this effect of temporal distancing can be observed in how it abbreviates the durational logic of autistic communication into visual motifs or bridges. The scenes of Rubin "zoning out" by watching tap water flow over a spoon, or the moments during FC when her attention drifts elsewhere, never remain on-screen long enough to assume the status of communication or events in their own right. The latter are edited out altogether. The former are employed as brief transitions between other scenes, with the camera often zooming in on Rubin's face as if to emphasize her humanity. The superimposition of Margulies's voice-over, in conjunction with Wurzburg's editorial and compositional choices, turns the scenes that might potentially open onto a different, autistic economy of voicing into a form of evidence that signifies interiority. In this way, all that is "out of time" or potentially "meaningless" about autistic communication is turned by Wurzburg's film into a timely, meaningful illustration that can be accommodated within the standardized duration of the television documentary.

A viewing of Baggs's "In My Language" makes it clearer that the autistic voice to which a film such as Wurzburg's lays claim is a casualty of the interventionist first-person voice-over rather than its referent. Structurally, this eight-minute-long video, which Baggs posted to YouTube in 2007, is the inverse of *Autism Is a World*. The illustrative sounds and images that serve mainly as supporting evidence in Wurzburg's film are the main event in the first half of Baggs's video, which consists entirely of a number of encounters resembling the transitory scenes where Rubin is shown "zoning out." These scenes are presented without explanatory commentary, accompanied only

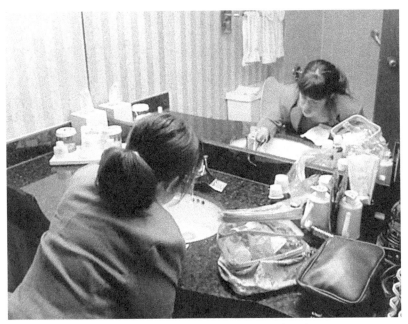

FIGURE 3.5 Still from *Autism Is a World* by Gerardine Wurzburg (2004)

by a wordless voice that hums meditatively to itself. The video opens with a medium shot of Baggs, backlit by a window, flapping hir hands and moving back and forth in hir living room. In the following scenes, Baggs interacts with a series of everyday items in hir home in ways that don't necessarily correspond to their uses as objects or their status as "things" that belong to a different ontological category than humans: sie strums hir fingers across a computer keyboard, pats and flicks at a beaded necklace, flutters a receipt in the wind, strokes the ridges of a griddle pan, vigorously fondles the knob of a drawer, smells and rubs hir face against a book, and waves and wags hir fingers before the camera.

As we move through these encounters, the camera framing becomes part of the textural world being explored, as Baggs zooms and reframes without concern for focalizing the "event" in each scene with any particular fidelity. Sie moves in or out to focus on the texture of the object or the movements of hir hand that interest hir, and at other times the camera looks awry so that the action is limited to a corner of the frame. Hir face is seldom in focus, so that the human face or its stand-in, the speaking voice, does not organize our relationship to the diegesis, as it does in *Autism Is a World*. The soundtrack

FIGURE 3.6 Still from "In My Language" by Amanda Baggs (2007)

FIGURE 3.7 Still from "In My Language" by Amanda Baggs (2007)

converges randomly and serendipitously with the image, as Baggs's humming sounds are occasionally punctuated rhythmically, and at other times drowned out, by the scratching, tapping, grating, and fluttering sounds produced through hir interactions with various materials. The camera, in hir hands, becomes a haptic, sonic eye, to borrow Laura Marks's description of this feminist video technique: rather than scrutinizing the object in each scene with a controlling, penetrating gaze, sie grazes the surface of the materials with which sie interacts, using the camera to immerse hirself in textures, sounds, and movements instead of abstracting hirself from hir environment.[30]

In the second half of the video, titled "Translation," these scenes are repeated with subtitled voice-over commentary in the first person by Baggs in which sie describes the previous part of the video as expressions of hir "native language." Since Baggs is almost entirely nonverbal and often communicates through text-based interfaces, hir voice-over consists of typed commentary vocalized using text-to-speech software. The speech-generating device through which Baggs's typed commentary is filtered renders hir words in an uncanny mechanical monotone that deflects the attempt to read it as an interior monologue or to scan it for signs of personality or gender. The point of hir video, Baggs tells us, is not to lay bare the "bizarre workings of the autistic mind" but to acknowledge "the existence and value of many different kinds of thinking and interaction in a world where how close you can appear to a specific one of them determines whether you are seen as a real person . . . [with] any rights."

Baggs's insistent use of first-person pronouns (*I, me, mine*) in hir "translation" might seem incongruous in light of this statement, in that Baggs uses them to claim and authenticate hir own unique form of subjectivity and voice. But the very point of Baggs's commentary—which is as complex in its logic as it is articulate—is to show how the modes of relationality implied by grammatical personhood and articulate speech forcibly mediate hir access to political recognition. Baggs's use of the genderless pronouns *sie, hir,* and *hirs* similarly comments on the restrictive and binary engendering of "proper" pronominal forms. Baggs's decision to withhold this commentary until the second half of the video, and to frame it as a translation, is a provocation: it points out that the autistic voice cannot be heard, seen, or acknowledged until it begins to speak in a recognizable tongue. The lure of authentic insight into the "native" autistic mind is one that Baggs's video never fulfills. Even as the label "translation" implies an interpretive key to Baggs's so-called native language, the scenes that continue to play alongside hir commentary remain beguilingly opaque. In one of the rare instances in which Baggs synchronizes hir explanation to an action (sie is moving hir fingers in a stream of water), hir only explanation is that the action has no symbolic content or hidden message. Sie comments:

> My language is not about designing words or even visual symbols for people to interpret. It is about being in a constant conversation with every aspect of my environment. In this part of the video the water doesn't symbolize anything. I am just interacting with the water as the water interacts with me. Far from being purposeless, the way that I move is an ongoing response to what is around me. Ironically the way that I move when responding to everything around me is described as "being in a world of my own" whereas if I interact with a much more limited set of responses and only react to a much more limited part of my surroundings people claim that I am "opening up to true interaction with the world."

Baggs insists that hir own spoken words are merely an impoverished translation of a mode of voicing that thoroughly exceeds any single signifying operation. Bearing out this critique, the content of hir voice-over refuses the explanatory charge conventionally assigned to the spoken word in documentary, as well as the interpretive finality that would otherwise be guaranteed by the location of hir verbal commentary "over" hir other audiovisual expressions.

The divergence between Baggs's "native language" and its voice-over translation is beautifully hinted at in a scene that soon follows. Baggs tells us, "I smell things, I listen to things, I feel things, I taste things, I look at things," and as if to illustrate these statements we see hir smelling hir hand, listening to a dreidel by spinning it near hir ear, rubbing hir face against a towel, tasting a pen, and turning hir eye sideways as if to look at hir ear. The fact that sie smells and tastes all the "wrong things" only indicates the dissonance of the singular "I" with hir perceptual and relational promiscuity, which sees a "you" not only in people but in everything around hir; sie continues, "It is not enough to look and listen and taste and smell and feel, I have to do those to the right things." At best, sie seems to be saying, a first-person voice can speak "near" and not "for" oneself, to invoke feminist scholar and filmmaker Trinh T. Minh-ha's description of a form of speaking that "reflects on itself and can come very close to a subject without, however, seizing or claiming it."[31]

FIGURE 3.8 Still from "In My Language" by Amanda Baggs (2007)

"In My Language" is evocative of Trinh's experimental films in its deconstruction of the documentary tropes of humanitarian intervention. Trinh is
well known for her critique of the totalizing language of ethnographic cinema, notably expository third-person narration and the observational conventions of wide-angle framing and minimal editing, for its way of disguis-
ing the filmmaker's subjective perspective as scientific or factual information
about non-Western cultures.[32] Her film *Reassemblage* (1982), a collage of fragmented images of Senegal, operationalizes the strategy of "speaking nearby"
in the form of a whispering, accented voice-over that acknowledges the futility of distilling the complexity of the African continent into a meaningful
soundbyte. Baggs's film arguably belongs within a corpus of feminist experimental filmmaking that includes Trinh, Leslie Thornton, and Patricia Gruben,
among others. Thornton and Gruben have both experimented with mute-
ness, inarticulateness, and aphasia as strategies that comment on the patriarchal exclusions of language, and the redoubling of these exclusions in classic
Hollywood films that depict female bodies as an unspeaking spectacle. Linda
Peckham's description of Thornton's film *Adynata* (1983) works just as well
as a description of Baggs's film: "The arrested articulation opens a space of

doubt and disturbance at the center of the film," Peckham writes, thus locating the enabling failure implied by the dual definitions of *adynata*: "a confession that words fail us" and "'a stringing together of impossibilities' as a means of speaking."[33]

But whereas Trinh's cinematic experiments aimed to alter the sensibilities of ethnographic film viewers, and Thornton and Gruben intervene in the habits of classical Hollywood spectators, Baggs's address is to humanitarian audiences. Baggs extends Trinh's critique to the humanitarian first-person voice-over, as the liberalized guise in which the so-called voiceless are turned into native informants observing and reporting authoritatively on their condition to their well-wishers. The mismatch of sound and image — between the clarity, authority, and immediacy of Baggs's verbal commentary and hir insistence on its poverty as a translation of hir expressive acts — powerfully reveals the inadequacy of the notion of interiority associated with the first-person voice-over, as a privileged humanitarian trope of having a voice. Baggs evokes a parallel, unspoken economy of voicing that cannot be "possessed" but that emerges through the conflict between linguistic signification and a more expansive, embodied communicative comportment. Hir choice of the first-person voice-over as the vehicle for this critique is both striking and counterintuitive: whereas the performative and expository functions associated with this mode of voicing are typically associated with the discursive liberation and legitimation of interiority, Baggs reveals that the humanitarian conception of interiority can in fact be seen as thoroughly confining from an autistic perspective.

In the following section, I situate Baggs's critique of language and verbalization in this video in the larger context of hir other writings as well as those of other autistic commentators. I argue that autistic accounts of language and communication contain the elements of a counterdiscourse of voicing that resonates with the work of cultural critics like Dolar and Barthes. These unlikely interlocutors mount a powerful critique of the logocentric notion of the voice that orients the humanitarian therapeutic discourse surrounding autism and its implied vision of humanity. As I go on to show over the course of the chapter, this critique is also deeply relevant to the history of documentary and its investments in the (speaking) voice as a marker of social and representational progress.

Autistic Counterdiscourses of the Voice

Autism has been regarded throughout its diagnostic history as a failure to communicate, and language and voice thus feature prominently in its diagnosis and treatment. The causes of autism remain in question, over seventy years after the pioneering research of Leo Kanner and Hans Asperger. The hypotheses that have propelled autism research at different historical moments are varied and controversial: they include maternal neglect, metabolic imbalances, vaccines, environmental toxins, genetic factors, and, most recently, neurological abnormalities in sensory perception and integration.[34] The common denominator of these diagnoses has been a fascination with autism as a communicative disorder that impacts language ability and speech. This is borne out in the recently released fifth edition of the *Diagnostic and Statistical Manual of Mental Disorders*, published by the American Psychiatric Association, which defines autism as a spectrum disorder involving impairments in social communication and interaction and a range of imaginative behaviors and interests.[35]

Overcoming this so-called deficit in communicative capacity remains, by and large, the goal of the growing list of customizable therapeutic interventions for autism spectrum disorders, which encompass various permutations of speech, occupational, and sensory integration therapies. Too numerous to systematize, the therapeutic approaches (e.g., behavioral, cognitive, psychopharmacological) currently employed in the treatment of autism spectrum disorders draw on different scientific models, employ different curricula, and activate different forms of relationships between the therapist and patient. However, the basic competencies they seek to cultivate—including eye contact, social interaction, compliance, attention, and imaginative-symbolic skills—are all implicitly or explicitly designed to cultivate a comportment toward human voices, faces, and language and to orient the cognitive, physiological, and affective supports of vocal sounding toward the production of words.[36]

It is precisely this conflation of language and speech with voice that Baggs disputes when sie writes, "Not everyone has words but everyone has a voice and a means of communicating. And not everyone who uses words sees words as their primary voice or their primary means of understanding things. . . . [M]ost people seem to miss these facts, and automatically see having a voice as the same as using speech or at least using language."[37] Baggs's statement is deceptively simple. On the surface it appears to correspond to the structure of a human rights claim in that Baggs claims that sie too has a voice and deserves, on that basis, to be recognized as human. In this regard, Baggs might seem to confirm the conservative, humanitarian vision of humanity that is grounded in essential characteristics (such as voice) and that progressively includes excluded subjects on the condition that they exhibit these characteristics. However, more careful parsing reveals that Baggs strategically uses human rights discourse to critique the confining form of humanity that humanitarian agents believe they liberate by giving autistics a voice. Baggs's insistence that autistics who cannot speak *already* have a voice suggests that what is "given" in such therapeutic interventions is not a voice per se but rather an attunement to the humanitarian—and, by extension, the documentary—conventions of articulate, persuasive speech.

Baggs suggests that we can grasp an alternative, autistic concept of the voice if we disarticulate the voice from language and speech—that is, if we approach the voice from the perspective of those who are thought *not* to have one in the first place. In so doing, sie calls into question one of the most enduring refrains of Western philosophy, dating back to Plato and Aristotle: the belief that humanity abides in the capacity for externalizing interiority through speech.[38] The metaphysical turn in post-Socratic philosophy, as Frances Dyson has noted, was characterized by the imperative to subject the body to a purification process that would banish its corporeality and etherealize its true inner substance: reason.[39] According to this narrative, the voice, or the capacity to produce physical soundings, exists to make meaning, specifically linguistic meaning. This is what is believed to set humans apart from other animals. Animals, Aristotle famously proclaimed, do not have a voice even though they produce sounds, for "voice is a sound *with a meaning*."[40] The meaning in question is thought to *already* reside within the body in the form of a soul, *logos*, or inner speech, the human bequest of the Word of God; the voice is merely the vehicle by which it may be exteriorized.

The imperative of humans "rising above matter" to achieve reason weighs on the voice in a particular way. In this logocentric mode of privileging the linguistic content of speech over its social, embodied modes of making meaning, the voice is treated as a "vanishing mediator" whose corporeal content evaporates in the act of utterance. Dolar's elaboration of this phenomenon is worth quoting at some length for its clear explanation of the paradoxical dualism between mind and body, subjectivity and corporeality, that structures metaphysical thinking. Dolar writes:

We can make various other sounds with the intention of signifying something, but there the intention is external to those sounds themselves, or they function as a stand-in, a metaphorical substitute for the voice. Only the voice implies a subjectivity which "expresses itself" and itself inhabits the means of expression. But if the voice is thus the quasi-natural bearer of the production of meaning, it also proves to be strangely recalcitrant to it. If we speak in order to "make sense," to signify, to convey something, then the voice is the material support of bringing about meaning, yet it does not contribute to itself. It is, rather, something like the vanishing mediator (to use the terms made famous by Fredric Jameson for a different purpose)—it makes the utterance possible, but it disappears in it, it goes up in smoke in the meaning being produced. Even on the most banal level of daily experience, when we listen to someone speak, we may at first be very much aware of his or her voice and its particular qualities, its color and accent, but soon we accommodate to it and concentrate only on the meaning that is conveyed. The voice itself is like the Wittgensteinian ladder to be discarded when we have successfully climbed to the top—that is, when we have made our ascent to the peak of meaning. The voice is the instrument, the vehicle, the medium, and the meaning is the goal. This gives rise to a spontaneous opposition where voice appears as materiality opposed to the ideality of meaning. The ideality of meaning can emerge only through the materiality of the means, but the means does not seem to contribute to meaning.[41]

In the philosophical scenario summarized by Dolar, the voice's sole purpose is as a vehicle for linguistic meaning: as a corporeal, bodily thing, it is both the medium of and an obstacle to the expression of divine speech. Dolar identifies a stance regarding the voice that is not clearly articulated in Jacques Derrida's famous critique of the metaphysics of presence surrounding the voice. Derrida argues that the metaphysical tradition as a whole is characterized by a phonocentric bias in which the voice covers over the work of the signifier, producing an illusion of self-presence: as a result, speech is privileged over written communication as the ground of unmediated interiority or consciousness. Dolar demurs that Derrida's discussion of the metaphysical bias and its enduring impact on contemporary humanistic inquiry renders consistent a complex philosophical history in which the voice was not always seen as the ground of presence. On the contrary, in post-Socratic discourses of voice and music, the materiality of the voice has often been understood as a potential threat to presence, sense, and metaphysical consistency.[42]

With these considerations in mind, Dolar redefines the voice as the counterintuitive, abjected remainder of Western thought's irreconcilable investments in the concept of a voice. Dolar proposes that the voice is the nonsignifying element within communication, or *"what does not contribute to making sense."* The voice, he writes, is "the material element recalcitrant to meaning," "that which cannot be said," "the non-linguistic, the extralinguistic element which enables speech phenomena, but cannot itself be discerned by linguistics."[43] This category would then accommodate all of the corporeal soundings that are believed by Aristotle not to have "soul" in them—for instance, vocal qualities like accent, intonation, and timbre; nonverbal expressions like song; and mechanical, involuntary utterances such as coughs, hiccups, laughter, sighs, breathing, echolalic babbling, and the like—although Dolar argues that even these are captured by language and turned into a mode of the articulate. At the same time, Dolar insists that while the voice is not a linguistic phenomenon, it cannot be situated in the body either: he proposes that while the voice stems from the body, it separates from the body in the manner of a missile; the voice therefore belongs neither to the body nor to the realm of language but remains recalcitrantly alien to both.[44]

Dolar's redefinition of a voice as an embodied, communicative comportment that precedes, exceeds, and eludes the confines of linguistic signification dovetails closely with the recent attempts of a number of autistic commentators to articulate how their modes of voicing remain at odds with the faculties of language and speech that contemporary treatments for autism spectrum disorders take as their goal. Baggs, who has written extensively about hir experiences with autism, explains, for instance, that hir mode of sensory perception consists of perceiving the world as a rich tapestry of patterns in motion. Sie explains that conventional language, which is based on abstract symbolic categories rather than patterns, is fundamentally inadequate for the fluid world of hir sensory impressions.[45] Baggs writes, "I don't have many buffers; to me the world comes in in such great detail that it is hard for me to put the easy interpretations on it that most people use; the way they divide it into pieces and make it abstract is foreign to me."[46] Here, Baggs refers to the broad range of neurological differences in processing, prioritizing, interpreting, and integrating sensory information from the environment and the body that make it difficult for those on the autistic spectrum to abstract the body from the environment, and subjects from objects. These differences, Baggs explains, pose particular difficulties when it comes to verbalization, which relies heavily on the faculty of abstraction.

The primatologist Dawn Prince, who was diagnosed with autism only well into adulthood, has similarly written with great insight about her inability to reconcile herself to the arbitrary abstractions of linguistic meaning. She describes her own encounters with language as a concrete, sensory horizon in its own right, where words resist being assigned to specific concepts or situations and instead have an elastic, mimetic potential. Prince explains her own fascination with repeating the word *hippopotamus*, which was capable of absorbing and bequeathing the associations of context and memory wherever she went. This word would bring familiarity and order to overwhelming new sensory situations, investing them with the reassuring associations of her grandmother's muted makeup colors, the smell of a cedar chest, or the sensation of loved ones nearby. Simultaneously, it would become a receptacle for singling out and collecting new sense impressions, such as the joyful sound and warmth of running bathwater. She writes, "To me, it was a completely valid response when someone asked me, 'Do you need to go to the bathroom?' to answer 'Hippopotamus.'"[47] Language, encountered in this way, is less a medium of communication than a living and malleable medium of existence that joins subjects and environments, and humans with other species—indeed, Prince attributes her ability to commune with animals and plants to this mimetic encounter with language.

Other autistics, including Temple Grandin, have attested to the extraordinary degree of muscular, sensorial, and cognitive focus demanded by listening to and producing meaningful speech. Grandin explains that an attunement to words sometimes requires tuning out phatic sensory cues, including the nuances of vocal tone and facial expression to which autistics are presumed to be impervious and which they themselves find difficult to produce.[48] Tito Rajarshi Mukhopadhyay, an autistic writer and poet who communicates using FC, finds speaking to be profoundly dissociative. He describes speech as a futile process of ordering a bundle of bodily sensations that resist being "zoned" as faculties or organs. The vocal faculty, he writes, is particularly elusive: "autism was making him feel that his voice was a distant substance that was required to be collected and put somewhere inside his throat. But he was unable to find it."[49] Typing or pointing to letters is often preferable, as D. J. Savarese reports. The calming presence of a facilitator assists Savarese in focusing his muscle movements on the act of typing, without which his body flaps and moves uncontrollably in response to the overwhelming sensory detail that comes at and pulls him in all directions.[50]

Drawing on autistic perspectives such as these, Erin Manning has noted that, unlike neurotypical individuals, autistics are not exclusively attuned to human language or faciality, as the two orienting coordinates of the voice. Autistic perception, she argues, is often immersed in the world as a system of entangled relations that encompass human, nonhuman, organic, and inorganic registers. In this unhierarchized "attunement to life as an incipient ecology of practices" that is constantly in the making, the abstractions involved in language are frequently experienced as an imperative of distilling an infinite mélange of sense impressions into the narrow channels of intersubjective relations and signification.[51] The body must similarly be subtracted from its exploratory environmental relations, and the vocal channel localized and differentiated from the other organs in order for speech to occur.

For all these "subtractions," it is undeniable that linguistic forms of communication, such as speaking, writing, typing, and FC, are vital translation tools for autistics—without these mediating forms, it would be difficult, if not impossible, to engage with autistic modes of voicing in the first place. However, the complex capacity of language to shape experience in socially meaningful ways means that the subtraction in question is often experienced as an awakening from a state of hibernation. Rubin, the protagonist of Wurzburg's film, has described her mind as "waking up" after lying "fallow" for years upon being introduced to FC. Prince, on the other hand, shows how language can behave as a kind of connective tissue linking different registers and dimensions of experience when it is relieved of its usual signifying functions. Taking both perspectives on language into consideration, Manning proposes that language can be "both more-than and less-than"—it can multiply and foreclose on, add to and subtract from expressive and receptive potential all at once.[52]

When we approach accounts such as these with Baggs's statement in mind, we find that they offer nothing less than an autistic counterdiscourse of voicing that complicates the logocentric humanitarian notion of having a voice. From a humanitarian perspective, the autistic dwelling in an infinite field of perceptual and relational possibilities is seen as disabled or trapped. However, when we look at speech from an autistic perspective, it is voicing in the "normal" sense, from which these possibilities have been subtracted, that is revealed to be disabled, lacking, closeted, and constrained—it would not be an exaggeration to call it thoroughly autistic. This is what Baggs argues when sie proposes that those who respond without hesitation in a recognizable tongue to the humanitarian call to have a voice are confined to a limited conception of humanity.

Baggs, Prince, and other autistic writers are attentive to the mimetic potential activated by the process of communication, before it is subordinated to the confines of sanctioned signifying forms. Their communicative comportment is one in which the affective and physical supports of vocal sounding resist being harnessed as a medium or channel for exteriorizing inner experience but participate instead in an ongoing merger with emerging fields of sensation. What is more, the voice, as autistic interlocutors invoke it, is not restricted narrowly to the production of sonorous soundings through the larynx, diaphragm, and mouth but refers more broadly to a more complex gestural paralanguage that includes some of the common behaviors attributed to autistics, such as staring vacantly, humming, echoing others' words, swaying, or flapping. As Baggs insists, autistics *do* communicate, even when they are accused of being uncommunicative (existing in a "world of their own," "avoiding eye contact," engaging in "obsessive or repetitive" activities) or when their communications are deemed to be failures (nonsensical, socially disruptive). We might propose as an alternative that these communiqués are not antisocial or uncommunicative. They represent an ongoing communion with the world ("an ongoing response to what is around," to borrow Baggs's words from "In My Language") rather than being oriented solely toward a neurotypical human subject. If these communications have an orientation, it is toward an audience that they hope to hail into being in their own image.

The autistic voice, understood in such terms, resonates with Barthes's notion of the grain of the voice. Barthes defines the grain of the voice as an erotic, prelogical, and corporeal element in communication that exceeds its coded, sanctioned forms of embodiment and signification, or "the materiality of the body speaking its mother tongue."[53] The autistic voice may seem at first to be at odds with the organicism of Barthes's concept, for which Barthes has been critiqued. As Grandin attests, the voices of autistics are frequently perceived as "flat with little inflection and no rhythm," or *lacking in grain*, a perception that is further exacerbated when autistics communicate using speech-generating devices that reduce vocalization to a depersonalized mechanical sound.[54] In other instances where their vocalization is echolalic, inappropriately pitched, idiosyncratically syntactic, socially disruptive, or stuttering, autistics resemble other minoritarian subjects whose voices are deemed *too grainy*. Like female voices, transgender voices, racially inflected or regionally accented voices, and the voices of the ill, the aged, and the disturbed, autistic voices are infrequently encountered in mainstream media forms.[55] Even in documentary films, which "typically demonstrate a wider variety of accents, dialects, and speech patterns than those found in fiction films," hyperembodied voices are routinely edited for clarity or subtitled, a measure that according to film historian Jeffrey Ruoff serves to maximize the intelligibility of their speech while minimizing the interference of its grain.[56]

Transgender filmmaker and artist Wu Tsang expresses her solidarity with these dilemmas of autistic voicing in *Shape of a Right Statement*, a video from 2008 in which Tsang re-performs the second part of Baggs's "In My Language." Tsang faces the camera, dressed plainly in a black top and nude skull cap, framed in front of a shiny silver curtain. The background is as flamboyant as Tsang's appearance is neutral, its shimmering surface seeming to reflect in turn the lack and excess that simultaneously mark her androgynous body and voice. Tsang repeats Baggs's "translation" word for word, replicating exactly the mechanical tones, pauses, and speech patterns of Baggs's electronically generated speech, but without subtitles. Tsang's face remains perfectly expressionless as she speaks, but the tears welling in her eyes and her occasional sharp intakes of breath betray the tremendous effort involved in her performance. The effect is disorienting. Without subtitles lassoing our attention to Tsang's words, we are invited to experience the texture and grain of her peculiar vocal delivery. It is as if Tsang attempts to inhabit precisely those registers of voicing that are usually subtracted, cast out, or subordinated in service of intelligibility. In addressing these communiqués to us, she asks us to become the audience with which the autistic voice seeks communion.

The complexities of the autistic voice are further illuminated if we turn to a less commonly cited definition of the grain of the voice. Barthes writes that the grain opens the voice to *signifiance*, which he defines elsewhere as "'the un-end of possible operations in a given field of a language.' Contrary to signification, *signifiance* cannot be reduced, therefore, to communication, representation, expression."[57] Barthes also writes that the grain of the voice inheres in "the very precise space . . . of *the encounter between a language and a voice*."[58] He would seem here to be describing the opening of signifiance, which has typically been interpreted as a textual encounter, whereby the reader or listener attempting to master language is ultimately undone by the slippage and slide of the signifier that perpetually defers the stabilization of meaning. But when we consider the aforementioned quote in conjunction with Barthes's evocation of the grain as the materiality of the body, we are able to envision signifiance in a different register, as a *temporal* encounter between corporeal and linguistic materialities. To rephrase Barthes, we might say that signifiance emerges in the existential interval between the plane of enunciation and the plane in which it is bounded and given shape as communication.

Reading Barthes's grain of the voice against its grain, as it were, we can focus on its temporal movement rather than its binary operation. This broadens our perspective beyond Barthes's own preferred example of song, turning his essay into an invitation to experience all vocalization, including speech, nonteleologically, from the perspective of the voice *as* voice, rather than retrospectively from the perspective of language.[59] Reconfigured in this manner, the grain of the voice offers a means of understanding the temporal, durational dimension of communication implied in the autistic counterdiscourse of the voice. The opening of signifiance provides a vocabulary for what writers like Mukhopadhyay, Baggs, Prince, and Rubin gesture to as the awakening of the body to communication—one that is experienced as a temporary suspension that diffuses the body in the environment before it must be gathered up and localized in the service of articulate speech (Mukhopadhyay's account of having to "collect" and put his voice in his throat is a vivid reminder). Thus, the grain as signifiance invokes those dimensions of vocalization that do not culminate in the destination of intelligible speech.

Returning to Baggs's statement that "not everyone who uses words sees words as their primary voice or their primary means of understanding things," one can locate the "primary voice" to which sie refers in this suspended time of communicative potential. The writings of Baggs and others, in conversation with Barthes and Dolar, enable us to see that the autistic voice does not belong exclusively to autistic individuals but is a spectral presence in *all* speech. The conditions of possibility of its emergence can now be understood in terms of the extent to which the conventions of voicing remain open to what we might, following Dolar and Barthes, call the nonsignifying element within communication, or the interval of signifiance.

The autistic counterdiscourse of voicing that I have laid out has implications for the study of documentary that go beyond the specific representational challenges of autism. At a more general level, the concept of the autistic voice urges us to revisit the role of the speaking voice as documentary's defining formal feature as well as the central metaphor of documentary studies. Documentary was once defined by Bill Nichols as a "discourse of sobriety" motivated by rhetorical rather than aesthetic goals and, hence, a genre organized around the spoken word rather than the image. Although it is now widely agreed that the horizons of the documentary genre have far exceeded these narrow interventionist parameters (Nichols has since rescinded his definition of documentary as a sober rhetorical genre), documentary scholars continue to reference Nichols's use of voice as a metaphor for the implied worldview or perspective of a documentary film, as well as a literal measure of the genre's inclusion of the perspectives of previously disenfranchised or voiceless subjects. For instance, a number of documentary critics, from Michael Renov to Catherine Russell, regard the emergence of documentary films featuring first-person vocal commentary (often by minoritarian subjects) as evidence of the genre's progression from an objective voice or worldview to one that is more reflexive and inclusive.

I argue that the seemingly innocuous metaphor of "the voice of documentary" can be seen as an indication of the enduring logocentric—and, by extension, humanitarian—investments of documentary studies in the speaking voice as a measure of humanity. The attention of autistic interlocutors like Baggs to the paralinguistic, embodied dimensions of voicing allows us to read these investments against their grain. Specifically, I propose that concept of the autistic voice activates a minor, feminist, register of Nichols's analysis of the voice of documentary. Whereas Nichols traces documentary's progressive evolution from totalitarian and univocal modes toward polyvocal and thus more inclusive modes of voicing, the autistic voice comments on how the reality effects of documentary are bound up with the documentary tropes of persuasive speech, and raises questions regarding the narrative of documentary's reflexive progress toward polyvocality. These questions also pertain to recent documentary scholarship on the first-person voice-over. Using my readings of the voice-overs in "I Am Autism," *Autism Is a World*, and "In My Language," I examine how the autistic voice can potentially unground the humanity that this vocal trope tacitly authenticates, and point toward its "regressive" openings.

In my introductory chapter, I noted that Grierson, writing in 1942, located the generic specificity of documentary in its "anti-aesthetic" vocation. Grierson is also known for pioneering the use of expository voice-over commentary, a technique of narration derided by fiction filmmakers as the "last resort of the incompetent" for its violation of cherished ideals regarding the visual focus and invisible discourse of film.[60] Grierson's promotion of this technique reflected an intuitive understanding of how the metaphysical attunement to the speaking voice as a bearer of linguistic meaning—rather than an embodied obstacle to its intelligibility—could be combined with the architectonics of documentary to achieve the rhetorical effect of immediacy. The "I Am Autism" video offers an excellent illustration of how expository voice-over narration functions as the quintessential "vanishing mediator," to quote Dolar's description of how voice is treated in the metaphysical tradition. The emanation of this disembodied voice from off-screen has the effect of "rising above" other sounds and images beneath it in the audiovisual hierarchy, as well as its own source, materiality, and embodiment, to forcefully assert its message.

Over half a century later, in his magisterial study of documentary, *Representing Reality* (1991), Nichols reframes Grierson's innate grasp of this metaphysical principle of voicing as a hypothesis regarding the pivotal role of the speaking voice in documentary's reality effects. Nichols claims that documentary's distinctive stylistic features emerge from its rhetorical motivations as a "discourse of sobriety" aiming to persuade spectators of the authenticity and credibility of its claims regarding social reality. Documentary films, Nichols proposes, are organized around an "informing logic" requiring a "representation, case, or argument about the historical world."[61] Since "arguments require a logic that words are able to bear far more easily than images," Nichols infers that the onus of documentary's representational burden rests on the sound track rather than the image, and specifically on speech.[62] He notes that "commentary by voice-over narrators, reporters, interviewees, and other social actors figure strongly in most documentary."[63]

In linking documentary with the oratory arts of persuasive speaking more than with the visual arts of composition and montage, Nichols highlights the rhetorical efficiency of the speaking voice in collapsing the ideological distance between text and spectator. His point is that documentary works on its audience through voices that explicitly (e.g., voice-over exposition) or implicitly (e.g., interview footage) argue its stance. Thus, the film invites an unspoken "yes" in response to the question it poses: "This is so, isn't it?" He writes that in those instances where documentary aims to mobilize its "*indexical* relation to the historical world" in support of factual claims, speech "adds flesh to fact," behaving as the material supplement by means of which the mute facticity of audiovisual evidence is shot through with social meaning and made credible.[64]

Nichols's account of documentary speech closely parallels Dolar's account of the spontaneous opposition between the materiality of voice and the ideality of meaning in the Western, logocentric tradition ("The ideality of meaning can emerge only through the materiality of the means, but the means does not seem to contribute to meaning").[65] In other words, the reality effects of documentary—that is, its authority, credibility, and persuasiveness—depend on its success in subordinating the "flesh" of documentary speech (its grain, or signifiance) in service of its rhetorical aims. When approached through the concept of the autistic voice, Nichols's ideas offer a suggestive commentary on how the rhetorical immediacy of documentary is achieved by both mobilizing and disavowing those registers of voicing that might potentially destabilize its intended meaning. Indeed, it would seem as though Nichols were referring to the ways in which the vanishing materiality of the speaking voice inspires documentary's reality effects when he employs the voice of documentary as a metaphor for the unique perspective or worldview of every documentary film.

This metaphor receives its most substantial elaboration in Nichols's essay "The Voice of Documentary," which predates *Representing Reality* by a few years. In a frequently cited passage from this essay, Nichols writes, "By 'voice' I mean something narrower than style: that which conveys to us a sense of a text's social point of view, of how it is speaking to us and how it is organizing the materials it is presenting to us. In this sense, 'voice' is not restricted to any one code or feature such as dialogue or spoken commentary. Voice is perhaps akin to that intangible, moiré-like pattern formed by the unique interaction of all a film's codes, and it applies to all modes of documentary."[66] Intriguingly, Nichols disavows any privileged connection between the voice of documentary and the documentary tropes of persuasive speech when he writes that voice is not restricted simply to dialogue or spoken commentary. In the second edition of his textbook *Introduction to Documentary*, published in 2010, Nichols employs speech as a general signifier of documentary's expressive possibilities, writing that the "voice of documentary speaks with all the means available to its maker."[67] In other words, documentary "speech" encompasses not only literal speech but every possible enunciative choice regarding the relationships between sounds and images (composition, selection, arrangement, inclusion, exclusion, mode of narration) through which a documentary can make convincing truth claims. Or, as Nichols explains in his 1983 essay, "we may think we hear history or reality speaking to us through a film, but what we actually hear is the voice of the text, even when that voice tries to efface itself."[68]

Nichols's use of voice as a metaphor for the elusive element that both holds together the message of a documentary and disappears in the act of its utterance insists on the very connection between voice and speech that he disavows. Voice has immense critical potential as a metaphor that identifies an enduring logocentric tendency in the genre's approach to mediation, especially in those instances where those who are represented by documentary appear to "speak for themselves." It is striking, therefore, that "The Voice of Documentary" argues the opposite. This essay identifies a series of roughly chronological documentary modes that progressively democratize and undermine the truth claims of the Griersonian expository mode through a more complex and inclusive distribution of voices and modes of address. These include an observational mode that eschews voice-over commentary in favor of social actors speaking indirectly among themselves, an interactive mode in which interviewees step up to the camera to report their testimony or engage in a dialogue with the filmmaker, and a reflexive mode of documentary that is self-conscious regarding the effects of its chosen modes of vocalization. Nichols has since updated this list to include a performative mode that typically involves a highly subjective voice-over and a poetic mode that avoids speech altogether.[69]

Some critics, like Stella Bruzzi, have criticized Nichols's genealogy of the evolving modes of documentary as an overly linear and schematic "family tree."[70] Since the publication of the first edition of her book New Documentary in 2000, Bruzzi has been a vocal critic of Nichols's chronology of the various modes of documentary, which she argues produces false dichotomies between ideologically regressive and progressive documentary approaches based on films that share formal features. However, Nichols's account of documentary's departure from its sober, rhetorical origins remains a gravitational force field in contemporary documentary studies, whose focus has overwhelmingly shifted from the rhetorical to poetic, subjective, spectacular, performative, or sentimental relations to the real.[71] One such example of the consensus around Nichols's narrative of documentary's "evolution" from the primitive, authoritarian days of Griersonian voice-of-God narration to more inclusive and reflexive modes of voicing can be seen in the enthusiastic critical embrace of documentaries featuring a highly reflexive first-person voice-over as one of the genre's most sophisticated approaches to the politics of representation. I turn now to these critical accounts, with the following proposal: the spectral—one might even say autistic—undertow in Nichols's metaphor of the voice of documentary urges us to examine how the reality effects of the first-person voice-over in the reflexive mode are powerfully bound up with our ideological attunement to speech and language as markers of humanity, or, in other words, with logocentrism.

A number of documentary scholars have addressed the proliferation of documentary films produced since the 1970s that are "spoken" from the (often but not always marginal) subject position of the filmmaker, who may also serve as a protagonist. Different names have been given to such films: Nichols groups such films under the rubrics of the performative and reflexive documentary modes, whereas Michael Renov, Laura Rascaroli, Catherine Russell, and Alisa Lebow respectively employ the labels "new autobiography," "the essay film," "autoethnographic film," and "first person film." These labels draw attention to different permutations and subsets of reflexive, personal documentary filmmaking. Rascaroli, for instance, is interested in the essayistic attempt to textually incorporate the process of reasoning and thinking, whereas Russell is concerned with films that deconstruct ethnographic vectors of oppression such as race, ethnicity, gender, and sexuality from either side of asymmetrical relations of domination and subordination. Renov and Lebow, on the other hand, are each interested in films that problematize subjectivity from an autobiographical perspective and in terms of the relation between the individual and their culture or community.[72]

While the emphases of these authors vary in important ways, they all isolate two common features of their overlapping, and continually expanding, documentary filmography. The first is a commitment to deconstructing the autonomous, unified, and objective subject position traditionally associated with the "sober" Griersonian mode of expository commentary. The second is the presence of a highly reflexive voice-over commentary in the first person that employs strategies such as irony, unreliability, contradiction, digression, and contrapuntality. As Russell notes, the voice-over remains the primary site of these deconstructions, even though they can also be expressed through the look of the camera or the image.[73] Not only does this type of first-person voice-over offer an economical means of centering the perspective of formerly marginalized or unacknowledged subjectivities—a politically reflexive act—but its formally reflexive mode of exposition means that the speaking subject is problematized as fragmented, multiple, incoherent, split, and, perhaps most important, *relational.* As Lebow writes,

> autobiographical film implicates others in its quest to represent a self, implicitly constructing a subject always already in-relation—that is, in the first person plural. As psychoanalysis teaches, and as others such as Emmanuel Levinas and Judith Butler have argued, the self is always a relational matter, never conceivable in isolation. First person film merely literalizes and makes apparent the fact that self-narration—not to mention autobiography—is never the sole property of the speaking self. It properly belongs to larger collectivities without which the maker would be unrecognizable to herself, and effectively would have no story to tell.[74]

To sum up, the reflexive first-person voice-over is widely regarded as a transgressive convention that not only grapples with who has the right to speak in documentary but also dismantles cultural preconceptions regarding the so-called voice or worldview of a given documentary film. The concept of the autistic voice pinpoints what remains underinterrogated in these accounts: the logocentrism of the first-person voice-over. If first-person film makes it apparent that "the self is always a relational matter," as Lebow argues, then the autistic voice argues that the subjectivity designated by the first-person pronoun—a linguistic designation of personhood—is necessarily constituted in relation to a linguistic collectivity. Whereas relationality, in this discourse, is more or less equivalent with interpersonal or interhuman relationality, the autistic voice joins feminist film critics like Trinh and Peckham in foregrounding the seemingly *impersonal, inhuman,* and *regressive* relationalities that escape such linguistic designations. The unspoken associations of the first-person voice-over with realist concepts such as honesty, truth, or stable interiority have already been successfully deconstructed. By adding interhuman relationality to the list of these realist concepts, the autistic voice urges documentary studies to re-examine its benchmarks of representational progress: it shows that even though documentary has seemingly been acquitted of its representational realism, a more entrenched form of realism inheres in the genre's insistent use of pronominal verbalization to demonstrate that "a human being is present."

The capacity of the first-person voice-over to reinforce interhuman relationality can be understood as an extension of the principle that Chion dubs *vococentrism*: a speaking voice, Chion argues, commands attention over other sounds, much as a human face is accorded a special privilege over other images.[75] The first-person voice-over similarly rises above the other audiovisual elements of documentary speech—including those nonverbal but nonetheless communicative and relational elements that I have described as the autistic voice—when it comes to the voice of documentary. We can witness this principle in action in the expository first-person voice-over of "I Am Autism" as well as in the interventionist first-person voice-over in *Autism Is a World*. In "I Am Autism," we see faces *and* hear an acousmatic voice speaking in the first person. But because the listless, silent, and unresponsive faces of autistic children are coded as nonfaces, and thus nonrelational, the acousmatic voice stands in as an implied human presence, even as it paradoxically speaks from the inhuman perspective of the "disease" of autism. The interpellative power of such an expository speaking voice is not simply a function of its place in the audiovisual hierarchy, as effected through a set of technical manipulations such as sound design, volume, and editing; it is also linked to its use of the first-person pronoun to constitute its subjectivity in relation to a logocentric human collectivity, with which the audience is invited to identify.

The relationship between the Rubin we hear in Margulies's first-person voice-over and the Rubin we see struggling with autism in Wurzburg's *Autism Is a World* clarifies that the relational bonds of this collectivity are defined by the exclusion of the nonverbal, "nonrelational" autistic. This relationship is not unlike that which exists between the voice of autism and the faces of autistic children in "I Am Autism." The Rubin who addresses us in the first person in Margulies's soft, mellifluous voice using unbroken, perfect English assumes the status of a subject, speaking about that abjected part of herself that suffers from "awful autism" as an object to be observed, described, and overcome. Even though the source of Margulies's voice-over is unseen, the quality of her voice conjures the mental image of a correspondingly coherent, able, feminine body that stands in as the absent "face" of the film and entreats our identification. The first-person voice-over comfortably claims the status of the film's voice, whereas this category and the humanity it connotes never seem appropriate to the incoherent sounds that pitch forth from Rubin's on-screen body.

Baggs's electronically generated first-person voice-over, on the other hand, suggests that the autistic voice is precisely what must be jettisoned from the speaking voice in order to evidence a recognizable mode of personhood. Hir use of this trope seems to exemplify the kind of reflexivity described by Rascaroli, Russell, Lebow, and others, in that Baggs's commentary self-consciously thematizes its own self-evidently positive value as a marker of humanity, interiority, and relational capacity. The difference is that Baggs critiques the epistemic limits of the first-person voice-over at a level that is rarely questioned: sie calls out the thoroughly limiting interhuman relationality that a speaking voice, particularly one speaking about itself, is thought to activate. Even as Baggs's words make a claim on behalf of hir humanity in the "translation," they also demonstrate how hir promiscuous mode of interacting with the world in the first part of the video is both activated by *and* paradoxically confined by the logocentric communicative logic of the first-person voice-over. In this way, Baggs urges us to consider the modes of communication, relationality, and representation that remain in the shadows of this convention as the starting point for an autistic approach to political and formal reflexivity in documentary. Baggs's use of the first-person voice-over to undermine the meaning of "coming to voice" returns us to Nichols's claim that speech makes documentary's truth claims credible. If a (speaking) voice is that elusive something that coheres documentary's disparate elements into a single overarching perspective that invites the spectator's tacit identification and approval, then the autistic voice, Baggs suggests, must be the dizzying multiplication and kaleidoscoping of that perspective.

Toward an Autistic Discourse on Humanitarianism

Thus far, I have considered the dynamics between three different types of voices speaking for autism as they pertain to the politics of documentary representation. I now expand my purview to address how these voices also animate the broader discursive history of autism. My analysis is guided by a reading of Foucault's *Madness and Civilization*, a book whose philosophical engagement with the prehistory of Western attitudes toward disability also offers a compelling commentary on what it means to produce an autistic discourse on humanitarianism.

The connections between autism and Foucault are far from accidental. Foucault's work on the institutional and discursive formations that have named and defined medical disorders (such as the asylum, psychiatric science, and the medical gaze) has been instrumental in shaping the field of sociological studies of science and technology, from which some of the most enabling contributions to contemporary research on autism have emerged. However, the more philosophical questions raised by Foucault regarding the outcasting of "unreason" from the space of Western civilization have not yet been substantially taken up in relation to autism. I turn now to these questions in order to tease out the stakes of the various claims regarding interiority and exteriority, confinement and emancipation, that animate contemporary medical as well as media interventions around autism. The exercise of mapping the discursive history of autism also allows me to unearth the often contradictory and ambivalent threads of Foucault's own ideas in this early book on the workings of power and subjection.

My proposal is that my three examples of documentary voices speaking for autism map more generally onto contemporary debates regarding autism in fields as wide-ranging as medicine, science and technology studies, and critical disability studies. In practice, these voices are thoroughly entangled and overdetermined, and the contentious status of autism means that any effort to schematize the positions it engenders can only fall short. The central facts about autism about which there is consensus, as many scholars note, are that we don't yet know much about it at all and that no two autistics are exactly alike. As Chloe Silverman notes, various interest groups remain in heated dispute as to how the existing empirical evidence about autism should be mobilized: for example, some (but not all) autistic self-advocates see the search for a cure as devaluing their own unique abilities, while psychologists use autism as a platform for constructing theories of cognition, and parent-advocates seek resources to pursue innovative therapies or genetic research.[76] Still, the clarity gained from describing the function of the three main voices that weave through these variegated positions makes this a worthwhile exercise.

The first voice (I will call this the dominant voice) emerges from the compulsion, mandated by the emergence of modern industrial capitalism, to envision the healthy, able-bodied, and able-minded individual capable of work as the norm of the human. This voice has its counterparts in the voices of the white man, the colonizer, the heterosexual, the anthropologist, and so on. Looking back at the previous chapters, we can locate the voice of the photojournalist, and the traditional voice of the television news anchor, as described by Margaret Morse, as iterations of this subject position. In the video "I Am Autism," the dominant voice is the humanitarian voice speaking in the guise of autism in a didactic expository voice-over. Fabian identifies the epistemological hypocrisy involved in such speech: the dominant voice speaks objectively about otherness while effacing its own subject position. This self-effacement authorizes the dominant voice to describe autism in positive terms as a psychological disorder, a behavioral deficit in empathy or relational capacity, a neurological disability, or a genetic disease. Autism has been treated alternately in all of these ways since Kanner's pioneering research in 1943, but the common denominator lies in its coding as a lack requiring correction. As previously noted, "impairment" has been a consistent theme in the ever-evolving diagnostic classification of autism.

Much of the contemporary critical literature on autism refers to this dominant voice as the "deficit" or "medical" model of thinking about autism. This voice is analogous to the voice of "scientific reason," whose development Foucault traces through the classical-era precursors of the nineteenth-century mental asylum. One of Foucault's most well-received insights in *Madness and Civilization* is that the voice of medicine, speaking at once in the eternal tones of the Father, Judge, Family, and Law, tells us more about its own genealogies and norms than about the object (the patient) that it seeks to define as a deviation from these norms. Along these lines, Amit Pinchevski argues that autism has attracted a disproportionate amount of scientific attention relative to its incidence because, as "a paradigmatic case of arrest in communication, socialization and development, and as the ultimate impasse, it constitutes the antipode against which the medical-scientific discourse measures its rational tools for accessing another mind."[77]

Foucault seeks to re-create the negative content of the positivist medical voice by paying attention to its economic, legal, and moral conditions of possibility. The current surge of social constructivist approaches to the study of autism consistently adopt an archaeological reading of Foucault that attends to the discursive architectonics shaping medical statements at different historical moments. Ian Hacking's work is a direct application of this strain in Foucault's thinking. Hacking's concept of the "looping effect," or the mutual shaping between classificatory categories and the behaviors, norms, and self-identifications of autistic individuals, has become a foundational critical standpoint from which to regard the "autism epidemic."[78] Autism Speaks's campaign is just one example of the popular use of this sensationalist phrase to emphasize the dramatic rise in the incidence of autism from one in two thousand in the 1970s to one in a hundred at the time of writing of this chapter. This increase in incidence is frequently explained in naturalistic terms that evidence the enduring force of the positivist medical voice: explanations include bad parenting by "refrigerator mothers," metabolic imbalances, environmental toxins, vaccines, weather-related phenomena, television watching, and, more recently, neurobiological or genetic factors.[79]

Hacking's work has been immensely influential in dissipating the popular, sensationalist preoccupations with autism and situating its emergence as a diagnostic category within a broad series of discursive transformations that together comprise what Foucault has called the biopoliticization and medicalization of life. A number of scholars have followed Hacking's lead, arguing that the so-called autism epidemic needs to be understood in light of mutually informing transformations in the scientific, technological, institutional, and social realms. Several studies have racked focus from the so-called deficits of autism to this discursive background, attending to phenomena ranging from the deinstitutionalization of mental retardation, to the broadening of diagnostic criteria to assess the condition as a spectrum, to improvements in medical technology, to increased knowledge and awareness of autism in medical and lay spheres.[80] Others focus on social aspects of the discursive matrix that shapes the autistic spectrum as a target in motion, including shifts in the status and social organization of expertise, the affective role of parents and communities of care, the growing influence of the self-advocacy movement, and the generic forms and conventions of depicting autism, including "conversion" or "recovery" narratives and stereotypes of savantism and dependency.[81]

Even as they acknowledge the immense value of these social constructivist interventions, some scholars argue that this approach reinforces a worldview in which the autistic person is seen as a passive receptacle of discursive forces.[82] This critique, which is often leveled directly at Foucault, misses some of the finer points of Foucault's analysis that tackle the difficult question of how to make unreason speak without destroying it. We can elaborate on these points by attending to a second, "resistant" voice that speaks out against the humanitarian deployment of the dominant voice by appropriating its techniques of legitimation. Zana Briski in chapter 1, Tia Lessin and Carl Deal in chapter 2, and Wurzburg in this chapter all attempt to enable such a voice to "speak out." Rubin's appropriation of the authority associated with a didactic, expository documentary voice-over to assert her own autistic perspective using an interventionist first-person voice-over is an example of this kind of resistant voice. Kimberly Roberts's harnessing of the testimonial codes of liveness and Briski's students' use of the humanitarian aesthetic of innocence are other examples.

Robert McRuer's seminal work in critical disability studies articulates the complexities of this appropriative mode of resisting the dominant mode of power. McRuer argues that the regime of able-bodiedness, that is, the dominant voice against which autistic critics have spoken out, "still largely masquerades as a nonidentity, as the natural order of things," even more so than its counterpart, heterosexuality.[83] McRuer contends that this order was organized until recently by a dialectic of visibility, whereby the invisible influence of the dominant identity was maintained by spectacularizing its others as pathological. The retrograde audiovisual politics of "I Am Autism" exemplify this waning representational regime, in which the normative status of the vocal, articulate speaking subject is tacitly reinforced by the visible *and* audible pathologization of the nonverbal autistic body. McRuer argues that the rigid binary between normality and pathology has become flexible and supple in our postmodern, neoliberalized climate, in which the boundary line between the two is perpetually redrawn to reflect the changing patterns of tolerance. The result, he explains, is new techniques of exclusion: "Neoliberalism and the condition of postmodernity, in fact, increasingly need able-bodied, heterosexual subjects who are visibly and spectacularly tolerant of queer/disabled existences."[84] "In many cultural representations, disabled, queer figures no longer embody absolute deviance but are still visually and narratively subordinated, and sometimes they are eliminated outright (or perhaps—in the flexible new parlance—laid off). Flexibility again works both ways: heterosexual, able-bodied characters in such texts work with queer and disabled minorities, flexibly contracting and expanding, while queer and disabled minorities flexibly comply."[85]

McRuer points out that under neoliberalism, the exclusion of disabled minorities need not take the form of outright exclusion: instead, the inclusion or tolerance of difference can serve to successfully maintain dominant identities. The increasing visibility of autistics in Hollywood films is an example of this strategy at work. Stuart Murray notes that an increasing number of fiction films feature autistic characters but that the inclusion of these characters frequently serves as a means of centering a neurotypical protagonist: the disabled character animates and enables the narrative trajectory of the (usually able-bodied) protagonist, either by providing savant-like assistance in the dilemma at hand or by serving as an emotional enigma that the protagonist must work through.[86] McRuer's point is that visibility or inclusion is not necessarily a viable strategy of resistance in such a context, since visibility is often the currency on which the dominant order thrives in the first place.

Thus, McRuer's analysis brings a certain complexity to the existential efforts of disabled individuals who desire access, agency, and visibility, while simultaneously critiquing the normative ideals of ability associated with such agency. He describes the political work of speaking out against normative notions of ability as "coming out crip": a practice that "at times involves embracing and at times disidentifying with the most familiar kinds of identity politics."[87] This idea builds on the queer theorist José Esteban Muñoz's notion of disidentification, which refers to the survival strategies available to minority subjects when navigating a phobic majoritarian sphere that punishes abnormality. For Muñoz too it is imperative that the minoritarian agent remain flexible in order to parry the fluctuating modalities of neoliberal power; he therefore describes disidentification as a series of counteridentificatory performative actions that mimic the mechanisms and tropes of power (such as, in our case, the dominant humanitarian voice) but with a difference, through practices of recycling, reformatting, reappropriating, remaking, repossessing, and mutating.[88] The growing intersection of queer and disability studies therefore conceives of the second, resistant voice as one that reflexively emulates the flexible structure of neoliberal power as a strategic mode of improving highly asymmetrical power relations.

The geometric (rather than archaeological) logics in Foucault's thinking about madness and reason usefully illuminate the present discussion of asymmetry and symmetry in "coming out crip"—especially the movement from interiority to exteriority implied by this concept. Michel Serres, one of Foucault's most discerning commentators, parses these logics as follows, in a dense but rich paragraph about Foucault's history of madness: "Far from being a chronicle, the history of madness is a history of the variation of dual structures . . . located in the two spaces of reason and nonsense . . . structures of separation, of relation, of fusion, of opening up, of foundation, of rejection, of reciprocity, of exclusion, or even of 'nourishment'—in short, all the structures imaginable and imagined, more or less unconsciously, in history, in this double unity, including the unending circle that allows moving from one domain into the other without interruption."[89] Serres is referring to Foucault's narration of the loss of madness as a voice in dialogue with reason as a series of epistemic breaks that variably closed, opened, or connected these two spaces. McRuer performs a similar type of maneuver when he deconstructs the strict binary between able-bodiedness and disability by reconceptualizing the hierarchical and static relation between normal and impaired bodies as one of interdependency and mutuality. He extends Butler's critique of heterosexuality as an "inevitable comedy"—a position that is impossible to fully inhabit—to the norm of able-bodiedness, by showing that no body operates at peak capacity.[90]

The Butlerian (or Foucauldian) maneuver in disability studies critique is enabling precisely because it permits a counterintuitive analysis of the dominant regime (in this case, the regime of able-bodiedness) as one that is crippled by its own compulsory and delusional exclusions. This is also the point of Serres's analysis of Foucault's history of madness. Serres shows that in every case where a line of exclusion is drawn—for instance, during the large-scale internment of the mad alongside other social "degenerates" across western Europe in the second half of the seventeenth century, or, subsequently, the practice of sequestering the mad from criminals in the eighteenth century—there is a regulatory logic at work on both sides of the line. One side protects, and the other excludes, but not necessarily in the manner that is apparent. In the latter instance of separating the mad from criminals as a humanitarian measure, it is the prisoners who are protected from the mad and not the other way around. "The pseudoliberation," Serres writes, "always hides a more obscure and more real enclosure."[91] This leads him to conjecture that the "liberation" of madness is not exempt from a coercive regulatory logic in which the essence of madness is always located in what is *ultimately excluded* in a process of ongoing epistemological clarification.

Serres's intervention protests the usual relegation of Foucault's history of madness as an early account of power operating purely through exclusion and repression—a position Foucault is thought to have revised in his later works. It also points to a central contradiction in the discourse among autistic self-advocates, where a common complaint and self-reproach is that the voices speaking out against the pathologization of autism are those of the vocal, "high-functioning" autistics, and not nonverbal autistics with serious disabilities. The subtext is always that the real, authentic voice of autism has not yet been heard and that further intervention is required to draw out its subjugated interiority. With each protest of this kind, the ostensible spectrality of disability represented by the resistant voice divides and subdivides into a structure that looks ever inward in search of its essential, excluded core. The "resistant" voice thus subscribes to a repressive hypothesis regarding power; it interprets McRuer's proposal that disabled individuals should "come out crip" as a call to liberate this excluded core, whereas McRuer's larger point that there *is* no "core," since identities are performatively (de-)constituted. Serres's conjecture regarding the so-called essence of madness identifies the aporia at the heart of this view of disability: the resistant or "crip" voice is always seen as that which has not yet come out, which is still locked up inside, and which can therefore be located only through a series of "coming out" acts in which otherness is endlessly refined, perfected, and recycled.

We can, finally, detect a third, autistic, voice that is attentive to the gridlock existing between the first two voices, in which the resistant voice is thought to represent the ever-elusive content abjected and excluded by the dominant voice. We can glimpse this third voice in Baggs's "In My Language." Baggs disidentifies with the dominant notion of the human and stages a performative "coming out" of sorts, but sie goes the extra step of acknowledging the *confinement* that paradoxically awaits hir resisting voice.[92] The two halves of Baggs's video beautifully illustrate this point. The first half of the video, which demonstrates an autistic mode of voicing, unfolds on its own terms. However, when Baggs grafts the explanatory commentary, or "translation," of the first-person voice-over onto this material in the second half of the video, the previous part of the video becomes retrospectively coded as autistic in relation to the "normal" mode of communication of the voice-over. Baggs brilliantly uses the content of hir voice-over to comment on the impoverishment of this normative documentary convention of "having a voice" in relation to those grainy, autistic registers of communication that it excludes and disavows. Hir choice of the first-person voice-over as the vehicle of this critique suggests that the documentary tropes of immediation used to give a voice to disenfranchised social subjects should be seen as a discursive closet or trap, rather than a path to liberation.

Baggs's video makes explicit the ironic commentary that is embedded in the pensive, erotic photographs analyzed in chapter 1 and in Roberts's cynical mobilization of liveness in chapter 2. The dominant, humanitarian perspective, which is attuned to normative human language, relationality, and voicing, sees the autistic, dwelling in an infinite field of perceptual and relational possibilities, as disabled, trapped, or lacking in relational capacity. Baggs's video reveals that it is not the autistic but the *humanity* that is sought for hir by humanitarian agents in the form of a resisting, articulate speaking voice that is limited, locked up, and confined—and in fact thoroughly autistic. This astonishing reversal is an extension of Serres's commentary on "pseudoliberation." Serres explains this reversal in terms of the way reason is limited by the exclusion of unreason: "for there to be clarification, analysis, and differentiation of unreason, for this differentiation to lead to an image of the rational, implies, all of a sudden, that one has to define, in their turn, both *reason* and *norm*. And, suddenly, it is they who are going to appear insulated and limited. Lock up madness behind a gate, but understand, in so doing, that you limit reason."[93]

If Baggs responds to Foucault's attempts to articulate what Serres calls "a discourse of unreason on reason"—or, apropos this chapter, to articulate an autistic discourse on humanitarianism—it is by acknowledging that an autistic voice can only be articulated within and against the confines of immedial conditions that are thoroughly compromised. But sie also issues the following, challenging questions: What it would mean to free documentary to inhabit an autistic voice? To what forms of mediation must we become accustomed in order to be able to hear and interpret these mute communications? These are questions that I take up further in the next and final chapter.

Chapter 4

THE DOCUMENTARY ART OF SURRENDER
HUMANE-ITARIAN AND POSTHUMANIST
ENCOUNTERS WITH ANIMALS

The Elephant's Self-Portrait

In early 2008 a YouTube video of an elephant painting what was repeatedly described as a self-portrait generated ripples of excitement across the Internet. Originally uploaded by a pair of tourist art entrepreneurs as a teaser for their online business venture, Exotic World Gifts, the video subsequently made the rounds of numerous social networking sites, accumulating millions of hits, tweets, and comments.[1] Shot at an unidentified Asian location, the video features an elephant bearing a trough of materials in its trunk being led by its mahout up to a canvas, where it proceeds to engage an audience of tourists in a somewhat novel circus routine: painting on an easel by gripping a paintbrush with its trunk.

The main event of the video takes place at around a minute and a half into the eight-minute clip, when the animal's single protracted gray brushstroke begins undeniably to resemble a crude outline of an elephant's torso and trunk, eliciting a marked escalation in the crowd's response from polite amusement to exclamations of astonishment. The camera zooms in at this moment to dramatize the remarkable spectacle of mimesis—an elephant's trunk painting an elephant's trunk—synchronizing our surprise with that of the on-site audience. It remains locked in this framing, then recedes slowly as the pachyderm laboriously completes its rudimentary portrait amid alternating gasps and cheers from the now offscreen onlookers. Finally, the animal stops, switches brushes, and adds one final flourish: in place of a paintbrush,

FIGURE 4.1 Still from "Original Elephant Painting" YouTube video (2008)

the raised trunk of the elephant in the portrait bears an orange flower complete with a green stem and leaves.

The motley array of comments generated by this video alternate between wonder and mistrust, awestruck defenses of animal intelligence and incredulous dismissals of the painting as a trick or a gag. But what unites believers and skeptics alike is the anthropocentric teleology of animal intelligence underpinning their shared question: is an elephant capable of producing a self-portrait?[2] Regardless of the answer, the terms of the question remain undebated: all agree that the capacity for selfhood and art separates human beings from the so-called lower animals. The elephant's ability to produce an iconic representation of itself consistent with the figural traditions of portraiture is venerated as a miracle because it seems to evidence consciousness and, hence, proximity to the human, as an evolutionary ideal.

Curiously, this humanizing narrative has become the legitimating framework for a number of animal welfare initiatives that advocate painting as a humane technique for rehabilitating former working elephants. In 1998 the Russian émigrés and conceptual artists Vitaly Komar and Alexander Melamid garnered financial support from various international philanthropic sources to establish the first "elephant art academy" in a training camp in Lampang,

Thailand. Komar and Melamid aimed to combine artistic provocation with humanitarian intervention: their plan was to rescue Thai draft elephants subjected to coercive and harmful working conditions in illegal log-poaching operations and tourist entertainment in the aftermath of Thailand's logging ban, implemented in 1990, and to gainfully reemploy them as working artists. In their coauthored book *When Elephants Paint*, Komar and Melamid describe the ironic spectacle of elephants painting on easels as a form of conceptual art that foregrounds the affective, creaturely basis of all artistic production. Melamid likens elephant painting to abstract expressionism: "Both are totally mindless occupations. Pollock, when he discovered drip painting, did he think about it? Even when I paint a realist painting, do I really think about what I'm doing as I'm doing it? If you think about it, it shows, and it's not good. Elephants are really the best Abstract Expressionists—they don't think too much."[3]

The conceptual thrust of Komar and Melamid's project has since been supplanted by its humanitarian zeal. A number of elephant training camps across the Asia-Pacific region are now united under the banner of Komar and Melamid's nonprofit initiative, the Asian Elephant Art and Conservation Project. The goal of these camps is to "supervise the gentle teaching of various painting techniques to elephants and caretakers using non-toxic art supplies."[4] The branding and sale of elephant paintings in the name of conservation serves a moral and an economic purpose at once: it furthers the cause of animal rights by demonstrating the elephants' worthiness for empathy, generates employment opportunities for mahouts, and sustains a thriving cottage industry of Asian elephant art purveyors. As an example, Exotic World Gifts advocates "compassion shopping," or the consumption of non-Western handmade goods by Western tourists, arguing that their fair-trade business model enables marginalized or at-risk Third World artists (including "starving elephant artisans") to support themselves using their own creative labor.[5]

The humanitarian infrastructure and rationale supporting elephant painting is reminiscent of the discourse of *Born into Brothels*, discussed in chapter 1, in more ways than one. Each elephant training camp has its star elephant artists, who "specialize" in different styles and color palettes, including brushstroke paintings, line drawings, and splatter paintings that are often compared to prominent works of abstract art. But the most popular and expensive of these elephant paintings are the realistic portraits of elephants produced in the Maetaman Elephant Camp in Chiang Mai, Thailand, the site attributed to the viral video. The high price reserved for realism suggests that the exchange value of elephant self-portraits has less to do with their artistry than with their status as documentary evidence of a self—a shift that is signaled by the exciting zoom-in on the elephant painting in the YouTube video, which emphasizes the spectacle of a nonhuman appendage wielding technology in the manner of a human hand. The visual coding of this video and of the self-portrait indicates that both are operating as a form of realist documentary art, whose purpose is to convince the audience of the presence, authenticity, and plausibility of the elephant's *self*.

The practice of training elephants as artists painting self-portraits can be understood as a variant of the participatory documentary interventions that I have explored throughout this book. In the previous chapters, which focus respectively on photography workshops among brothel children, disaster journalism by Katrina survivors, and first-person films featuring autistic protagonists, I have argued that the gesture of handing over the camera invites dehumanized subjects to evidence their humanity in the form of innocence, liveness, or voice. The elephant's self-portrait similarly insists on its humanity: it protests the axiomatic understanding of animals as beings without a self and calls humanitarian attention to the suffering of these elephants on the basis that they, like humans, have a self and therefore have humanity. The curiosity of the elephant self-portrait raises a number of compelling questions regarding the humanitarian ethic of participatory documentary. For instance, what theories regarding incarceration, freedom, and progress underpin the ethical imperative of liberating animals from the zoo or factory and moving them to the art academy? If we approach the elephant's self-portrait from the perspective of media theory, what are the conventional codes of looking, recognizing, framing, interfacing, and editing that predispose one to interpret it as a self-portrait? What modes of relating to the world, or power relations, are implied by this notion of selfhood? If selfhood is the portal through which animals can assume a positive subjectivity or agency in the eyes of human beholders, then what modes of relationality are exercised in evidencing that agency and, conversely, what types of power relations might be said to function at its limits?

In this chapter, I contemplate how larger philosophical questions such as these are bound up in the reflexive gesture of handing over the camera (or in this case the paintbrush) to the so-called dehumanized other as a prosthetic means of humanization. *Reflexivity* has a specific set of meanings in documentary studies. Bill Nichols uses this term to describe two different sets of operations in documentary—formal and political—that aim, respectively, to upset formal norms and conventions and to transform the viewer's consciousness regarding the social issues and power relations surrounding the text.[6] *Formal reflexivity* refers to films that offer self-conscious metacommentary regarding the received forms, styles, status, strategies, structures, conventions, expectations, and effects of documentary, using techniques such as stylization, deconstruction, irony, or parody.[7] *Political reflexivity* also aims to "make familiar experience strange" but begins with the "materiality of social practices" rather than with form.[8] As an example of the latter, Nichols cites Julia Lesage's seminal work on feminist documentary films, whose strategies of consciousness-raising were less concerned with challenging realist conventions than with empowering formerly excluded subjects as authors of their own self-representations.[9] *Reflexivity* therefore describes the practice of unsettling the received frames of documentary, whether the genre's formal conventions or its representational ethics.

These two aspects of documentary reflexivity do not always coincide in participatory documentary interventions. As I have shown throughout this book, formally or medially reflexive inquiries regarding the received ideological and formal frames of documentary are often bracketed in favor of a politically reflexive humanitarian ethic that leaves intact a conservative notion of humanity. This is true, for instance, of what I call the "resistant voices" of humanitarian subjects who "speak out" against those who speak for them by appropriating their techniques of legitimation and end up perpetuating the vicious circle of immediation. Nichols, approaching the problem from the opposite direction, notes that it is equally common for formal reflexivity to bracket ethical questions. As he writes, "one of the oddities of the [formally] reflexive documentary is that it rarely reflects on ethical issues as a primary concern, other than with the sigh of a detached relativism readier to criticize the choices of others than to examine its own."[10] I have attempted to tease out an element of this critique in my reading of Mel Baggs's "In My Language" in chapter 3, suggesting Baggs's dissatisfaction with the complacency surrounding the formally reflexive first-person voice-over as a stable and ethically irreproachable ground of politics.

This chapter maps the concepts of political and formal reflexivity in documentary onto two different approaches to animal art that I will call "humane-itarian" and "posthumanist." I argue that both of these approaches to reflexivity are fundamentally tied up with the figure of the human, which remains their unthought, obstinate ideological framework, even when their stated aim is to estrange or decenter the human. I begin by introducing the term *humane-itarian* as a descriptor for the mode of intervention characterized by my opening example, tracing its roots to the merger of two post-Enlightenment discourses: humanitarian reason and humane reform. I argue that the politically reflexive documentary gesture of installing animals as authors of their own self-representations should not be considered a liberatory discourse. Rather, the elephant's self-portrait operates in this context as a documentary immediation: a regulatory capture apparatus that reinforces a particularly anthropocentric and perceptually normative mode of being in the world. Michel Foucault's work enables us to grasp the biopolitical import of humane-itarian documentary practices, and the stakes involved when animals are made to mimic the generic forms of human selfhood in order to justify the value of their lives.

Recently, a number of scholars have proposed a "posthumanist" critique of the ethical stance that I call humane-itarianism, arguing that it subscribes to a liberal discourse of civic inclusion that is fundamentally anthropocentric and humanist. Posthumanism seeks not merely to include the nonhuman but to fundamentally decenter the human from its privileged position in relation to cognition, reason, and meaning making. Whereas posthumanism would position itself as a more rigorously reflexive alternative to humane-itarianism that operates at a formal and not merely political level, I propose that the critical strategies used to defamiliarize or disillusion the received frames of anthropocentrism—strategies that are regarded as the cardinal virtues of formal reflexivity, in and beyond documentary—are complicit in the larger discursive structures that hold the human in place. The early twentieth-century surrealist scholar Roger Caillois is a challenging interlocutor of posthumanist reflexivity. Caillois's writings on the seemingly irrational or "suicidal" acts of mimetic insects who willfully lose themselves in their environment offers a provocative critique of the posthumanist technique of defamiliarizing anthropocentric frameworks by bringing to light formerly imperceptible and invisible nonhuman modes of existence that make up the human's constitutive outside.

I turn to Caillois in this final chapter in an effort to reassess and push the limits of the previous chapters. Caillois urges us to see mimetic surrender as the repressed counterpart of the dialectic of defamiliarization that I advocate in my reading of *Through Navajo Eyes* in the first chapter. His ideas regarding mimesis closely parallel the yielding mode of relating to the world that I describe in chapter 3 as an autistic counterdiscourse of voicing, and he speculates regarding the potential of mimesis for reimagining human-animal relations, as well as the fundamental openness of the category of the human. I argue that Caillois points us toward new techniques of reflexivity that abandon the humanitarian ethical values of visibility, selfhood, and identity in favor of an ethic of indistinction, affinity, and surrender informed by mimetic modes of inhabiting the world. The implications of Caillois's theories for participatory documentary, while not immediately evident, are profound. I tease these out through an engagement with the feminist media scholar Laura U. Marks, who has expounded on the significance of Caillois's work on mimesis for documentary studies. Marks's concept of the haptic image urges us to examine how Caillois's embrace of mimesis might translate in visual terms into a noninterventionist approach to mediation that surrenders to rather than mastering difference.

Finally, I consider a series of human-animal documentary experiments that model the attitude of mimetic surrender articulated by Caillois and Marks. In each of these examples, the documentary medium is released from its humanist vocation as an intervening force between subjects who speak about an object who is excluded from their dialogic exchange and reconceived as an environment that supports unexpected interspecies encounters. These works innovate a set of mimetic gestures, sensations, and modes of relation that together constitute the medial vocabulary of a documentary art of surrender. We glimpse in them a radical ethic of documentary and an approach to mediation that abandons the humanitarian discourse of immediation and its inherited preconceptions regarding the human and the less-than-human.

Humane-itarianism as a Capture Apparatus

The elephant self-portrait has become a symbol of sorts for the animals' liberation from a state of imprisonment: elephant painting advocates celebrate their voluntary artistic output as agential acts of self-expression of a kind deemed impossible for zoo animals in captivity. In this section, I propose that "humane-itarianism," or the ethical orientation driving this narrative of liberation, emerges from a coalition between two post-Enlightenment discourses of humanism: the humanitarian media intervention and humane re-form. I situate the uncertain implications of this merger for animal subjects in light of Foucault's analysis of the modern prison as a site of humanitarian in-tervention and humane reform. Using Foucault's analysis of illumination as a means of tacit biopolitical control, I argue that the selfhood that the elephants are trained to represent functions as a version of what I have called a docu-mentary immediation, or an anthropological machine for the reproduction of the human. I propose that the evidentiary logic of the animal self-portrait behaves as a "capture apparatus," to borrow information theorist Philip Agre's term—one that reaffirms the restrictions and exclusions of the zoo or prison while purporting to liberate animals from captivity.[11]

To begin, I will briefly recap what I mean by the humanitarian media in-tervention, a topic that I have already introduced in the previous chapters and that I will now reframe as one of the discursive precursors of humane-itarianism. I refer to the practice of saving the lives of individuals who have been stripped of their political status and rights—owing to war, a hostile state, disaster, illegal trafficking, disease, and so on—by bearing witness to, exposing, or illuminating their condition. Whereas the nineteenth-century definition of humanitarian action by the International Committee of the Red Cross focused exclusively on the punctual, brief, and politically neutral work of life-saving relief, humanitarian organizations have more recently expanded their purview to include the protracted political work of media witnessing. As Thomas Keenan has noted, the work of humanitarian witnessing is rou-tinely articulated through visual metaphors ("the eyes of the world, the light of public scrutiny, the exposure of hypocrisy") that reveal its Enlightenment faith in the power of media visibility as a means of enacting change.[12] The tropes of documentary immediacy, as elaborated in chapter 2, partake of and extend this narrative regarding media exposure.

The other progenitor of humane-itarianism is humane reform, a discourse that has progressively sought to eliminate suffering that results from cruelty or neglect by appealing to the notion of humanity. Didier Fassin writes that the term *humanité*, which emerged in the context of pre- and post-Revolutionary France, incorporates two meanings: humankind, the "ethical category encom-passing all human beings, forming the basis for a shared experience," and hu-maneness, or an "affective movement toward others, manifested as sympathy with them."[13] Fassin argues that the moral sensibility of humaneness, which relates to an "intelligence of emotion," derives from this dual etymology and lineage of *humanity*, understood as reason and compassion in the "attitude held toward the other as vulnerable human being."[14] The notion of shared vulnerability has since been extended to animals: whereas in its earliest inception, the Royal Humane Society was founded to resuscitate drowning victims who were presumed dead, Humane Societies in most countries are now devoted exclusively to protecting animals in distress. Jeremy Bentham's famous rhetorical question—"Can animals suffer?"—now forms the basis of the modern animal rights movement.[15] As Matthew Calarco notes, "uncovering some sort of fundamental identity (for example, sentience or subjectivity) shared by all animals" is the modus operandi of the contemporary animal rights movement, which merges the utilitarian schema of animal sentience with the Kantian ethical framework described by Fassin to obtain membership for animals within the moral sphere of rights.[16]

Foucault's *Discipline and Punish* yields unexpected insights regarding the implications of the merger between humanitarianism and humane reform. This book undertakes an analysis of the modern prison as a site where this merger led to a number of humane-itarian reforms that have lingering consequences for our current inquiry into animal lives. Foucault emphasizes not only the openness of modern prisons to the light of public scrutiny but also their adoption of humane and benevolent reformative measures focused on the soul rather than the body of the prisoner. One of Foucault's central arguments in this book is that even though the light-filled design of the modern prison (as seen in Bentham's diagram of the panopticon) exemplifies the values of enlightenment and progress, illumination in this context operates as a means of entrapment and tacit control. Rather than subjecting criminals to repression, punishment, and death, the modern, humane prison enlists inmates in their own self-governance without laying a hand on them, using the mere suggestion of surveillance. This is just one of the ways in which the supple thematic of humanism turns the very medium of enlightenment— light—into a vehicle of control. "Visibility," Foucault concludes, "is a trap."[17]

When we view Foucault's argument in concert with his subsequent writings on governmentality and biopolitics, we can see how the humane alternative to killing participates in a biopoliticization of life—one in which entities marked for extermination are instead turned into self-governing sites of surplus value. Although Foucault does not refer directly to animals in his work on incarceration, the elephant training camp parallels the epistemic shift traced in *Discipline and Punish*. As an economically profitable, legal, and humane alternative to the cruel and repressive world of coerced animal labor, the elephant art academy symbolizes Asia's transition from barbarism to modernity. The movement of elephants from the dark world of illegal logging to the spotlight of the art gallery explodes the discursive scope of Foucault's insights regarding the biopolitics of humane reform. Instead of being put out to pasture or exterminated, the vagrant animals "laid off" by the illegalization of logging are reoccupied as cultural producers who are put to work in the cultivation of their selves. The rehabilitation of Asian draft elephants as artisanal painters therefore confronts us with the unusual ways in which humanitarian media exposure extracts social and economic value from nonhuman lives.

From a humane-itarian perspective, the spectacularization of elephants as artists is seen as a benign alternative to the torturous conditions of captive animals. The histories of literature and film abound with melancholy reflections on the latter: Akira Mizuta Lippit has written, for instance, about Topsy, the errant circus elephant whose death by electrocution was famously filmed by Thomas Edison, ensuring that this animal would live on as a spectacle even in its death throes.[18] "Elephant artisans" seem to be engaged in relatively unalienated acts of self-expression in comparison with Vladimir Nabokov's doleful description of an ape at the Paris zoo who, "after months of coaxing by a scientist," is alleged to have sketched a charcoal drawing of the bars of its cage.[19] Nabokov's ape offers an apt illustration of art historian John Berger's belief regarding the alienation of animals in captivity. Inhibited by the bars of a cage, Berger argues, the captive animal can never return a human look; its glassy gaze can only reflect its utter marginalization. Berger argues that zoo animals become a mirror for the human, or a screen onto which humanist fantasies of integrity, diligence, or nobility can be projected. As a result of this manufactured overidentification, the animal's commonality with and difference from its human onlooker are both distorted, "like an image out of focus."[20]

Elephant painting advocates celebrate the volitional artistic output of pachyderms in art training camps as proof that humane reform can counter this distortion effect.[21] That the highest price tag (and therefore the highest exchange rate of compassion) is reserved for the self-portrait genre of elephant paintings over and above the many other styles attributed to the star elephant artists at each academy reveals the high value attached to the self as a humane-itarian commodity, as well as a signifier of freedom from captivity. But from what standpoint can the paintings of the elephants, especially those that are said to portray their selves, be described as an authentic expression of nonhuman agency? If we consider the Cartesian adage that animals, unlike humans, do not possess a soul or consciousness of a self, alongside Foucault's cautionary account of the captive soul as a site of biopolitical value, then what apparatuses of capture can be said to await these animal artists and those who gaze, captivated, on their display?

Online commentators are preoccupied with the iconic self-portrait in the viral video, for its realistic color palette and figurative qualities, and tend to ignore the more abstract elephant paintings sold on some websites, which are tellingly never referred to as self-portraits. The interpretive rationale of reading the elephant's crude figural rendering as a representation of its self is indebted to a well-known psychoanalytic account of self-formation. The elephant, painting its own visible figure as a photorealistic icon, is applauded for displaying an imaginary grasp of its self, not unlike the infantile human's misrecognition of itself in a mirror image. Jacques Lacan's account of the "mirror stage" pinpoints the act of identifying with one's own image as the moment when the child distinguishes the visible borders of its (reflected) body from the surrounding milieu, including its mother's enveloping presence.[22] The difference is that the infant later accedes to language and the symbolic order, while the painting elephant is arrested in a primordial stage of development. Since the elephant can only draw, not write, it is restricted to a limited form of subjectivity, rehearsing the well-worn dictum that language evidences a more advanced consciousness. The elephant's self-portrait comprises the barest of line drawings and contains no identifying features whatsoever that might indicate the singularity of its author. The characterization of this image—which could really be a portrait of *any* elephant—as a self-portrait also suggests that the selfhood of the elephant is of a different order than that of the human. Coupled with the conservationist claim about the impending extinction of the Asian elephant species, the multiplicity or anonymity of the animal's self seems to affirm that the meaningfulness of death as an event is applicable to animals only when an entire species is exterminated.[23]

Even though several mammals and birds are known to recognize their mirror images, the painting elephant is enlisted in the more complex task of *reproducing a structure of self-recognition*. We can grasp the significance of this task by approaching Lacan's theory of the mirror stage as an example of what Giorgio Agamben calls an "anthropological machine" or a machine for the reproduction of the human.[24] Agamben points to Carl Linnaeus's taxonomic categorization of the human as an example of this machine at work. In *Systema naturae* Linnaeus issues a cryptic imperative in lieu of any specific identifying characteristic of the generic name *Homo* (which he later changed to *Homo sapiens*): *nosce te ipsum*, or "know yourself."[25] Agamben interprets this message as follows: since the human has no positive content, the reflexive act of self-knowledge requires constant verification in the eyes of another, that is, in a reflective screen. Lacan's theory of the mirror stage describes an identificatory structure for reproducing a form of life that has no positive content. The elephant's self-portrait serves as such a mirror for its humanitarian onlookers: whether or not the elephant recognizes itself is beside the point; what is important is that it is (mis)recognized as having a self and, thus, humanity, and this misrecognition affirms the humanitarian equation of self-recognition with humanity.

The normative coordinates of selfhood, in which membership is sought for the painting elephant, come into sharper focus when we consider that Lacan's theory not only is oriented toward "normal" human psychic development but was evolved in a specifically European context. After all, not all animals employ trichromatic, binocular vision, and not all humans privilege vision as a means of organizing sensory information. Interlocutors in feminist, queer, and disability studies have protested that Lacan's emphasis on a visual metaphor excludes consideration of how tactile, aural, or multisensory perceptual orientations might complicate his narrative of subject formation. Lisa Cartwright, for example, has argued that "empathetic identification," a type of emotional attunement that interanimates empathy (which relies on emotion and perception) and identification (which relies on vision and unconscious psychic processes), can provide an alternate route to radically intersubjective and multisensory coproductions of selfhood.[26] Erin Manning's account of autistic perception as an "attunement to life as an incipient ecology of practices," discussed in chapter 3, similarly posits an account of self-formation that departs from Lacan's account of the mirror stage. Although nonocular avenues of emergence are not beyond the purview of control, we can note for now that the mapping of selfhood onto the elephant's representation of its image as seen by the visually oriented subject normalizes a perceptual regime that is not only anthropocentric but also paradigmatically Western and neurotypical.[27]

The artistic discourse surrounding the elephant paintings is similarly conservative, despite its claims to radicality. For instance, Melamid, one of the two Russian artists who founded the Asian elephant art initiative, celebrates conceptual and abstract art as the "ultimate democracy" that undermines the institutionalized artistic principles of authorship, intentionality, and cultural capital.[28] Melamid's affiliation of art with lowly, unskilled, unpredictable, or bestial impulses as opposed to an exclusively human capacity would seem to infuse the Kantian designation of art as antiutilitarian with a Deleuzian sensibility. The feminist scholar Elizabeth Grosz has mounted a sophisticated argument of this type by proposing that the ornamental displays and mating calls of animals and birds should be regarded not as a functional aspect of natural selection but as excessive, redundant, artistic performances that expend libidinal energy to no predetermined end. Grosz insists on these grounds that animals are artistic, "if by that we understand that they intensify sensation (including the sensations of their human observers), [and] that they enjoy this intensification."[29]

Even as Melamid gestures in this direction, he reoccupies a conservative position with his claim that the nonfigurative paintings rendered by elephants deserve attention because of their resemblance to existing works by Jackson Pollock, Franz Kline, and other prominent modernist artists. The back cover of the volume coauthored by Komar, Melamid, and the New York–based curator Mia Fineman prominently displays an image of the artists holding up an illustrated volume about Marcel Duchamp before an elephant. The humor of Komar and Melamid's ironic commentary that "even" elephants can produce conceptual art turns on the tacit consensus that *we*, unlike the animal, know in advance what conceptual art is and are in on the joke. Fineman speculates in a catalog essay for the Asian Elephant Art and Conservation Project that, having proven themselves in the domain of the realist portrait, elephants might explore "Elephant Abstraction . . . Elephant Impressionism, Elephant Surrealism, [and] Elephant Conceptual Art."[30] Here, even as Fineman celebrates elephant paintings as "the ultimate Outsider Art" and "a frenzy of interspecies collaboration" between mahout and elephant, she reaffirms art as a known set of historically stable Western generic conventions, whose amateurish imitation by trained elephants and their naive helpers ensure that their paintings are regarded paternalistically in the manner of primitive art or *art naïf.*

It is not necessary to enter into the debate of what constitutes art in order to note how its restriction by elephant painting enthusiasts to creative work with a display function reinstates, in liberalized form, another version of the zoo's distortion effect. Scholars like Thomas Sebeok and Tim Ingold have striven to disaffiliate art from display by focusing on the world-forming creative activity of animals like beavers and bees, who collaborate purposively with their own species, or the affective and physical labor of domesticated animals in more dubious forms of human-animal collaboration such as sport, hunting, companionship, surveillance, agriculture, and transportation.[31] Their perspective is another that reveals how celebrating the achievements of painting elephants (as opposed to logging elephants) reaffirms the exclusions on which the stability of our definitions of art and humanity depend. Conversely, looking at the elephant's self-portrait from the perspective explored in chapter 1, we can see how this documentary immediation functions, just like the aesthetic of feral innocence, to dematerialize the labor of the painting elephant.

The conundrum of the painting elephant is one that Rey Chow argues is unavoidable for marginalized constituencies who are bestowed with the rights, privileges, and passcodes of liberal selfhood: the benevolent gaze that scrutinizes their displays of agency coercively installs its own view of such agency as an impossible standard that marginal entities must mimic in order to be immediately legible to their well-wishers.[32] Since the normalizing forms taken by this type of reflexive gaze (such as the self or art) inevitably mediate the ways in which minoritarian entities evidence their agency, the evidence in question is always found to be lacking; the elephant's demonstration of self-consciousness is only as successful as its capacity to function as a poor replica that confirms the ontological and moral superiority of those who recognize it as a self-portrait. This means that the humane-itarian gesture of "recognizing" the humanity of animals is ultimately a narcissistic gesture in which a dominant group, in this case, the human, installs its so-called others (animals) as a mirror in which it can repeatedly look for evidence of its own uncertain ontological superiority.

To sum up, the documentary value of the elephant's self-portrait has to do with its capacity for immediately evidencing and reinforcing a particularly normative, anthropocentric discourse of selfhood and art. The work of the animal self-portrait as a documentary immediation closely approximates what the information theorist Agre calls a "capture apparatus." In an update to Foucault's work on surveillance and Gilles Deleuze's notion of societies of control, Agre argues that surveillance-based technologies have been replaced by algorithmic technologies of "capture" to which human users voluntarily submit. These capture apparatuses include digital interfaces whose inscribed grammars recalibrate and reorganize the activities that they claim to merely represent, even as the users' feelings of volition and mobility deliver them even more efficiently as data that can be captured and mined. In such a context, Agre warns, our metaphors of entrapment can themselves become a trap that keeps us from noticing forms of control based on mobility and freedom rather than enclosure.[33] Agre's analysis of capture offers a valuable rubric through which to understand the metaphors of enlightenment and liberation driving the discourse of animal art. Rather than seeing the politically reflexive gesture of equipping the elephant with a paintbrush as a means of superseding the structures of entrapment that characterize our relations with animals, the concept of capture urges us to see this gesture, as well as the selfhood that it liberates, as a trap.

Posthumanist Visibilities and Mimetic Indistinction

I have argued so far that the practice of elephant painting recenters the human despite its apparent interest in the self-representations of animals. The limitations of the humane-itarian approach to reflexivity can be productively understood in terms of Cary Wolfe's critique of "humanist posthumanism." Wolfe uses this term to refer to intellectual or artistic formations that may be ethically committed to undermining the ontological divide between the human and the animal, but whose internal disciplinarity, which is drawn from "the liberal justice tradition and its central concept of rights, in which ethical standing and civic inclusion are predicated on rationality, autonomy, and agency," is centered by a normative concept of the human that grounds discrimination against animals in the first place.[34] Wolfe locates his own efforts among those of other scholars who have attempted to enact a "posthumanist posthumanism" by turning to theoretical paradigms and figures that are oriented not by the human but by the horizon of externality or finitude that binds the human with the nonhuman.[35]

Below I assess the stakes of Wolfe's attempt to theorize a more rigorous approach to posthumanism that inhabits the charge of reflexivity at an ideological and not merely ethical level (or at the formal and not merely political level, to use Nichols's terms) by defamiliarizing the received frames of anthropocentric thinking. Although scholars like Wolfe have done much to deconstruct the persistent strains of humanism in contemporary thought, their reflexive maneuver ends up perpetuating a regime of visibility that upholds the very form of life that posthumanism intends to unsettle. I develop this argument through an engagement with Caillois, whose work is an early precursor of posthumanist scholarship that also challenges contemporary models of posthumanist reflexivity.

Currently, a whole host of critical tendencies are grouped under the loose umbrella of posthumanism, including new materialism, critical animal studies, disability studies, object-oriented ontology, and speculative realism. These different approaches identify and disidentify with the term *posthumanism* for various reasons that it is beyond this chapter's scope to assess, but Wolfe's working definition of this term explains why it nonetheless identifies their shared conditions of possibility: "Posthumanism names a historical moment in which the decentering of the human by its imbrication in technical, medical, informatic, and economic networks is increasingly impossible to ignore, a historical development that points toward the necessity of new theoretical paradigms (but also thrusts them on us), a new mode of thought that comes after the cultural repressions and fantasies, the philosophical protocols and evasions, of humanism as a historically specific phenomenon."[36] Despite their very different methodologies and philosophical antecedents, posthumanisms share an interest in the phenomenology or ontology of entities that are difficult to assimilate within humanist frameworks of thought — such as animals, insentient objects, or disabled individuals — as a way of mapping the coordinates of a posthumanist theoretical paradigm. A common procedure in such works involves defamiliarizing, deconstructing, or otherwise unsettling humanist assumptions and dogmas by bringing to light modes of being, knowing, and feeling that they cannot accommodate.

For example, Wolfe has attempted to stage a dialogue between nonhuman and autistic modes of perception by troubling the normative, humanist coordinates of vision, both as a perceptual mode and as a metaphor for thought. In one chapter, he mobilizes the animal rights advocate Temple Grandin's reflections on her experiences with autism — including her claim that the "blinding" hypervisuality of autistic persons, combined with an extreme sensitivity to touch, enables a peculiar understanding of and resonance with nonhuman perception — to speculate regarding "new lines of empathy, affinity, and respect" that may be forged between humans and nonhumans, above and beyond Grandin's own innovation of humane animal-holding and rendering facilities.[37] In another, he offers a reading of the artist Eduardo Kac's uses of visuality to subvert the conventional training of the human sensorium. In both instances, Wolfe's goal is to decenter vision as a normative marker of human ability by revealing its constitutive blindness. As he puts it, "what we think of as 'normal' human visuality does *not* see—and it does not see that it does not see."[38]

Along similar lines, Jussi Parikka asks how the biology of insects offers "lessons of 'nonhuman perception'" that can open human ways of approaching the world to as yet unknown or underexplored registers of experience.[39] Parikka proposes that envisioning the perceptive and organizational worlds of insects as media theory reveals a "whole new world of sensations, perceptions, movements, stratagems, and patterns of organization" that remains invisible and imperceptible to a view of technics that focuses narrowly on human communication.[40] The Estonian zoosemiotician and ethologist Jakob von Uexküll is one of the scholars repositioned by Parikka as a media theorist. Uexküll counters the Heideggerian dismissal of animals as "poor in world" by arguing that every species, including the human, exists in a perceptual world (*Umwelt*) that forms a "bubble [that] represents each animal's environment and contains all the features accessible to the subject," even though those features, or "carriers of significance," may be irrelevant or imperceptible to other species.[41]

In one of his favorite examples, Uexküll describes "a stroll on a sunny day before a flowering meadow in which insects buzz, and butterflies flutter."[42] But each organism's experience of the meadow's idyll is limited to its *Umwelt*: "As soon as we enter into one such bubble, the previous surroundings of the subject are completely reconfigured. Many qualities of the colorful meadow vanish completely, others lose their coherence with one another, and new connections are created. A new world arises in each bubble."[43] Parikka likens Uexküll's theories regarding the mutually noncommunicating yet contrapuntally synchronized perceptual worlds of animals to those of other early twentieth-century modernist scholars and artistic avant-gardes who aimed to denaturalize the human sensorium. Following from their example, Parikka asks how media technologies may be deterritorialized from the human body as their primary locus of organization and opened up to "the durations of animals, insects, stones, matter, technology, etc."—that is, to perceptual worlds that may otherwise remain closed to a human perspective.[44]

I cite these two texts by Wolfe and Parikka to call attention to a more general tendency. Broadly speaking, the reflexivity of posthumanist critique, that is, the manner in which it enacts its awareness of its epistemic limits, has its origins in the high modernist tradition of defamiliarizing and dialectically rejuvenating the habituated frames of perception and cognition. The modernist avant-gardes' fascination with primitive cultures as a source of philosophical inspiration and modernization (as exemplified by Sol Worth and John Adair's desire for a "uniquely Navajo" film grammar, discussed in chapter 1) can also be seen in the source material (animals, autistics, inanimate objects) through which posthumanism aims to reinvent humanist dogmas. There is no doubt, however, that posthumanism is explicitly critical of modernist primitivism and insists that minoritarian ontologies are products of complex historical and material processes, not representatives of some authentic norm or prior "original" condition—a fantasy that Worth and Adair subscribe to in regard to their Navajo film students. We also observe a striking departure from the Brechtian commitment to desensationalized alienation in the emphasis among posthumanist scholars on sensorial affinity and affective becoming as avenues of cross-species entanglement. What these two seemingly disparate critical tendencies do share, however, is an investment in a mode of reflexivity that seeks to make the invisible preconditions and the constitutive outside of its own thought visible.

Posthumanist reflexivity involves a methodological paradox: even though it argues that the status of visuality, or the relationship between seeing and knowing, must be rethought to reflect the shortcomings of humanism, this critique goes hand in hand with the move of recovering formerly imperceptible and unknown agencies and bringing them into a metaphorical field of visibility. We might say that the nonhuman agencies or existences made visible by posthumanism are *visibilities* in the Deleuzian sense. Deleuze uses this term to highlight a conceptual maneuver in Foucault's readings of disciplinary institutions such as the clinic and the prison. Instead of treating the empirically visible "facts" of enlightenment placed on display by these seemingly progressive, modern institutions as self-evidences, Foucault focuses on them as products of illumination, as a medium that works on and transforms social relations. For Deleuze, Foucault demonstrates a novel way of thinking about visibility. Visibility, for Foucault, is not a preexisting quality, state, or characteristic of an object that shows up under light. Instead, visibilities are "forms of luminosity which are created by the light itself and allow a thing or object to exist only as a flash, sparkle, or shimmer."[45] To transpose this idea back into our current discussion, the nonhuman agencies or existences made visible by posthumanism are not its referents but products of its modernist approach to reflexivity.

Wolfe's formulation applies here: posthumanist critique "does not see that it does not see" its mode of reflexivity as a form of illumination of the very kind that Foucault describes as a modern medium of entrapment. In his example of the humane, light-filled prison, being exposed to light turns the most intimate and inaccessible aspect of the prisoner—their soul—into a site of value, information, and control. Ironically, the moment when the prisoner is acknowledged as having humanity is when they are most decisively subject to control. Foucault's argument regarding the repressive internal logic of liberal discourses of enlightenment poses an important challenge for the posthumanist approach to reflexivity: if humanity functions as a ruse in discourses of enlightenment, then is a "posthuman condition" also a ruse when it comes to the reflexive gesture of exposing, bringing to light, making distinct, and giving a positive identity to the negative content or constitutive outside of the human? How might this gesture of inclusion end up doing violence to modes of being in the world that resist distinction altogether? To what extent does the repressive internal logic of posthumanist reflexivity parallel the humane-itarian approach to reflexivity in drawing nonhuman lives into a biopolitical regime of visibility?

This is where Caillois's work is helpful. Rather than defamiliarizing anthropocentrism by making nonhuman modes of existence visible, Caillois's study of mimetic insects that exhibit radically passive and even suicidal behaviors explores what it would mean to submit to the mimetic logic of invisibility, self-renunciation, and indistinction. I argue that Caillois offers a critique of the humanitarian ethical orientation that is sustained by the reflexive maneuver of making the invisible visible. I ask how his interest in mimesis can pave the way toward a more radical ethic of reflexivity in participatory documentary that surrenders to and takes its cues from the relational modes of the other, instead of bringing them into the humanist enclosure of the politics of visibility, and its implied vision of subjectivity and agency.

In 1935, at around the same time that Lacan penned the first version of his mirror-stage essay, Caillois wrote an article entitled "Mimicry and Legendary Psychasthenia," which paints a very different picture of what a self-portrait might look like from a nonhuman perspective. Caillois is concerned not with charismatic megafauna who are able to abstract themselves as an image but with the representational acts of mimetic insects that "play dead" by merging morphologically with their surroundings. Among his examples are mantises whose curled feet simulate the petals of flowers, and butterflies whose wing markings resemble the mildew on lichens or perforated leaves, or whose folded wings in repose approximate the major vein of a branch's outermost leaf.[46]

The morphological features of these creatures, Caillois notes, are supplemented by seemingly automatic or instinctual gestures that permit them to "become assimilated into the environment," such as the cataleptic swaying of the mantis, which imitates the effect of a gentle wind passing through flowers, or the mechanical manner in which sea spiders garb their shells in a disguise of seaweed and polyps gathered from their habitats.[47] Caillois rejects functionalist explanations of why such insects imitate their natural environments, observing that morphological mimicry is not always effective as a mode of self-preservation or self-defense, as is usually assumed with forms of camouflage. Far from enabling them to elude predators, many of whom detect their prey primarily through smell or changes in motion or color, not through their visibly discernible borders, the act of visual fusion with their environment actually *incites* death for mimetic insects. "Hiding in plain sight," they are often crushed by larger animals or inadvertently eaten by herbivores—and, in the extreme case of some leaf insects, even cannibalized by their own species.

To account for this bizarre reflex, which he understands as a "disorder in the relationship between personality and space," Caillois turns to abnormal psychology, borrowing the term *psychasthenia*, which was popularized in French psychiatric parlance in the 1930s by the psychotherapist Pierre Janet. Janet uses this term, which refers to a general nervous "weakness" that causes a proclivity toward obsessions and compulsions, to describe the compulsive spatial behaviors of schizophrenics. Caillois's meditation on psychasthenia in relation to mimetic insects demonstrates a conceptual maneuver that we now affiliate with posthumanist inquiry. He employs abnormal and nonhuman ontologies—in this case, the impulse to do something even when it is obviously not in one's self-interest—to decenter the normative, anthropocentric coordinates of cognition and subjectivity. The following passage contains the kernel of Caillois's discussion of psychasthenia:

When asked where they are, schizophrenics invariably reply, *I know where I am, but I don't feel that I am where I am*. For dispossessed minds such as these, space seems to constitute a will to devour. Space chases, entraps, and digests them in a huge process of phagocytosis. Then, it ultimately takes their place. The body and mind thereupon become dissociated; the subject crosses the boundary of his own skin and stands outside of his senses. He tries to see *himself, from* some point in space. He feels that he is turning into space himself—*dark space into which things cannot be put*. He is similar; not similar to anything in particular, but simply *similar*.[48]

Lacan references Caillois's ideas about psychasthenia in his discussion of the mirror stage, in which he suggests that entities that lack the perceptual ability to visually distinguish the spatial borders of their selves from their milieu suffer from "the derealizing effect of an obsession with space."[49] The "abnormal" case of the schizophrenic, as described by Caillois, buttresses Lacan's argument regarding the importance of spatial identification with one's image for the emergence of the normal human subject—a process that hinges on abstracting the borders that separate inside from outside, and self from milieu.

Although the mimetic propensities of schizophrenics and certain classes of insects are undoubtedly subtended by very different neurobiological and discursive determinants, Caillois suggests that they suffer from a similar sensory predicament: vision does not provide the vital sensation of spatial abstraction from the body and milieu that is necessary for the body to function normally. This is why schizophrenics cannot experience themselves from either the first- or third-person perspectives. Instead of being set apart from their milieu by their sense of vision, they are disjointed from vision itself and "[stand] outside of [their] senses" at the threshold of their own skin. They "[try] to see [themselves], from some point in space" in order to gain some sense of spatial orientation, but they can only "feel" that they are turning into something indistinguishable from space itself.[50]

Where psychoanalysis regards the incapacity of vision to discern borders as pathological, abnormal, or disabling, Caillois reframes it as an enabling condition that permits the mantis or schizophrenic to experience an intimate, *haptic* relationship with the tactile dimensions of their landscape that is unknown to their visually oriented counterparts. It appears to be a consequence of such "fascinated" haptic looking that mimetic insects give in to what Caillois calls the "veritable *lure of space*" and become absorbed into the contours of their surrounding environment.[51] Caillois's account of this haptic relationship with the world closely parallels those of the autistic writers mentioned in the previous chapter, several of whom describe their difficulties in abstracting their bodies from their surroundings as one that nonetheless enables unusual and generative modes of relating to the world.[52] Caillois writes, "Morphological mimicry could then be genuine photography, in the manner of chromatic mimicry, but photography of shape and relief, on the order of objects and not of images; a three-dimensional reproduction with volume and depth: sculpture-photography, or better yet *teleplasty*, if the word is shorn of all psychic content."[53]

Caillois's observations are nothing less than an attempt to reconceptualize the structure of identification from a psychasthenic vantage point. In Lacan's theory of the mirror stage, the neurotypical subject identifies with the visible borders of their own form and abstracts themself as a subject. According to Caillois, the schizophrenic and the mimetic insect identify instead with the tactile contours of the surrounding landscape, and appear to transform into objects. Thanks to this haptic attunement, these creatures enjoy a unique communion with the aesthetic and spatial contours of their milieu: their bodies appear not to exist on a separate plane but withdraw to an inorganic state and blend imperceptibly into their environment. They perform teleplastic acts of photorealistic and sculptural impersonation that dissolve rather than resolve the visible borders between their bodies and their surroundings. The results of this haptic mode of identification, as Caillois explains, are utterly disorienting if we privilege forms of identification and representation that rely on the normal functioning of vision and that result in the emergence of selfhood or subjectivity in the normative sense. Soon after the previous passage, he notes:

> This assimilation into space is inevitably accompanied by a diminished sense of personality and vitality. In any event, it is noteworthy that among mimetic species, the phenomenon occurs only *in a single direction*: the animal mimics plant life (whether leaf, flower, or thorn) and hides or gives up those physiological functions linking it to its environment. *Life withdraws to a lesser state. . . .* alongside the instinct of self-preservation that somehow attracts human beings to life, there proves to be a very widespread *instinct d'abandon* attracting them toward a kind of diminished existence; in its most extreme state, this would lack any degree of consciousness or feeling at all. I am referring, so to speak, to the *inertia of the élan vital*.[54]

Many commentators have accurately identified Caillois's statement regarding the suicidal tendencies of mimetic insects, in tandem with his description of the mimetic faculty as a "dangerous luxury," as an endorsement of something resembling the Freudian death drive.[55] The ethical consequences of such a statement are certainly vexing, as is Caillois's sentimental and feminized description of mimesis as a viscous, seductive force that eventually consumes the ego libido. Caillois's romantic tone regarding the mystique of the natural world is typical of modernist and avant-garde scholars of the time — one is reminded of Lacan's nostalgic musings about the medium of art as naturally embodied by the life cycles of animals.[56]

Dismissing Caillois on these grounds, however, would be to miss his larger point. It is important to note that Caillois rejects the available biocentric explanations for understanding suicidal mimesis, including rationalistic and traditional Darwinian theories, which posit that survival is the goal of all species. From this standpoint, the mimetic "instinct of renunciation" can be regarded only as a tragic act of madness or masochism.[57] But if we set aside these biocentric explanatory frameworks and their systems of value, as Caillois does, it becomes possible to see his fascination with suicidal insects as a repudiation of the interventionist attitude that aims unquestioningly to save or preserve animal lives — and, relatedly, the attitude that aims to rescue autistics from their "prison of silence." Where the humane-itarian intervention stops the killing of animals in the name of their alleged humanity, Caillois suggests that the more radical stance would be to surrender the ultimate humanitarian principle: life itself.

Caillois's exegesis on mimesis contains the elements of a radically noninterventionist ethic that runs counter to the ethic of humane-itarian intervention. Specifically, Caillois asks what it would mean to relinquish "humanity," or the humanitarian mode of illumination that endows "mere life" with a form of visibility and meaning. The implications and extensions of this ethic when it comes to representational politics receive unexpected elaboration in Gayatri Chakravorty Spivak's critique of liberal feminist interventionism in her essay, "Can the Subaltern Speak?" In her discussion of sati, or widow suicide, Spivak identifies a common slippage that takes place when Western intellectuals represent the acts of non-Western groups to themselves: this is the slippage between representation in the aesthetic sense (representation as portrait or tropology) and representation in the political sense (representation as proxy or persuasion).[58] Spivak illustrates of the effects of this slippage at the end of her essay, where she tells the story of Bhuvaneswari Bhaduri, a young Indian female revolutionary who employed the signs of her body to reinscribe the political script of widow suicide. By committing suicide during her menstrual period, she showed that she was taking her life for her own political reasons, and not because she was driven to do so by religious or patriarchal custom.

Spivak notes that this woman's grammar of political action would have been incomprehensible as such to the liberal Western feminist focused on self-empowerment or self-expression as the de facto code of political representation.[59] Such a universalizing gaze would inevitably abstract Bhaduri's minoritarian expression from the complexities of its rhetorical context and misrecognize it as a symptom of oppression. Through this example, Spivak encourages us to understand liberatory Western feminisms as humanitarian interventions. Caillois's discussion of suicidal mimesis mounts an analogous critique of humanitarian agents who would wish to interpret the mimetic insect's act of isomorphic merger with its environment (an expressive or aesthetic representation) as a tragic sacrifice or sign of weakness (an act of political representation). Doing so would necessarily fold these "abnormal" entities into a normalizing field where the possible meanings of life are prescribed in advance. Instead, Caillois invites us to contemplate the mimetic insect's self-destructive behavior on its own opaque terms: to confront the fact that they may not "think about" their sacrifice as such, or even experience their departure from life in any anthropomorphically politicized sense.

It is clear why modern scientific and philosophical discourses have avoided mimetic thinking, given its drastic implications. Foucault argues that mimetic ways of understanding the world based on relations of similitude (such as resemblance, adjacency, proximity, contact, emulation, analogy, and sympathy) have been replaced in modernity with an emphasis on identities and differences.[60] His analysis remains applicable for much of twentieth-century theory, including the deconstructive tradition, which rejects mimesis for its premodern associations with realism and verisimilitude.[61] Caillois himself acknowledges at the outset of his essay that the mimetic characteristics of indistinction, sameness, and imperceptibility are fundamentally discordant with the values of distinction, difference, and visibility that preoccupy twentieth-century critical procedures—this includes the reflexive procedures through which thought makes its preconditions known.[62]

Many of Caillois's critical contributions come from his recuperation of the mimetic principles of similarity and correspondence. Mimetic thinking leads him to connect morphological mimicry not just with the way schizophrenics represent their relationship to space but also with the "sympathetic magic" of primitive cultures, and modern scientific representations of abstract space and hyperspace that displace organic life as the privileged organizing principle of space. In this way, mimesis allows Caillois to articulate a minoritarian epistemology that is attentive to various peripheral representational practices that undermine the sensory, geometric, and ideological principles of Renaissance perspective and Euclidean space. In later works, Caillois describes his approach as the basis of a "diagonal science," or an open series of experimental or poetic analogies and correspondences conceived in opposition to the abstract and binarizing taxonomies of the structuralist human sciences.[63]

Caillois's influence on scholars like Wolfe and Parikka is undeniable. The latter's articulation of the unexpected solidarities that exist between non-human, non-Western, neurologically atypical, and scientific epistemologies aptly engages the mimetic principles of adjacency and sympathetic resonance.[64] At the same time, there is an unreconciled tension between Caillois's fascination with similarity and the posthumanist strategy of defamiliarizing anthropocentric interpretative frames. The modernist tactic of defamiliarization involves exposing the veil of illusion represented by the dominant perspective in order to reveal the true difference of what it conceals. This is not only a thoroughly antimimetic maneuver but one that goes hand in hand with the gesture of bringing to light, uncovering, and making distinct those lifeways that were previously hidden from sight. The technique of reflexivity favored by posthumanist thinking implicitly follows a humane-itarian politics of visibility that reinstates the very form of life that posthumanism strives to displace. Caillois, on the other hand, insists that to fully realize a posthumanist mode of reflexivity, it would be necessary to surrender the values of distinction and visibility altogether, and to yield to the unfamiliar logic of mimesis, even if the outcome of such yielding seems unthinkable.

Caillois's provocation anticipates those of a number of prominent feminist cultural critics who have extended Spivak's critique of humanitarian feminisms, including Rey Chow, Erin Manning, and Lisa Cartwright, whose work I have discussed previously. These scholars have employed rubrics that resonate with the themes of withdrawal and weakness implied by psychasthenia—such as coercive mimeticism, autistic perception, and empathetic identification—as feminist or nonimperialist epistemologies.[65] These scholars challenge the positive values of visibility, vitality, difference, and individuality that are attached by default to the liberal discourse of rights, as a result of which minoritarian representational practices and approaches to agency that stress sameness, multiplicity, or mutuality are routinely viewed in a distorted light.

Given Caillois's rejection of the prevailing representational and political registers through which agency is apprehended, we can now see how he was attempting to develop a distinctively nonnormative vocabulary for explaining the atypical behavior of mimetic insects, by stressing the relationship between minor sensory registers (hapticity), representational strategies (mimesis), and political affects (weakness, withdrawal, abandonment, giving up, diminishment, and surrender). Through the mimetic insect, he illustrates an immersive way of engaging the world that dissolves the sharp distinction between subject and object, resulting in a less assertive, radically passive form of life, rather than an abstraction from the environment whose ultimate product is an individual or subject.

Surrendering Documentary

The questions raised by Caillois regarding the reflexivity of critique are highly pertinent to our current inquiry into the humanitarian impulse in participatory documentary. His work shows that the technique of defamiliarizing the conventional frames of discourse and exposing what these frames obscure relies on antimimetic philosophical protocols that participate in complex ways in maintaining the normative construction and status of the human. His insights are especially relevant to documentary, as a discourse in which reflexivity, both formal and political, is understood in precisely such antimimetic terms. Caillois's turn to mimesis for an alternative urges us to reconsider the derogatory associations of documentary with mimetic verisimilitude and indexicality. He prompts us to ask: What if, instead of making dehumanized subjects visible by "giving" them selfhood or a voice, the reparative, political orientation of documentary reflexivity were mimetically attuned toward those agencies that elude the coordinates of liberal selfhood? What if formal reflexivity in documentary sought not to distinguish the image from its referent but to make the two indistinct? How might embracing mimesis enable an approach to mediation that aims to *become similar* to the so-called nonhuman or the less-than-human, rather than making the latter legible to a humane-itarian radar?

In this final section, I approach these questions through feminist film scholar Laura U. Marks, who uses Caillois's discussion of mimesis to elaborate on the significance of a tactile rather than visual approach to the documentary image. I argue that Marks's notion of the "haptic image" allows us to imagine a radically noninterventionist ethic of participatory documentary based on the mimetic principle of surrender. I conclude with readings of three artistic experiments that demonstrate the possibilities and vexations of such an ethic in practice. Beatriz da Costa, Simon Starling, and Sam Easterson each immerse visual media within nonhuman milieus, inviting animal collaborators to physically interact with, touch, manipulate, inscribe, and alter them. Although these practitioners would not necessarily identify as documentary filmmakers, their work powerfully exemplifies what it would mean to engage in a participatory documentary practice that gives itself over to an unfamiliar logic, instead of seeking to "give" humanity to its beneficiaries. Da Costa, Starling, and Easterson explore the mimetic relations of indexicality, proximity, and hapticity as avenues for a noninterventionist, yet thoroughly reflexive, mode of engagement that nonetheless takes mediation as its necessary point of departure. In the process, they cultivate an attunement to the documentary medium as a milieu of mutual becoming and transformation, rather than as an intervening force that distinguishes between subject and object, human and nonhuman.

Reflexivity in documentary tends to be understood as an antimimetic enterprise. According to Nichols, the aim of reflexivity is to defamiliarize the naive but nonetheless obdurate associations of documentary with mimetic illusionism, using techniques such as stylization, deconstruction, irony, or parody. As he puts it, reflexive documentaries raise suspicion regarding notions such as "realist access to the world, the ability to provide persuasive evidence, the possibility of indisputable argument, [or] the unbreakable bond between an indexical image and that which it represents"—in short, regarding the status of the documentary image as a transparent reflection of the world.[66] The dismissal of mimesis in documentary studies can be seen as part of what Chow calls the poststructuralist legacy of a Platonic philosophical tradition: the image produced in the act of imitation is seen as deceptive because of its way of confusing reality and the act of representation; thus, it is thought to require deconstruction. Properly speaking, Chow notes, the poststructuralist suspicion of the mimetic image should be described as iconophobia, but the phobia in question tends to be extended beyond the image to the process of mimesis more generally, without necessarily inquiring into how mimetic processes can yield representational practices that are not visual, imagistic, or iconic in any traditional sense.[67]

In her book *The Skin of the Film*, Marks undertakes precisely this inquiry. Marks uses Caillois's account of the mimetic insect's teleplastic imitation of its environment to explore a parallel account of mimesis that takes its point of departure not from the iconic relationship of resemblance but from an indexical relationship that involves a haptic transfer of material. Marks's approach, I will suggest, inspires a new way of imagining the possibilities of participatory documentary as a practice of surrender. Marks argues that the Platonic repudiation of mimesis as illusionistic representation has unspoken investments in a regime of visuality that she dubs "optical visuality." Optical visuality describes a normalizing regime of visuality that assumes the universality of vision as a "distance sense" that emphasizes the separateness of the seeing subject from what it sees, without necessarily interrogating how this experience of vision is informed by historically specific symbolic conventions and structures of identification.[68] Cartesian dualism, Renaissance perspective, and the optical structure of identification described by Lacan are all examples of visual discourses that cultivate the capacity for visual discernment—a capacity that also informs the reflexive act of discerning representations of reality.

With Caillois as one of several points of historical reference, Marks excavates a parallel, minor discourse of mimesis that is rooted in a synesthetic, tactile form of visuality that "yields to the thing seen" rather than attributing a position of mastery to the viewing subject.[69] Marks argues that normative "optical" visuality, which "sees things from enough distance to perceive them as distinct forms in deep space," exists on a spectrum with a "haptic" mode of visuality, in which "the eyes themselves function like organs of touch."[70] Elsewhere, Marks describes haptic visuality as "a form of visuality that muddies intersubjective boundaries" and "a kind of visuality that is not organized around identification, at least identification with a single figure, but that is labile, able to move between identification and immersion."[71] For Marks, haptic visuality initiates the dynamic process of becoming that is at the core of the concept of mimesis (one recalls Caillois's description of the schizophrenic's sensation of formlessness or "turning into" nothing in particular) before vision resolves the distinction between the sensing being and its environment.[72] By focusing on touch, Marks adjusts our attention to the mutually transformative material exchange involved in the representational process of mimesis, prior to its objectification in the seemingly stable form of the image.

Marks maps this distinction between optical and haptic visuality onto two different approaches to the cinematic image: optical compositions that invite the viewer to regard and assess the image from an external vantage point, and haptic images that do not resolve immediately, if at all, into figuration. Haptic images pull the viewer in close, inviting a haptic look that surrenders to the image and takes on its tactile and labile qualities.[73] As examples, she cites film and video techniques, common to experimental work, that amplify the graininess and ambiguity of the image and invite a caressing and erotic look, such as overexposure, underexposure, multiple exposure, optical printing, scratching, soft focus, and blurred motion.[74] Haptic images, she writes, have a way of dissolving the hierarchical relationship between subjects and objects, and thereby cultivate a mimetic, tactile knowledge of the world. She describes this "tactile epistemology" as an "immanent way of being in the world, whereby the subject comes into being not through abstraction from the world but compassionate involvement in it" such that "erstwhile subjects take on the physical, material qualities of objects, while objects take on the perceptive and knowledgeable qualities of subjects."[75]

The haptic image has applications that extend well beyond Marks's descriptions of experimental diasporic film and video techniques that appeal to sensorial and embodied knowledge. In chapter 3, I suggested that the haptic image offers a useful description of autistic modes of perception and mediation. The haptic image is equally useful as a description of documentary practices that employ the indexical, rather than iconic, properties of audiovisual media to cultivate a mimetic relationship with the world. In Charles Sanders Peirce's tripartite semiotic system, the index differs from the other two categories of signs, icons and symbols, in that it is "really affected" by its object. Peirce elaborates, "In so far as the Index is affected by the Object, it necessarily has some Quality in common with the Object, and it is in respect to these that it refers to the Object. It does, therefore, involve a sort of Icon, but an Icon of a peculiar kind; and it is not the mere resemblance of its Object, even in these respects that make it a sign, but it is the actual modification of it by the Object."[76]

Peirce notes here that the index and the icon are both signs of a mimetic order, but that they belong to different categories of mimesis: the icon resembles its object, while the index shares an existential or material connection with the object, having been actually modified by it. This explains why Mary Ann Doane characterizes the indexical sign as being "perched precariously on the very edge of semiosis," given that "the disconcerting closeness of the index to its object raises doubts as to whether it is indeed a sign."[77] Indeed, the iconicity of an image, or its resemblance to its object, as perceived by the human beholder, is a necessary supplement to the interpretation of an indexical sign such as the documentary image as realist or objective. Without this explanatory supplement, the indexical sign merely points blindly toward its object but otherwise mutely resists interpretation by a human subject.

To put it somewhat differently, we might say that the indexical properties of a visual medium cultivate an interpretive modality that is more haptic than optical, urging the interpreting subject to participate in the admixture between sign and object rather than standing outside it. The works to which I now turn are all engaged in different ways in collaborative documentary practices that activate the indexical, haptic properties of media as carriers of significance within animal Umwelten, to borrow Uexküll's terms. The manner in which da Costa, Starling, and Easterson surrender the semiotic, narrative, and technical protocols of their media to their nonhuman collaborators enables the medium to take on the qualities of its nonhuman handlers. Unlike the elephant's self-portrait, which employs the iconicity of the documentary image as a humanizing interpretive supplement, da Costa's *PigeonBlog*, Starling's *Infestation Piece*, and Easterson's *Animal Cams* draw inspiration from the psychasthenic insect's haptic mimicry in their way of making the medium similar to the so-called lesser or weaker forms of organic and inorganic life. This process results in documentary sounds and images whose legibility for or orientation toward a human subject is not immediately evident. These works do not share a common genre, medium, or mode of address; in fact, their practitioners vary substantially in terms of their production and exhibition contexts, spanning the domains of new media art, conceptual art, and video art. But in Caillois's own boundary-crossing spirit, I am not concerned so much with the situations of these works within the disciplinary formation of documentary as I am with the diagonal correspondences and openings that emerge from their mimetic attitude of surrender.

PigeonBlog

PigeonBlog, a San Jose–based amateur science initiative by the late new media artist Beatriz da Costa, inverts the uses of biomimicry in military aeronautic reconnaissance by repurposing aerial surveillance technologies to improve the environmental conditions of urban birds. In a chapter about her project, da Costa briefly references an early twentieth-century military experiment in

FIGURE 4.2 Pigeon outfitted with *PigeonBlog* equipment. Courtesy of Beatriz da Costa and Robert Nideffer.

enlisting camera-carrying pigeons as agents of surveillance, writing that this novel mode of reconnaissance served as both inspiration and foil for her civilian "grass-roots scientific data-gathering initiative."[78] As da Costa explains, the miniature panoramic camera technology in question was designed by German court pharmacist and engineer Julius Neubronner in the early 1900s for taking time-lapse photographs during the flight of homing pigeons. Although Neubronner intended his technology to be used in aerial reconnaissance, it was never used for this purpose because there were difficulties in getting the pigeons to return to dovecotes displaced during battle and, perhaps more important, because the images taken by the pigeons provided no information of strategic value.

Da Costa developed a technological prosthesis that would emulate the native flight patterns of homing pigeons rather than retraining them to serve human purposes. Having observed that California air pollution–monitoring stations currently monitor only specific bands of air in low-traffic areas, and therefore produce skewed projected data for the surrounding highly polluted minority neighborhoods, da Costa employed the low-altitude flight patterns of urban pigeons to inexpensively gather air pollution data at levels that fixed-location state instruments do not monitor. To this end, she collaborated with a team of engineers to produce GPS-enabled electronic air pollution–sensing devices that could be carried as "backpacks" by trained urban homing pigeons. These devices sent real-time location information to an open-access online server and blogging environment. Here, viewers could access a minute-by-minute air pollution index from a pigeon's perspective, presented in the form of an interactive map. By transforming pigeons into mobile "reporters" working on behalf of the city's poor, da Costa hoped not only to complement the gaps in official scientific pollution data but also to contest the reputation of pigeons as urban parasites.[79]

The conceptual sophistication of *PigeonBlog* lies in the tactical "uselessness" of the pollution data visualized on the blog, with which spectators are encouraged to interface. As da Costa notes, these data have little value from a scientific perspective, since few other birds inhabit the specific atmospheric band at which pigeons fly, and the data are irrelevant to the lived experience of humans at ground level. Given the characterization of pigeons as an urban menace, the improvement of their environmental conditions ranks even lower than those of other animal species in the pecking order of civic priorities. Against this context, da Costa's recognition of the scientific uselessness of the data gathered by pigeons pinpoints the anthropomorphic bias of environmental and animal rights conversations. Crucially, by noting the analogies and affinities between pigeons and other disposable populations whose living conditions do not merit monitoring or improvement, *PigeonBlog* questions the biopolitical logic that governs the priorities of civic administration, in which the enhancement and securitization of some lives comes at the cost of letting others decline.

PigeonBlog dramatizes the messy ethical and aesthetic conflicts of involving animals in any so-called participatory project. In installation, audiovisually striking images and sounds captured by "embedded reporter" pigeons who flew alongside the "reporter" pigeons carrying cell-phone cameras and microphones were used to entice spectators to engage with the data visualized on the blog-based interface. The mismatch between the iconic spectacle of prosthetically enhanced pigeons in flight and the useless pollution data indexed during their flight is one that hangs over the project, as a reminder of the humanizing protocols of mediation, translation, and visualization through which the lives of animals are made meaningful to humans.

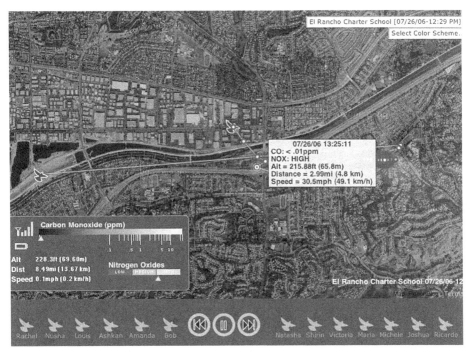

Inside the image (labels and readouts):

El Rancho Charter School [07/26/06-12:29 PM]

Select Color Scheme.

07/26/06 13:25:11
CO: < .01ppm
NOX: HIGH
Alt = 215.88ft (65.8m)
Distance = 2.99mi (4.8 km)
Speed = 30.5mph (49.1 km/h)

Carbon Monoxide (ppm)

.1   .5   1   5 10

Alt   228.3ft (69.60m)
Dist   8.49mi (13.67 km)   Nitrogen Oxides
Speed 0.1mph (0.2 km/h)   LOW   MEDIUM

El Rancho Charter School 07/26/06-12

Rachel Nusha Louis Ashkan Amanda Bob   Natasha Shirin Victoria Maria Michele Joshua Ricardo

FIGURE 4.3 Pollution visualization on *PigeonBlog* interface. Courtesy of Beatriz da Costa and Robert Nideffer.

Infestation Piece

Like da Costa, English conceptual artist Simon Starling employs allegory in his artistic practice to invoke the mutually generative interplays between human and nonhuman territorial concerns. Starling produced *Infestation Piece (Musselled Moore)* (2006/2008) by staging an encounter between his sculptural medium and underwater animal participants. The first step involved creating a steel replica of Henry Moore's bronze sculpture *Warrior with Shield*, a work produced by Moore in 1953–1954 with the support of public funds from the Canadian government. At the time, Canada's patronage of Moore was met with intense opposition from Toronto-based artists, who resented the English artist's encroachment onto the Toronto art scene (which was doubly illicit in that he was introduced to the city by British art historian and Soviet spy Anthony Blunt). Starling then submerged his steel replica in Lake Ontario for eighteen months, with the intention of evoking

FIGURE 4.4 Simon
Starling, *Infestation
Piece (Musselled
Moore)*, in progress
(being retrieved from
the water), 2006/2008.
Commissioned by
the Power Plant
Contemporary Art
Gallery, Toronto,
Canada. Photo by Rafael
Goldchain.

another ecological accident in the aftermath of the Cold War: the colonizing presence of eastern European zebra mussels in the Great Lakes since approximately the mid-1980s, when they were inadvertently introduced into the lakes in the ballast water of cargo ships arriving from the Black Sea toward the end of the conflict. The deleterious impact of this predatory species of mussel on the ecological balance of the Great Lakes is well known: the rapid consumption of algae by zebra mussels deprives native mussels of their food source, and they also immobilize these native species by attaching to their shells.

Starling's piece urges us to read this parable on the dangers of border crossing against its usual grain. Substituting Moore's original medium (bronze, which is toxic to mussels) with steel, Starling surrendered his sculpture to the invasive zebra mussels as a hospitable breeding ground.[80] This act of submersion activated the indexical rather than iconic signifying capacities of the sculptural medium, in that various underwater species were invited to touch, rub against, and attach themselves to the steel structure—a choice that is all the more interesting when we consider the injunction against touch that frequently structures spectatorial engagements with artworks in a gallery or museum context.

When *Infestation Piece* was retrieved from the water in 2008, it was covered with a patina of rust and mussels, having been "completed" by the combined work of water erosion and the life cycles of the resident mussels. The dried mussel shells encrusted on the corroded frame of Starling's steel replica hauntingly index a less well-known fact regarding the ecological gifts of this unwelcome immigrant species: zebra mussels filter algae and other pollutants from the water, resulting in increased sunlight penetration and plankton growth at greater depths. By literally plunging a work of high art into a new environmental context, Starling reconfigures the artistic medium— ordinarily a material or technical material for aesthetic expression—as a set of conditions that can carry an entirely different set of meanings within the *Umwelt* or environmental milieu of another species. In the process, *Infestation Piece* transforms an art-historical anecdote regarding the transnational ecological impact of art into a conduit for identifying the generative possibilities of ecological accidents.

Animal Cams

Video artist Sam Easterson turns cameras from tools of surveillance into a means of surrendering the conventions of the wildlife documentary genre, thereby fostering minor modes of encounter with animals. His "animal cams" call into question the spirals of power and pleasure involved in the practice of animal surveillance, from its earliest inceptions in Eadweard Muybridge's zoopraxographic experiments with animal locomotion, to more contemporary iterations such as the television nature documentary and the Internet pet video. Easterson has since 1998 collected video footage from the point of view of animals, which he exhibits online and in gallery, museum, and educational contexts under the banner *Animal Cams*.[81] The subjects of his experiments cut across taxonomic orders, encompassing an idiosyncratic range of nonhuman entities: *Animal Cams* prominently features charismatic mammals (such as sheep, wolves, buffalo, armadillos, alligators, and moles) but also arachnids (tarantulas), birds (falcons, turkeys, and chickens), carnivorous plants (pitcher plants), and even insentient objects (a tumbleweed).

On first glance, *Animal Cams* may seem like little more than soft surveillance, since Easterson's practice consists of fastening diminutive custom-modified helmet-mounted cameras onto the heads or bodies of his subjects that capture video footage as the carriers go about their day. The name of his project signals the parlance of early surveillant web videos, like *JenniCam*, and indeed, Easterson literalizes the gesture of burdening figures of "bare life" with a watchful humanitarian superego that mediates and autocorrects their every move. The literal nature of its execution also makes *Animal Cams* extremely productive to think with. After mounting his meticulously crafted cameras onto his understandably uncooperative collaborators (which he says is "ninety percent of the battle"), Easterson is obliged to simply let them go: that is, to surrender his cameras to the whims of their bearers, who routinely disrupt his intervention by shrugging off their intrusive headgear.[82] The fate of these cameras—which are jostled, scratched, licked and bitten by other animals, and dunked in water and mud before being shaken off or destroyed—accounts for the brevity of the videos, typically between a few seconds and several minutes long.

The image that indexes this act of surrender is a far cry from the smooth harmony suggested by the notion of immersive media, for it stages a visceral conflict between Easterson's vulnerable camera apparatus and a hostile environment that is thoroughly indifferent to its predicament. This palpable conflict and loss of control is perhaps what makes the experience of *Animal Cams* most distinct from its high-tech counterpart, National Geographic's *Crittercam*. The latter has a similar conceit of attaching digital cameras and other research instruments onto endangered marine and terrestrial animals to "witness the lives of animals from the animals' own perspectives."[83] Although it subscribes to a discourse of immersion that erases its own mediating effects—as if the camera were somehow capable of transmitting experience in an unmediated fashion—*Crittercam* relies on a highly produced narrative frame and expert audio commentary to compensate for the indecipherable and uneventful quality of the visual information in the video footage. Easterson emphasizes rather than minimizes the disjuncture between the perceptual worlds of animals and the narrative codes of the wildlife documentary genre. His *Animal Cams* reveal how conventional representations of animals suture over the elements of mediation that structure our glimpses into the "authentic" lives of animals, including the surreptitious surveillance of the camera, and strategic edits that eliminate uneventful "lag time" and dramatize the temporality of animality as one of spectacular action.[84]

The most striking aspect of *Animal Cams* lies in Easterson's deactivation of such anthropomorphic narrative conventions, from the humanistic framing centered on the subject's face to the camera's omniscient, panoramic presence, as well as shot/reverse-shot editing as a way of structuring our identification with animals as characters in a drama of survival. Since Easterson mounts his cameras on the heads or necks of his subjects, the image signifies indexically rather than iconically, with the digital prostheses registering both the movements and the stases of their often reluctant subjects.

Easterson's practice is evocative of the recent film *Leviathan* (dir. Lucien Castaing-Taylor and Véréna Paravel, 2012), which was filmed using dozens of GoPro cameras that were either attached to the deck of a commercial shipping vessel or released into the ocean. *Leviathan* unmoors the sounds and images registered by these cameras from a human perspective and scale, which the filmmakers sought to "relativize" by "resituat[ing] them in a much wider ecological sphere."[85] But if *Leviathan* provides an "extraterrestrial vision" of the world that situates the viewer in the position of the fish, the sea, the boat, or the sky, as Paravel puts it, the vision of *Animal Cams* is subterranean.[86] In stark counterpoint to the fantasy of distance afforded by the wildlife genre, the image burrows close to the ground, or points downward as the animal forages for food, toggling in and out of focus as objects pass haphazardly into the camera's shallow field of focus. We are rarely granted the plenitude of a panoramic landscape shot or a studied close-up that inventories the visual spectacle of the subject's body and sensory environment. Instead, the bulk of the videos are out of focus, pixelated, and convulsive, giving little evidence as to the identity of the animal in question, and the jostling of the camera registers on the audio track as a jarring series of static disturbances.

As spectators, we are made to feel the extent to which the coded surveillant pleasures of watching animals hinge on what Marks calls optical visuality, that is, an all-perceiving, distant gaze that perceives forms in illusionistic depth and in which figures are made available for identification and self-recognition. Depth and clarity are rarely a feature of *Animal Cams*. More often than not, we are privy to haptic images that are so close to their object as to be undifferentiated from it—images that fail to resolve into distinct shapes that we can visually identify.[87] Since so much of the footage is chaotic and

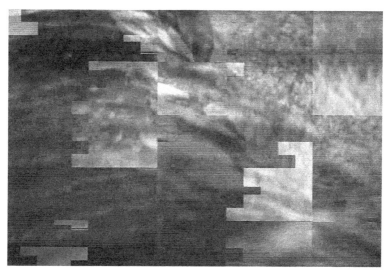

FIGURE 4.5 Still from "Turkey Cam" by Sam Easterson (2008)

illegible, the pleasure we take in the punctuating moments when we catch a glimpse of something recognizable is inordinate: whether the reflection of a bison in a pool of water, the rare intact view of a fellow sheep, the framing of a pair of armadillo ears, or a pair of paws suggesting a wolf at rest after a long day. The unexpected hermeneutic weight borne by these moments urges us to confront the extent to which our understanding of animal lives is oriented by narcissistic narrative tropes.

It is arguably moments just like these, including several breathtaking upside-down (we might even call these reverse-aerial) shots of seagulls in flight, that represent the ultimate payoff of *Leviathan*. These moments reward the spectator for submitting to the sensory trauma of being plunged into and out of the water like a fish for ninety minutes by reminding them of the simple pleasures of regarding nature at a distance. The "gasp" that these moments call forth from the audience is not unlike the gasp orchestrated by the YouTube video of the elephant painting when it zooms in on the elephant's trunk painting an elephant's trunk. It is a gasp of misrecognition. Castaing-Taylor and Paravel disavow the humanizing effects of these interpretive frames, claiming that their film "exists before interpretation intervenes" (the film's near-total avoidance of words also disavows these frames; both techniques partake of the discourse of immediation).[88] Easterson's obtusely minimalist titles ("Farm Cams," "Wild Animal Cams," "Bison Cam,"

FIGURE 4.6 Still from "Wolf Cam" by Sam Easterson (2008)

etc.) dangle these interpretive frames before us, but withhold the explanatory supplement in whose absence the audiovisual index only points blindly, bereft of any stable meaning. As a result, his *Animal Cams* are as disturbing to watch as the video of the elephant painting a portrait of itself is pleasing. The elephant, like Dr. Itard's wild boy in Truffaut's film and Zana Briski's star pupil Avijit in *Born into Brothels*, obligingly performs its "gratitude" toward its humanitarian benefactors by supplying an image that holds a screen to their humanity. Easterson's surrendered cameras do not oblige his collaborators to respond in any predetermined fashion. Instead, we are obliged to witness the surrendered humanitarian gift of documentary being "returned to the sender" in the form of thoroughly alien, ineffable, and abortive images from which we may be cut off at any moment.

The makers of *PigeonBlog, Infestation Piece*, and *Animal Cams* are all complicit in the humanitarian gesture of "handing over the camera" to marginalized entities. At the same time, their radically passive comportment toward minoritarian modes of existence and their willingness to allow the medium to be repurposed in unforeseeable ways embody a noninterventionist ethos that works against the grain of this interventionist gesture. Da Costa, Starling, and Easterson all explore the mutually transformative process of mimesis—allowing the documentary medium to become similar to its new handlers and vice versa—as a reflexive technique of rejuvenating the anthropocentric narrative and visual conventions of humane-itarian documentary forms. Their experiments confront mediation as an ethically compromised but nonetheless generative field of action, without which there cannot be an encounter with alterity. Their attitude of surrender gives in to the unpredictable outcome of this encounter. Far from serving as screens that verify our humanity, the compellingly illegible haptic images and sounds that they generate point toward the potentiality of the medium to support altogether new meanings and subject positions that are more capacious than either the human or the animal but that emerge from the messy and ethically fraught encounters between them.

These projects invite us to imagine what it would mean to become the addressee of these meanings. Their open-ended address goes beyond critique and refusal; it is genuinely affirmative. It calls on us to see a positive value in existences that humanitarianism, perhaps threatened by the exposure of its own limited worldview, can only see in terms of lack—to experience the exhilarating openings of nonhuman modes of being in the world, even if this means giving up our humanist modes of viewing, interpreting, and reading documentary as a discourse of immediation.

THE GIFT OF DOCUMENTARY

I began this book with the question: what does endangered life do for documentary? I would like to conclude the book by reflecting on this question in another form that offers one final reframing of the humanitarian impulse of "giving the camera to the other": *what is at stake in the gift of documentary?* What does documentary give the other, and what, if anything, does the other give back to documentary?

My question, what is at stake in the gift of documentary?, is informed by Thomas Keenan's meditations on a logical contradiction in the discourse of claiming human rights. In *Fables of Responsibility*, Keenan points out that the idea of claiming a right would seem to suggest that the right in question belongs to the person who is claiming it and that the loss of this right is merely accidental or contingent. But if this is the case, he asks, why *claim* what is one's own? He continues:

Why even open up the relation to the other that the linguistic act of claiming implies, when my relation to my rights is essentially a relation to myself without mediation through, or openness to, an other? This claim could only be a statement, the constative declaration of a fact which had fallen into temporary oblivion. Is this act of claiming necessary? For if rights must be claimed, then (1) the relation to [the] other, and the supposed "loss" of rights in the other, cannot be merely contingent, and (2) the rights claimed cannot simply pre-exist the claim that is made for them.[1]

Keenan reverses the customary understanding of human rights claims as a means whereby dispossessed individuals demand to be recognized as possessing the attributes of humanity by others who already possess these attributes. He proposes that the "fact" of a common humanity shared by the claimant and the addressee—or the guarantee of a relation between the "I" and the "you"—cannot be taken for granted until and unless it is claimed. Keenan reframes such claims as a *hail*—an interpellative call for help, action, or response that exposes the addressee to the originary nature of the experience of "dispropriation" and dispossession, or to the condition of being an other for the other, "an other *like* others."[2] In other words, human rights claims locate what is held in common not in preexisting attributes of humanity but in the experience of dispropriation that is necessarily and not contingently implied by the relationship with the other. Keenan points out elsewhere that human rights is a *general* claim on behalf of everyone, one that insists that the rights in question can exist only when the possibility of the claimant's suffering can be extended to all of humanity.[3]

The humanitarian gesture of giving the camera to the other can be read as a literal manifestation of what Keenan describes as the experience of dispropriation in the face of the other. Like the act of claiming rights, this gesture enacts the Levinasian contention that the primary relationship that constitutes being is the ethical relationship with the other, whose vulnerability suspends one's own "natural" right to exist and replaces it with the moral obligation to respond. The ethical principle of "giving up" the right to speak (for oneself and the other) is *potentially* radical in that it prioritizes the other's right to exist over one's own. Or, to paraphrase Didier Fassin's summary of humanitarian ethics, the potential sacrifice of one's own rights reasserts the sacredness of those of the other.[4]

In practice, however, such a sacrifice or gift is never free. In his anthropological study of economies of total gift exchange, Marcel Mauss argues that there is no gift or sacrifice that does not obligate the recipient to reciprocate. Gifts are given and sacrifices are made (whether sacrifices to deities or the sacrifice implied in giving up one's belongings to another) with the expectation of a return. Mauss's account of the obligation to give, receive, and reciprocate is strongly evocative of Keenan's proposals regarding the obligations surrounding human rights claims, which compel both claimant and addressee to acknowledge their relationship of mutual dispossession. Mauss writes, "To refuse to give, to fail to invite, just as to refuse to accept, is tantamount to declaring war; it is to reject the bond of alliance and commonality. Also, one gives because one is compelled to do so, because the recipient possesses some kind of right of property over anything that belongs to the donor."[5] Mary Douglas interprets this to mean that gift cycles engage the giver and the recipient in social bonds, alliances, or "permanent commitments that articulate the dominant institutions."[6] This is another way of saying that the gift, for Mauss, operates as a form of ideological hailing that interpellates the giver and the recipient as members of a shared social institution or community into which they are born from the start but whose bonds must be ritually rearticulated and reproduced. The exchange of gifts is a ritual that enacts their belonging to this community. Like the act of claiming rights, the act of giving is both performative and constative at once: it calls into being the "fact" of the relationship between giver and receiver.

I have argued throughout this book that the humanitarian impulse of giving the camera to the other operates as just such an ideological hailing. This "gift" invites the so-called dehumanized other to identify with, claim, and take up their place as a member of the community of "humanity." Immediations, I have proposed, are the ritualized representational tropes or conventions through which these claims of belonging are articulated. We might think of these conventions—from the aesthetic of feral innocence adopted by Zana Briski's students in *Born into Brothels*, to the televisual codes of "bare liveness" performed by Kimberly Roberts, the first-person voice-over that speaks for Sue Rubin in *Autism Is a World*, and the elephant's iconic self-portrait—as the eminently precoded and culturally ordained conventions that dictate how the recipient should engage with and operationalize the camera so as to maintain the social institution of humanity. These conventions are analogous to the elaborate but often implicit social conventions that Mauss argues dictate the exchange of gifts. To free the debtor, Mauss writes, the reciprocal gift, or the "clinching gift" that seals the transaction, must be equivalent to the first gift: the return gift must replicate the hail of the first.[7]

In practice, however, such hailing is not always guaranteed, or secure in its symmetry. As Keenan reminds us, the very functioning of ideology is dependent on misdirection and misrecognition.[8] To put it in Mauss's terms, the gift may be seized by someone for whom it was not intended, the cultural codes inscribed in it might be misread, or it might be reciprocated in a form that rejects the bonds that the gift was originally intended to cement. The same uncertainty is built, I have shown, into the gesture of giving the camera to the other. Once the camera is handed over, there is no guarantee that the ideological messages, codes, and conventions of documentary immediacy will find their mark. This opens a potentially productive gap: it is entirely possible for the encounter between the medium and the recipient to generate an unexpected response that undermines the documentary logic of immediations and their embedded visions of humanity. For instance, Manik's *Puja* and Tapasi's *Dressing* are examples of photographs that sidestep the unary aesthetic of innocence expected of children in the film *Born into Brothels*. The blind field activated by these images calls on the viewer to identify with a more complex vision of humanity that accommodates the eroticism and labor of non-Western childhoods. Mel Baggs's "In My Language," on the other hand, demonstrates a promiscuous, haptic approach to mediation that addresses *humanity* itself, as imagined by the documentary tropes of "having a voice," as fundamentally dispossessed and dispropriated—that is, as a confining, autistic, and limited form of relationality.

These responses to being given the camera operate as a *counter*hail that is issued alongside the hail of immediations. They borrow the structure of hailing that interpellates individuals as humans to interpellate humans as that which is excluded from the definition of human, that is, as *not yet* normatively human. They return the gift of the camera with images and sounds inscribed with a trace of themselves, and of their mode of being in the world—one that invites the viewer to engage anew with the medium and to cultivate an attitude regarding mediation that is informed by this trace. This open-ended attitude regarding mediation is what I have called a radically noninterventionist ethic of participatory documentary informed by the principle of mimetic surrender. Surrender is implied in giving, but so is the expectation of a return. When I refer to a participatory documentary practice informed by surrender, it is not because I believe that an altruistic practice that is unmotivated by the expectation of a return is possible. Rather, I refer to a practice that is open to the gift returning in an unexpected, "improper," minor form that opens up new vistas of relationality—a minor form whose possibility is nonetheless inscribed in the normative functioning of the gift.

Is this openness not the defining quality of documentary—and, indeed, the gift that documentary keeps on giving? This is what Dai Vaughan suggests, in his beautiful reading of one of the first-ever filmed "actualities," to which I would like to return, as a closing gesture. Vaughan finds in the very first films screened by the Lumière Brothers in 1895 some of the formal conventions that we now identify with documentary, including the distinction between those who are granted subjectivity, and permitted the right of direct address, and those that are regarded dispassionately by the camera as unspeaking objects. But the film that he finds most evocative of the future potential of documentary—*A Boat Leaving Harbor*—does not announce its documentary status in any of these conventional ways. The film, less than a minute in length, features the simple action of two men pushing off to sea in a rowboat from a jetty where two women and children stand. Just as the boat passes beyond the jetty it is caught in a light swell that turns it around, threatening to capsize it. The men struggle to control the boat, and one of the woman turns to look toward them. Here, the film ends.

This little film captivates Vaughan not because it allegorically evokes departure and return on the high seas but because the *sea itself* escapes the efforts of the filmmaker and protagonists to perform a scripted action and absorbs them in the challenge of the moment: "when the boat is threatened by the waves, the men must apply their efforts to controlling it; and by responding to the challenge of the spontaneous moment, they become integrated into its spontaneity."[9] For Vaughan, the greatest achievement of this film lies in its harnessing of spontaneity, that is, what is not predictable by, or under the control of, the filmmaker or the actors—a spontaneity that defines the potential of documentary. The promise of this film remains untarnished because it captures something of a moment when "cinema seemed free, not only of its proper connotations, but of the threat of its absorption into meanings beyond it."[10] Every fulfillment of this promise, he concludes, can only be a betrayal.

To me, there is something of this promise embedded in the gesture of giving the camera to the other. The iterations of this gesture that I have examined are, in many ways, driven by what Vaughan calls the inevitable betrayal of documentary: in Briski's *Born into Brothels* or Tia Lessin and Carl Deal's *Trouble the Water*, for instance, the rhetoric of documentary immediacy is one that seeks to turn the spontaneous encounter with alterity into a coded convention of authenticity. *Rhetoric*, Keenan reminds us, is another word for force.[11] Rhetoric coerces the other to yield in a manner that evokes a loaded gun (hence the interventionist metaphor of the camera as gun). The rhetorical force of documentary immediations is one that attempts to regain the control that is lost in the gesture of giving up control of the camera, or surrendering one's arms. In Sam Easterson's "Turkey Cam," the bird escapes

FIGURE C.1 Still from *A Boat Leaving Harbor* by the Lumière Brothers (1895)

Easterson's efforts to represent it much like the sea overcomes the Lumière Brothers and their actors. In the clash between the bird and camera, which culminates not in a scripted spectacle but in an equally captivating digital blur, one glimpses the yielding of rhetoric and, in that yielding, the reopening of the gift of documentary that returns to absorb the camera, and us, in the spontaneous moment of the encounter.

NOTES

Introduction: Immediations

1. *Oxford English Dictionary*, s.v. "immediate," accessed March 24, 2016, http://www
.oed.com/view/Entry/91838?redirectedFrom=immediate.
2. Per John Corner, Grierson's first use of the term *documentary* is in a review of
Robert Flaherty's film *Moana* for a New York newspaper in 1926. Corner, *Art of
Record*, 2. Corner notes that the phrase "creative treatment of actuality," which is
commonly attributed to Grierson, is actually difficult to find in Grierson's most
commonly cited writings; its first usage is likely in the article "The Documentary
Producer," written by Grierson for *Cinema Quarterly* in 1933. Corner, *Art of Record*, 13.
3. See Hardy, Introduction, 18. Hardy quotes from the *Fortnightly Review* (August
1939), where Grierson writes that "the basic force behind [the documentary film
movement] was social not aesthetic."
4. Grierson, "The Documentary Idea: 1942," 250.
5. Grierson, "The Documentary Idea: 1942," 257.
6. Kahana, *Intelligence Work*, 7. Kahana reads Grierson's review of *Moana* in 1926
as an ambivalent document that is less certain about the meaning and potential
value of documentary than his later manifestos. Kahana notes, "In fact, Grierson
emphasizes that the instrumental elements of Flaherty's film do not inhibit what
is truly admirable about the film: its capacity to link us to the timeless values of
nature, human and otherwise" (5). Kahana views this ambivalence as evidence of
an allegorical tendency in the documentary form—one that he argues cultivates
an interpretive attitude that continually articulates the particular to the universal,
while retaining the specificity of the particular (7–8).
7. See Scarry, *Thinking in an Emergency*; and Calhoun, "Idea of Emergency."
8. Winston, *Claiming the Real II*, 46.
9. For example, Michael Renov writes that "at the level of the sign, it is the differing
historical status of the referent that distinguishes documentary from its fictional
counterpart not the formal relations among signifier, signified, and referent." "Introduction," 2.
10. See Trinh, "Mechanical Eye," 57; and Rony, *Third Eye*, 102.
11. See, for example, Juhasz and Lerner, *F Is for Phony*; Beattie, *Documentary Display*;
Lebow, *Cinema of Me*; and MacDonald, *Avant-Doc*.

12. See Foucault, *History of Sexuality*, vol. 1.

13. Chow, *Protestant Ethnic*, 29.

14. See Chow, *Protestant Ethnic*, esp. chaps. 1 ("The Protestant Ethnic and the Spirit of Capitalism") and 4 ("The Secrets of Ethnic Abjection") and "Introduction: From Biopower to Ethnic Difference."

15. In a different context, legal scholar Ruti Teitel writes, "Today as before, humanity posits the core defining line; in law as in morals, it circumscribes the legitimate exercise of force in the international realm." "For Humanity," 225.

16. Agamben, *Homo Sacer*, 115.

17. Teitel, "For Humanity," 225. Teitel locates the discursive origins of the term *humanity* in "an amalgam of natural law, the law of human rights, and the law of war" (225). Also see Thomas Laqueur's "Mourning, Pity, and the Work of Narrative in the Making of 'Humanity,'" which traces the modern usage of the term *humanity* to the late eighteenth century, in conjunction with sentimental humanitarian narratives of suffering.

18. Pettman, *Human Error*, 2.

19. Agamben, *Open*, 26; also see p. 25.

20. Agamben, *Open*, 37.

21. Scarry, *Thinking in an Emergency*, 7.

22. Calhoun, "Idea of Emergency," 30.

23. Honig, "Three Models," 46.

24. See Cartwright, "Images of Waiting Children."

25. See Chouliaraki, *Spectatorship of Suffering*; and Doane, "Information, Crisis, Catastrophe."

26. Richard Rorty refers to this as the "sentimentalist thesis" of human rights. Quoted in Laqueur, "Mourning," 31.

27. See Rancière, "Who Is?"; and Keenan, "Where Are Human Rights . . . ?," 65–66.

28. Honig, "Three Models," 59.

29. Levinas and Kearney, "Dialogue with Emmanuel Levinas," 24.

30. Fassin, "Humanitarianism," 508.

31. I discuss Fassin in greater detail in chapter 2.

32. Butler, *Precarious Life*, 143.

33. As Butler notes, Levinas associates the face with a prelinguistic vocalization that exceeds translation. *Precarious Life*, 134, 161. The connections between face and voice in Levinas require further parsing beyond what I can provide here. I merely note that he employs these terms in a manner that retains both their literal and metaphorical significance.

34. Butler, *Precarious Life*, 147.

35. Sina Kramer points out that both Butler and Levinas take for granted Spinoza's law of nature as self-preservation, which Levinas rewords as overcoming selfishness in order to prolong the life of the other. See Kramer, "Judith Butler's 'New Humanism.'"

36. See, for instance, Moeller, *Compassion Fatigue*; and Cohen and Sue, "Knowing Enough Not to Feel."

37. Cartwright, "Images of Waiting Children," 206. Also see Chouliaraki, *Spectatorship of Suffering*; and Chouliaraki, *Ironic Spectator*.
38. Sliwinski, *Human Rights in Camera*; Torchin, *Creating the Witness*; and Hesford, *Spectacular Rhetorics*.
39. Keenan, "Publicity and Indifference," 107–8.
40. Nichols, *Representing Reality*, 3. This is a point also made by Elizabeth Cowie in the introduction to her excellent book on documentary style and form; see Cowie, *Recording Reality*, 4.
41. See Agamben, *Homo Sacer*.

Chapter 1: Feral Innocence

1. All quotes are transcribed from my viewing of the films in question. For *The Wild Child*, I transcribed the English subtitles from the DVD version of the film.
2. See Linnaeus, *Systema naturae*, 1:21. Rousseau's enthusiastic positive regard for the vigor, robustness, and tenaciousness of "natural man" and his imaginative description of a "serene, sylvan, solitary" state before speech, sociality, and culture are frequently contrasted with his predecessor Thomas Hobbes's pessimistic view of life in the state of nature as "nasty, brutish, and short." See Rousseau, *Social Contract*, 90–107; and Hobbes, *Leviathan*, 186.
3. See Yousef, *Isolated Cases*; Murray, *Autism*, 40; and Pinchevski, "Displacing Incommunicability," 165.
4. As Michel Foucault has noted, the same "parental complex" would soon be adopted by Pinel at Bicêtre, and by his contemporary Samuel Tuke at the York Retreat, in their pioneering efforts to develop a humane method of "moral treatment" that would "liberate the insane from their chains" by enlisting them as wardens of their own supervision. See Foucault, *Madness and Civilization*, 253. Later, Foucault elaborates, "[Tuke and Pinel] did not introduce science but a personality, whose powers borrowed from science only their disguise, or at most their justification. These powers, by their nature, were of a *moral or social* order; they took root in the madman's minority status." The physician was "Father and Judge, Family and Law. . . . Pinel was well aware that the doctor cures when, exclusive of modern therapeutics, he brings into play these immemorial figures" (271–72; italics added).
5. See Yousef, *Isolated Cases*, 109.
6. Worth and Adair, *Through Navajo Eyes*, 138.
7. Briski received her training in photography at the University of Cambridge and the International Center for Photography in New York City. After winning the National Press Photographers Association Pictures of the Year Award in 1995 for her photojournalism on female infanticide in India, she initiated the Sonagachi photography project in 1997, for which she received the Open Society Institute Fellowship (1999), the World Press Photo Foundation Award for "Daily Life Stories" (2000), and the Howard Chapnick Grant for the Advancement of Photojournalism (2001). *Born into Brothels* was produced with the help of grants from the Jerome Foundation, the Sundance Institute, and the New York State Council

on the Arts. It was subsequently awarded the Academy Award for Best Documentary Feature in 2005, in addition to winning numerous other awards. See "About Us" page on the Kids with Cameras website, http://kids-with-cameras.org/ (site discontinued, accessed August 13, 2014).

8. See, for instance, Ebert, "Review." Ebert describes Briski as "a good teacher" who "brings out the innate intelligence of the children as they use their cameras to see their world in a different way."

9. Nichols, *Representing Reality*, 44.

10. Nichols, *Representing Reality*, 56; also see Nichols, *Introduction to Documentary*, 179–94. In *Introduction*, Nichols uses "the participatory mode" to refer to what he calls "the interactive mode" in *Representing Reality*.

11. Berlant argues that the spectacle of the violently exploited child traffics in a fetishized form of affective and sentimental citizenship that produces a "universal response." She writes, "It claims a hard-wired truth, a core of common sense. It is beyond ideology, beyond mediation, beyond contestation. It seems to dissolve contradiction and dissent into pools of basic and also higher truth." "Subject of True Feeling," 57–58.

12. Although Briski and Kauffman share credit for the film's cinematography and direction, my analysis reflects the film's diegetic and nondiegetic emphasis on the primacy of Briski's authorship and Kauffman's supporting role. See, for instance, Kauffman's comments in Lavallee, "Making of *Born into Brothels*."

13. Arora, "Production of Third World Subjects."

14. Mosquera, "Media, Technology, and Participation," 45.

15. Barthes, *Camera Lucida*, 51, 43.

16. Hesford, *Spectacular Rhetorics*, 166. Hesford writes at length about the film's marginalization of the history of women's activism around sex work—including the headway made by Calcutta's first sex worker cooperative, the Indian Commercial Sex Workers, in reducing the rates of sexually transmitted disease and ensuring fair wages for sex workers—as well as its tacit advocacy of the criminalization of prostitution (168–70).

17. Svati Shah argues that the film's criminalization of prostitution and suppression of regional histories of activism rehearses an orientalist drama of white savior–brown victim that ultimately favors increased police and state enforcement rather than nongovernmental organizing efforts. See Shah, "Saving Brothel Children."

18. Burman, "Innocents Abroad," 241; also see 248–49. Burman writes, "The abstraction of childhood invites the application of inappropriately homogenized or culturally chauvinistic development models. . . . Ironically, such special treatment can tend to disqualify them from the social world around them—so that they can be literally lifted from it" (243). Lisa Cartwright, who has theorized projective identification from the standpoint of empathy, building on the work of Melanie Klein, makes the important distinction that "feeling for" the other (something that both the projecting subject and the recipient of the projection may experience) is not to "be" the other or to "feel like" the other, that is, to "feel as and what [the other]

feels." Cartwright, *Moral Spectatorship*, 34, and also see chap. 1 ("Moral Spectatorship: Rethinking Identification in Film Theory").

19. K. Brown, "Pain of the Other," 187.
20. Hesford, *Spectacular Rhetorics*, 169.
21. See Head First Development's website (http://headfirstdevelopment.org/) for a narrative history of the inception and progress of the Hope House project. This Calcutta-based humanitarian foundation has taken over the planning of the project from Kids with Cameras. Head First Development reports that construction on Hope House had begun as of March 2014, and a fundraising video on their website suggests that construction is now nearly complete at the time of writing (2016).
22. See Althusser, "Ideology."
23. Construction site photographs can be seen on Head First Development's website, and architectural renderings of Hope House can be seen on the Kids with Destiny website at http://dev.kidswithdestiny.org/.
24. Ariès, *Centuries of Childhood*, esp. 128–33, 329–36, 405–15.
25. See Valentine, "Angels and Devils," 583; see also Wall, "Fallen Angels."
26. Warner, "Little Angels, Little Monsters," 57.
27. Warner, "Little Angels, Little Monsters," 55.
28. Malkki, "Children," 62.
29. Malkki, "Children," 65.
30. Malkki, "Children," 77.
31. Higonnet, *Pictures of Innocence*, 117–19, 206–7.
32. See "Kids' Gallery," "Kids' Prints," and "Kids' Book" on the Kids with Cameras website (site discontinued).
33. Briski, *Born into Brothels*, 9; italics added.
34. The fascination of the child for the artistic and cinematic avant-gardes as a means of dialectically rejuvenating habitualized and exhausted ways of looking has been well documented. See, for instance, Rachel Moore's analysis of the figure of the child in relation to the primitivist tendencies of modern art and in early film theory, including Walter Benjamin, Siegfried Kracauer, Sergei Eisenstein, and Jean Epstein (Moore, *Savage Theory*), and Marjorie Keller's monograph on the metaphors of childhood in European and American avant-garde cinema (Keller, *Untutored Eye*).
35. Fineberg, *Innocent Eye*, 2.
36. Batchen, *Burning with Desire*, 56. Later on the same page, Batchen cites Louis Daguerre's description in 1839 of the photographic process as a paradigmatic instance of this aspiration: "This process consists of the spontaneous reproduction of the images of nature reflected by means of the Camera Obscura, not in their own colors, but with a remarkable delicacy of gradation of tints."
37. Sontag, *Pain of Others*, 28.
38. Broomberg and Chanarin, "Unconcerned but Not Indifferent," 98.
39. Higonnet, *Pictures of Innocence*, 33–35.

40. See Fabian, *Time and the Other*, 32.

41. Higonnet, *Pictures of Innocence*, 73–76.

42. Barthes, *Camera Lucida*, 40–41, 55–57.

43. Higonnet, *Pictures of Innocence*, 77.

44. See ZoomUganda's website at http://zoomuganda.org; Ninos de la Amazonia's website at http://ninosdelaamazonia.org; and Plan International, "Bangladesh Street Children."

45. See Charleston Kids with Cameras's website at http://charlestonkidswithcameras .org (site discontinued, accessed March 11, 2010); Hertz, "Children"; and Engelbrecht, *Please Read*.

46. Some of the early precursors of the Kids with Cameras model from the 1960s to the 1990s have been cataloged by anthropologist Richard Chalfen, who served as a research assistant to Worth and Adair during the Navajo Film Themselves Project:

> 8 mm film with third graders in Harlem (Bigsby 1968) and teenage street gangs in New York (Barrat 1978, Fraser 1987), video with immigrant children (Delgado 1992), still photography with mentally handicapped children (Cox 1984), Polaroid photography with a toddler in Boston (Cavin 1994), videos made by students at a Massachusetts high school (Gray 1990), and video in a "teen dreams" project (Jetter 1993) . . . and a model for introducing photography to children . . . in a project entitled "Shooting Back" (Hubbard 1991) [where] [h]omeless young people between the ages of eight and seventeen living in a shelter were helped to make their own 35 mm photographs.

> Chalfen, "Afterword," 294–95.

47. See Renov, *Subject of Documentary*, 176. Renov reads the growing popularity of personal and autobiographical documentary genres since the mid- to late 1990s, in which subjectivity serves as "a kind of experiential compass guiding the work toward its goal as embodied knowledge," as a sign that "the representation of the historical world is inextricably bound up with self-inscription." *Subject of Documentary*, 176.

48. See, for instance, Post, "Conceiving Child Labor."

49. See Cullen, "Child Labor Standards," esp. 87–94. ILO C182 lists the following among the "worst forms" of child labor, which are to be immediately prohibited as violations of children's rights: "(a): 'all forms of slavery or practices similar to slavery, such as the sale and trafficking of children, debt bondage, and serfdom and forced or compulsory labor, including forced or compulsory recruitment of children for use in armed conflict'; (b) 'the use, procuring, or offering of a child for prostitution, for the production of pornography or for pornographic performances'; (c) 'the use, procuring, or offering of a child for illicit activities, in particular for the production and trafficking of drugs as defined in the relevant international treaties'; and (d) 'work which, by its nature or the circumstances in which it is carried out, is likely to harm the health, safety, or morals of children.'" Cullen, "Child Labor Standards," 94.

50. In *Child Labour and Child Work* (1990), her ethnography of child textile laborers in Chinnallipatti, India, Ivy George argues:

Child Labour [*sic*] is the employment of children and the extraction of their productivity for the economic gain of another, with debilitating ramifications on the psychological and physical development of the child. The *working* child, on the other hand, enters work arrangements that offer freedom and independence. Working children cease to be mere means to another's ends; instead they actively participate in decision making and the appropriation of resources and in that sense the whole work process is a learning experience, entered into willingly. . . . I do not oppose children *working*; in fact, from a social and economic standpoint it may very well be a viable alternative for all the children who are driven to inhumane conditions of labour today. The provision of work settings which foster the development of children, and which are unexploitative, is of utmost importance in alleviating the problems that beset the children and their kin. My suggestion for an alternative approach rests on the earlier differentiation of work and labour. (22–23)

Victor Karunan advocates a "human-rights/child-centered approach [that] seeks to view working children as change makers" by positioning them not as "innocent, vulnerable, and susceptible beings, but also as active social actors who can make a positive contribution, as children, to social development and change." Karunan, "Working Children," 303.
51. See Mizen, Pole, and Bolton, "Why Be a School-Age Worker?"
52. See Nieuwenhuys, "Anthropology and Child Labor," 238–40. Nieuwenhuys suggests that the Western view of childhood (which has become the norm for defining childhood in modernity) stems from a misreading of the abolitionist discourses surrounding child factory labor during the Industrial Revolution. The elimination of child factory labor, she insists, had less to do with humanitarian motives than with the economic and ideological requisite of protecting the mechanized textile industry from the competition of a youthful labor force.
53. Lazzarato, "Immaterial Labor."
54. For an example of this critique, see P. Rosen, "Border Times."
55. Virno, *Grammar of the Multitude*, 54–55.
56. This is the vision presented by Penny Marshall's classic comedy film *Big*, from 1988, in which a man-child is portrayed as a corporate genius creating innovative products. This portrayal is in more ways than one the precursor of the "expansive playspaces" that characterize contemporary work cultures in the Silicon Valley. I thank Genevieve Yue for bringing this to my attention.
57. Edelman, *No Future*, 2.
58. Ginsburg, "Indigenous Media," 95.
59. Worth and Adair, *Through Navajo Eyes*, 7.
60. Worth and Adair, *Through Navajo Eyes*, 25.
61. Worth and Adair, *Through Navajo Eyes*, 138; see also Pack, "Uniquely Navajo?"

62. See, for instance, Ginsburg, "Indigenous Media"; and Peterson, "Reclaiming Diné Film."

63. Worth and Adair, *Through Navajo Eyes*, 50–51.

64. See Pack, "Indigenous Media," 274.

65. Worth and Adair write, "We reasoned that if a member of the culture being studied could be trained to use the medium so that with his hand on the camera and editing equipment he could choose what interested him, we would come closer to capturing *his* vision of *his* world." *Through Navajo Eyes*, 14.

66. Worth and Adair, *Through Navajo Eyes*, 152.

67. Peterson summarizes Worth and Adair's analyses as follows: "The Navajo filmmakers are understood to have documented their own group in constant motion, and in balance and harmony with their environment, illustrated by long shots in some of the films of 'journeys' on foot—to find silver for jewelry, to gather plants for wool dyes, to herd sheep, or to collect medicine for a ceremony. Such shots were considered intertextual references to Navajo creation stories, which often include journeys." "Reclaiming Diné Film," 33.

68. See Peterson, "Reclaiming Diné Film," 33. For Worth and Adair's analyses, see *Through Navajo Eyes*, 204, and 199–207.

69. Ginsburg, "Indigenous Media," 95.

70. Ginsburg, "Indigenous Media," 95–96. This anecdote is also recounted in Worth and Adair, *Through Navajo Eyes*, 4–5.

71. See Feitosa, "Other's Visions." Feitosa writes, "'Through Navajo Eyes' expresses a scientific experiment centered on the researchers instead of the 'makers'" interests. The project did not by itself give rise to any further Navaho film projects; it neither led to Navaho empowerment nor provided a viable means of self-representation through visual media" (48).

72. Ginsburg, "Indigenous Media," 98. See also Michaels, "Social Organisation."

73. Ginsburg, "Indigenous Media," 96. Also see Turner, "Defiant Images"; Ginsburg, "Shooting Back"; and Frota, "Taking Aim."

74. Moore, "Marketing Alterity," 127.

75. It is worth noting that, prior to the Navajo project, Worth had conducted a similar film experiment among "eleven- to fourteen-year-old Negro dropouts in Philadelphia." Worth and Adair, *Through Navajo Eyes*, 24.

76. Worth and Adair, *Through Navajo Eyes*, 168, also see 169.

77. See Trinh, "Mechanical Eye," esp. 60, and "Totalizing Quest."

78. Worth and Adair, *Through Navajo Eyes*, 170–71.

79. Chow, *Primitive Passions*, 21.

Chapter 2: Bare Liveness

1. See "TeleGhetto Pre-elections Interview," available on the Global Nomads Group YouTube Channel, and "Teleghetto—Election Part 2"; "Tele Ghetto: One Year Anniversary"; and "Tele Ghetto: Kokorat (Street Children)," available on the Students Rebuild YouTube channel. A description of Global Nomads Group can be found on their website: http://gng.org/. In most of Tele Geto's videos, Romel

Jean Pierre and Steevens Simeon are the cameramen, and Alex Louis is the reporter.

2. See "Tele Ghetto: Guerilla Media." More information about the Ghetto Biennale can be found at http://www.ghettobiennale.com/. Also see the Atis Rezistans website, http://www.atis-rezistans.com/.

3. In a recent essay profiling the Atis Rezistans collective and its three founders, André Eugene, Jean-Hérard Céleur, and Frantz (Guyudo) Jacques, art historian Katherine Smith proposes that their salvage aesthetic extends to their recycling of both Haitian cultural-spiritual history and Western representations of their work. Their practice, she contends, draws inspiration on multiple levels from Gede, an eroticized trickster figure, the ubiquitous spirit of the Vodou pantheon, and a "cosmic recycler of life and death." By channeling Gede's excessive, inappropriate masculinity in their works, Smith shows, the Rezistans artists assert and renew the creative potential of *vagabondaj*, a term generally employed to derogate economically and politically disenfranchised youth in urban Haiti. See Smith, "Atis Rezistans."

4. Katherine Smith, personal communication, April 9, 2011. Atis Rezistans's youth group are known as Ti Moun Rezistans. Smith suggests that the smaller scale of Ti Moun Rezistans's sculptural works in comparison with the large-scale installations of their mentors (some of which reach over two stories in height) is deliberately designed to attract casual buyers.

5. In this regard, Tele Geto's fake camera is reminiscent of anthropologist Michael Taussig's description of fetish objects as a means of "sympathetic magic" whereby colonized indigenous people have sought to gain power over their colonizers by producing replicas of them, such that "the representation shares in or takes power from the represented." Tausig, *Mimesis and Alterity*, 2; also see p. 55. Dennis Hopper's *The Last Movie*, made in 1971, portrays a similar incident: the protagonist, a stunt coordinator for a Western film being shot in rural Peru, is upstaged by Peruvian natives acting out scenes from the film using fake camera equipment made out of sticks and twine.

6. "Tele Ghetto: Guerilla Media."

7. See Morel and Harris, "This Isn't Show Business." In this interview, Morel explains the circumstances surrounding his presence in Port-au-Prince at the time of the quake, including his profile of Ti Moun Rezistans. This article also features images shot by Morel on January 12, 2010.

8. For instance, the AS IF Gallery in Manhattan exhibited Morel's photographs of Ti Moun Rezistans "in the throws [*sic*] of the Haitian earthquake" alongside Ti Moun's artworks: http://www.asifgallery.com/info/children-of-rezistans.htm (site discontinued, accessed April 14, 2011).

9. See Cotter, "Haiti's Visionaries."

10. Cussans writes, "Tele Geto was created by Ti Moun Rezistans of the Grand Rue area in Port-au-Prince during the Ghetto Biennale. In light of the lack of video news coming from the ground in Haiti after the earthquake I sent a basic video recording kit so that the children of the Grand Rue could document life there

after the quake." See Cussans, "Tele Geto Project." Cussans's blog, *Zombi Diaspora* (http://codeless88.wordpress.com/), contains several entries devoted to his involvement with Tele Geto.

11. All six videos can be seen on Cussans's YouTube channel; see "Tele Geto" videos 1–6. The following quotes are excerpted from these videos.

12. See Popplewell and Laughlin, "Global Voices in Haiti."

13. See Bazin, "Ontology of the Photographic Image," 8.

14. Cussans, "From the Archives."

15. See Margesson and Taft-Morales, "Haiti Earthquake."

16. Fassin and Pandolfi, "Introduction," 12–13. Fassin and Pandolfi differentiate old and contemporary intervention (exemplified respectively by Kosovo in 1999 and Iraq in 2003) as follows: previously, moral arguments were encountered in support of intervening to defend a weak state or to support a liberation movement, but in recent decades protecting a population and saving lives has become a specific, new justification for intervention.

17. Calhoun, "Idea of Emergency," 30.

18. See Barnett and Weiss, *Humanitarianism in Question*; and Rieff, *Bed for the Night*.

19. See Feher, "The Governed in Politics."

20. See Fassin and Vasquez, "Humanitarian Exception."

21. Agamben argues, "In the final analysis, however, humanitarian organizations—which today are more and more supported by international commissions—can only grasp human life in the figure of bare or sacred life, and therefore, despite themselves, maintain a secret solidarity with the very powers they ought to fight." *Homo Sacer*, 133. In "The Sovereign, the Humanitarian, and the Terrorist," Adi Ophir elaborates:

> Humanitarian organizations, in Agamben's words, "maintain a secret solidarity with the powers they ought to fight." . . . [When they] provide aid and relief to refugees, invoking the sanctity of their lives, [they] act as a substitute for the political authorities and under their auspices, contribute to the reinstitutionalization of a false (ideological) distinction between the realm of bare life and the realm of politics. . . . They depoliticize the disaster, obstruct understanding of its local and global contexts, and tend to represent its victims as passive objects of care, devoid of political will and organizational capacities—if they do not actually make the victims so. (168)

22. Fassin, "Humanitarianism," 519; also see p. 515.

23. Fassin, "Humanitarianism," 516–17.

24. Keenan, "Where Are Human Rights . . . ?," 65–66.

25. See Feuer, "Live Television," 13–14.

26. Doane, "Information, Crisis, Catastrophe," 222.

27. Doane, "Information, Crisis, Catastrophe," 232.

28. Morse, "Television News Anchor," 62–63.

29. Doane, "Information, Crisis, Catastrophe," 228.

30. Doane, "Information, Crisis, Catastrophe," 229–30. In this regard, the televisual

rhetoric of catastrophe has not changed much in the decades since the publication of Doane's essay in 1990, except that the spectator is now encouraged to consult the network's website for even more up-to-date content, infographics, and data analysis.

31. Van Meter, "Unanchored."

32. Classen, "'Reporters Gone Wild.'" Cooper's skyrocketing ratings following his on-location Katrina reports won his show, *Anderson Cooper 360°*, a devoted fan following among Internet bloggers, as well as a coveted two-hour prime-time slot on CNN in November 2005, replacing anchor Aaron Brown's *NewsNight*.

33. Classen, "'Reporters Gone Wild'"; also see Morogiello, "Anderson Cooper 360°'s Coverage," 39; and Van Meter, "Unanchored."

34. See Zelizer, *About to Die*, 25.

35. See CNN, "CNN Live Today," transcript 1.

36. VIPIR stands for "volumetric imaging and processing of integrated radar." Kagan's announcement that this is "the same technology that we used to bring you the invasion of Iraq" invokes Lisa Parks's insight that the "view from nowhere" of satellite images conceals a conglomeration of military-industrial interests. CNN, "CNN Live Today," transcript 3; and Parks, "Digging into Google Earth," 542.

37. CNN, "CNN Live Today," transcript 3.

38. CNN, "CNN Live Today," transcript 1. Referring to Zarrella's live camera feed from downtown New Orleans, Myers elaborates, "On the north side of the causeway where the police had actually been blocking the causeway off, there was nothing on that camera at all. Not because the camera is broken, because the rain and the wind are going so quickly there's literally nothing to see. Visibility there, [is] less than about 100 feet."

39. CNN, "CNN Live Today," transcript 1.

40. CNN, "CNN Live Today," transcript 1.

41. CNN, "CNN Live Today," transcript 1.

42. CNN, "CNN Live Today," transcript 2.

43. Cooper, *Dispatches from the Edge*, 128–29.

44. Sturken, "Desiring the Weather," 169. Also see Sturken, "Weather Media."

45. The Stewart quote is from "Mess O'Slightly-to-the-Left O'Potamia," transcribed from personal viewing. In his memoir, Cooper writes, "In Baghdad most major American news organizations contract with private security firms. Big guys with thick necks meet you at the airports and give you a bulletproof vest before they even shake your hand." *Dispatches from the Edge*, 56–57. On a related note, the much-publicized kidnapping and murder of *Wall Street Journal* reporter Daniel Pearl in Pakistan in 2002 and, more recently, the death of photojournalist and filmmaker Tim Hetherington while documenting the conflict in Libya in 2011 exemplify rather than detract from Fassin's point that the lives of professional Western humanitarian volunteers are evaluated on a different scale than civilian lives lost in non-Western disaster zones.

46. CNN, "CNN Live Today," transcript 1.

47. Dayan and Katz, *Media Events*. Also see Fleetwood, "Failing Narratives, Initiating

Technologies." Fleetwood analyzes the conjunction of racialized discourses of risk and choice and predictive discourses (such as the weather report), as they played out around Katrina, in which those without the resources to heed the weather forecast were regarded as victims of their own delinquent choices rather than of their impoverished circumstances.

48. To cite just one example, correspondent Drew Griffin, stationed in Meridian, Mississippi, reported to Kagan later in this edition of *American Morning* that "the hotels are just packed. In fact, we got in late last night, and there was a stream of refugees going from hotel to hotel, desperately trying to find a room." See CNN, "CNN Live Today," transcript 2.

49. Doane, "Information, Crisis, Catastrophe," 223.

50. Chun, "Crisis, Crisis, Crisis," 95.

51. Chun, "Crisis, Crisis, Crisis," 96.

52. See the website of Born Hustler Records at http://www.bornhustlerrecords .com/.

53. Turan, "Eyes of the Storm."

54. All quotes are drawn from my transcript of the film.

55. Walker, "Rights and Return," 85; also see 100.

56. Morse, "Television News Anchor," 64.

57. See Hartl, "*Trouble the Water* Captures Katrina."

58. Doane, "Information, Crisis, Catastrophe," 229.

59. Elizabeth Castelli's work offers a useful critique of the deployment of religious frames in discourses of natural disaster. In a recent essay, "Theologizing Human Rights: Christian Activism and the Limits of Religious Freedom," Castelli argues that discourses that frame human rights as the product of divine authority rather than of ongoing political struggles and debates ignore the historical roots of human rights in secular Enlightenment-era discourses.

60. See Berlant, *Cruel Optimism*, esp. chaps. 1 ("Cruel Optimism") and 3 ("Slow Death (Obesity, Sovereignty, Lateral Agency)").

61. Describing racism as the "pre-condition for exercising the right to kill," Foucault writes that racism has two functions: "introducing a break into the domain of life that is under power's control: the break between what must live and what must die," and establishing a positive "relationship between my life and the death of the other that is not a military or warlike relationship of confrontation, but a biological-type relationship" wherein the death of the inferior race is seen to make life purer for the rest. *"Society Must Be Defended,"* 254–56.

62. See Fassin, "Humanitarianism"; also see Ticktin, *Casualties of Care*; and Redfield, "Sacrifice."

63. See Agamben, *Homo Sacer*.

64. Hardt and Negri, *Empire*, 26.

65. Giroux, "Reading Hurricane Katrina," 175.

66. Giroux, "Reading Hurricane Katrina," 186.

67. Giroux, "Reading Hurricane Katrina," 179 (quoting Hardt and Negri), 191; and Giroux, *Stormy Weather*, 111; also see *Stormy Weather*, 15, 20–21.

68. Giroux, "Reading Hurricane Katrina," 188.
69. Giroux, "Reading Hurricane Katrina," 173. In *Stormy Weather*, Giroux compares Katrina and the murder of Emmett Till as follows: "While the murder of Emmett Till suggests that a biopolitics structured around the intersection of race and class inequalities, on the one hand, and state violence, on the other, is not new, the new version of biopolitics adds a distinctively different and more dangerous register to the older version of biopolitics. . . . [It] also relegates entire populations to spaces of invisibility and disposability" (21).
70. Giroux, "Reading Hurricane Katrina," 172, 191; and Giroux, *Stormy Weather*, 113.
71. Keenan, "Mobilizing Shame," 437–38.
72. Bernstein, "Bare Life, Bearing Witness." Also see Didi-Huberman, *Images*, 159; and Guerin and Hallas, introduction to *Image and Witness*, 4–6. Georges Didi-Huberman, Frances Guerin, and Roger Hallas argue that the iconoclastic view of images, which invests images with the ability to pierce through the real, can be regarded as the counterpart of another equally prevalent and instrumentalizing position, which sees images as a Platonic veil that forever conceals the real.
73. Fuqua, "'That Part of the World.'"
74. Hardt and Negri, *Empire*, 24.
75. Hardt and Negri, *Multitude*, 146.
76. Hardt and Negri write, "It seems to us that, in our age of the hegemony of immaterial production, *the poor* designate the paradigmatic figure of production. . . . In the paradigm of immaterial production, in production based on communication and collaboration, 'the poor' . . . also highlights the contradictory relation of production to the world of value: 'the poor' is excluded from wealth and yet included in its circuits of social production. 'The poor' is the flesh of biopolitical production. We are the poors." *Multitude*, 151–52. In their more recent book, *Commonwealth*, Hardt and Negri elaborate on this theme, arguing that "as modes of life characterized by mobility, flexibility, precarity are ever more severely imposed by capitalist regimes of production and exploitation, wage laborers and the poor are no longer subjected to qualitatively different conditions but are both absorbed equally into the multitude of producers" (55).
77. See Hardt and Negri, *Empire*, 393–413; and Žižek, "Have Michael Hardt and Antonio Negri Rewritten?"
78. See Rancière, "Who Is?"
79. Keenan, "Where Are Human Rights . . . ?," 65–66.
80. Ghosh, "Subaltern," 459.
81. Hardt and Negri, *Multitude*, 152.
82. Hardt and Negri, *Empire*, 393; italics added.
83. Nicholas Mirzoeff has argued that "the photograph became a prime locus of the performance of the racialized index" in the late nineteenth century and functioned as an important cornerstone of modern practices of visualizing and exhibiting difference that "created and sustained a desire to see racially." "Shadow and Substance," 111–12.
84. In a separate context, media scholar Meg McLagan has warned against assum-

ing the transparency of human rights testimonies, arguing that the attachment of humanitarian advocates to the medial conventions of journalistic realism prevents them from fully engaging media as a constitutive element of their political and identitarian goals. See McLagan, "Human Rights," 304–9.

85. Foucault, *Discipline and Punish*, 200. Also see chapter 4.

86. Timothy Campbell and Adam Sitze explain that this is "why, despite so many painstaking attempts at inclusion, certain populations nevertheless seem permanently incapable of achieving flourishing lives within those institutions." "Introduction," 19.

Chapter 3: "Having a Voice"

1. A chronicle of the autistic community's objections to this video can be found in Biever, "'Poetic' Autistic Film." Autism Speaks's response to these objections is noted in Wallis, "'I Am Autism.'"

2. See Ne'eman, "Disability Community Condemns."

3. The "I Am Autism" video can currently be viewed at https://vimeo.com /112235562. It is no longer available through the Autism Speaks website. Unless otherwise noted, all future quotes from the individual films are transcribed from my personal viewing of the films.

4. See L. Brown, "Responding to Autism Speaks." Also see M. Rosen, "Autism Speaks PSA."

5. See Biever, "Voices of Autism 'Silenced.'" Others have criticized Autism Speaks for mobilizing stereotypes of autistics as violent or destructive as a way of emphasizing the urgency of their cause, and expressed hurt at being stigmatized as a source of hardship and torment for their families. See, for instance, Rose, "So, What's the Problem?" Dana Commandatore, the mother of an autistic child, argues, "Whatever the challenges that autism may bring, my son deserves better than being presented as a burden on society. Autism Speaks' misrepresentation makes my life and the life of my child more difficult." Quoted in Ne'eman, "Disability Community Condemns."

6. See MMadmin, "AspieWeb Being Bullied." AspieWeb protests that the "silencing" of autistic voices was redoubled when Autism Speaks took legal action against them.

7. Cartwright, *Moral Spectatorship*, 6.

8. I discuss these therapeutic approaches at greater length later in the chapter.

9. See L. Brown, "Responding to Autism Speaks." Brown writes,

Autism Speaks's ultimate goal is to cure autism and create a world where Autistic people like myself no longer exist. Most Autistic adults and youth strongly oppose the idea of "curing" ourselves because we do not believe that we are defective, broken, diseased, or in need of being fixed. Having a disability does not mean that there is something wrong with us. Yet because Autism Speaks does not represent Autistic people or speak for us, they can put their efforts into looking for something that most of us do not want. This includes Autistic people who are visibly disabled, severely disabled, and non-speaking, as well as Autistic people who do not present as very disabled. . . . The majority of people do not know that there is such controversy with Autism Speaks because most people assume that any organization dealing with autism must be doing good things for the community.

10. See Schalk, "Metaphorically Speaking."

11. Fabian, *Time and the Other*, 91.

12. By denial of coevalness, Fabian means "*a persistent and systematic tendency to place the referent(s) of anthropology in a Time other than the present of the producer of anthropological discourse.*" *Time and the Other*, 31.

13. Rony, "Taxidermy and Romantic Ethnography," 100–104.

14. Quote from Baggs's video "In My Language." Baggs describes hirself as genderless and uses the pronominal forms *sie, hir,* and *hirs*. See Baggs, "Glossary." Baggs has published under the names Amanda Baggs and Amanda Melissa Baggs, but has formally changed hir name to Amelia Evelyn Voicy Baggs, and refers to hirself as Mel Baggs. I follow this nomenclature.

15. See the video "I Am Autism Speaks (Now with Added Sub-titles)" on YouTube.

16. See the video "I'm Autistic: Parody of Autism Speaks Video 'I Am Autism'" on YouTube.

17. See Charles Wolfe, "'Voice of God.'" Also see Nichols, *Introduction to Documentary*, 167-68.

18. Chion, *Voice in Cinema*, 17–29.

19. Chow, "After the Passage," 35.

20. Charles Wolfe, "'Voice of God,'" 150.

21. Although I cannot explore this connection in this chapter, the normalizing cultural logic through which this purposeful, opinionated voice eradicates other voices that might detract from its purpose might also be productively analyzed in terms of the notion of compression, as elaborated by Jonathan Sterne. Sterne has argued that postmodern media forms tend to operate not through fidelity but through compression. His main example, the MP3, works by discarding sonic material that cannot be detected by the human ear and is therefore deemed irrelevant or extraneous—but it gains through the very process of compression an enhanced and pared-down intelligibility. See Sterne, MP3, 1–3.

22. Charles Wolfe, "'Voice of God,'" 151. Wolfe argues that "Voice of God" narration of the prototypical variety associated with *The March of Time* is a myth in two senses: (1) such narration did not have the desired mythical effect on the listener, and (2) more often than not, even classical documentaries that employed off-screen vocal narration tended to complicate and experiment with its omniscient and omnipotent qualities.

23. Disability studies scholar Jessica Evans has argued in this regard that disability and childhood are both employed interchangeably as coded ciphers of dependency in the visual culture of charity. See Evans, "Making Up Disabled People."

24. Quote from *Jam Jar*.

25. See Nichols, *Introduction to Documentary*, 167–71, 199–209.

26. Lebow, *First Person Jewish*, xxiii.

27. Bissonnette and Williams, the protagonists of *My Classic Life* and *Jam Jar*, employ different metaphors to articulate how communication therapies have molded their perceptions of space and time in socially meaningful ways: Bissonnette describes the touch-based method of FC as a "potholder" or "ladle of doing language meaningfully" that allows him to collect and order his "spatial awareness." Williams, who has written several autobiographical texts about living with autism, explains that she could not understand her own actions until she "automatically," compulsively, wrote about them and "listened" to the pages of her books as they talked to her. Here, Williams gestures to the capacity of narrative forms for ordering and working through everyday experience: while Williams favors linguistic forms, painting helps Bissonnette to "frame," "order," and "clear up mysteries."

28. See Cartwright, *Moral Spectatorship*, 7–9, and chap. 3 ("'A Child Is Being Beaten': Disorders of Authorship, Agency, and Affect in Facilitated Communication"). Also see Engber's "Anna Stubblefield," which recounts a recent criminal case that has contributed to the controversies surrounding FC techniques.

29. These descriptions of Margulies's voice work, by Wurzburg's production company, State of the Art, can be seen in numerous news articles about *Autism Is a World*. See "*Autism Is a World* Nominated."

30. See Marks, *Skin of the Film*. Marks's concept of "haptic visuality" is discussed at length in chapter 4.

31. Trinh describes her commitment to a form of "speaking that does not objectify, does not point to an object as if it is distant from the speaking subject or absent from the speaking place. A speaking that reflects on itself and can come very close to a subject without, however, seizing or claiming it." Trinh, "'Speaking Nearby,'" 87.

32. See, for instance, Trinh, "Mechanical Eye."

33. See Peckham, "Not Speaking with Language," 183; 186. Also see Armatage, "About to Speak."

34. A number of recent books offer contextually rich accounts of historical phases and approaches in the diagnostic history of autism. Chapters 1 and 2 of Chloe Silverman's *Understanding Autism* offer an informative and nuanced reading of the pioneers in autism research, including Kanner and Asperger, as well as the impacts and controversies around Bruno Bettelheim's psychoanalytic approach. Gil Eyal, Brendan Hart, Emine Onculer, Neta Oren, and Natasha Rossi's *The Autism Matrix* offers a wide-ranging account of behavioral therapies involving parents and autistics in active roles in the aftermath of the deinstitutionalization of mental retardation in the 1960s and onward (see chaps. 4, 5, 7, and 8), while Majia Holmer Nadesan pays particular attention to the emergence of cognitive and biogeneticist paradigms (see chaps. 5 and 6 in Nadesan, *Constructing Autism*).

35. The American Psychiatric Association also explains the nature and significance of the revised diagnosis of autism spectrum disorder in the fifth edition of the *Diagnostic and Statistical Manual of Mental Disorders*; see American Psychiatric Association, "Autism Spectrum Disorders."

36. Contemporary behavioral, developmental, occupational, psychopharmacological,

and neurological treatment approaches to autism in the past fifteen years are reviewed in numerous recent books, many of which focus on the American context and are oriented toward the parents of autistic children. See, for instance, Simpson, de Boer-Ott, Griswold, Smith Myles, Byrd, Ganz, and Tapscott Cook, *Autism Spectrum Disorders*. At the time of writing, a variety of therapeutic approaches are employed in combination in the treatment of autism, including the Joint Attention, Symbolic Play, Engagement, and Regulation Model (JASPER), Applied Behavioral Analysis, Developmental, Individual-differences, and Relationship-based Model (DIR), Treatment and Education of Autistic and Related Communication Handicapped Children (TEACHH), the Early Start Denver Model, and Occupational Therapy Sensory Integration. Simpson, de Boer-Ott, Griswold, Smith Myles, Byrd, Ganz, and Tapscott Cook discuss these therapies in conjunction with psychopharmacological approaches.

37. Baggs, "Bunch of Stuff."
38. See Dolar, *Voice and Nothing More*, esp. chaps. 1 and 2.
39. See Dyson, "Genealogy of the Radio Voice," 168–72. Dyson situates the dematerialization of the voice within a broad cosmological shift that occurred in the period 500–300 BCE, where a worldview organized around flux and becoming (accommodating impermanent, corporeal, and unstable modes of knowledge, as seen in the work of the pre-Socratic philosopher Heraclitus) was restructured by the philosophies of being found in the works of later philosophers including Plato, Aristotle, and René Descartes (in which stability, endurance, transcendence, and permanence were favored as characteristics of true knowledge). The shift traced by Dyson from cosmologies of aurality and instability to those of visuality and stability demands to be read as the longer prehistory of the denigration of mimetic modes of knowledge discussed in chapter 4. I hope to further discuss the rich connections between aurality and mimesis, which cannot be easily accommodated within the scope of this chapter, in a separate work.
40. Aristotle, "De Anima," 573.
41. Dolar, *Voice and Nothing More*, 14–15.
42. Dolar, *Voice and Nothing More*, 42–52.
43. Dolar, *Voice and Nothing More*, 15.
44. Dolar, *Voice and Nothing More*, 70; also see all of chap. 1 ("The Linguistics of the Voice"). For Dolar, Lacan's theory of the object provides the key to that intractable alterity of the voice (the voice of the other) that interrupts its function as an "acoustic mirror" facilitating the illusion of self-presence. The obdurate objectivity of the voice, he proposes, offers a positive counterweight, however elusive, to the signifying operation that yields the subject as a purely negative entity. Nevertheless, relying solely on Lacan compromises our inquiry if we are to follow Baggs's indication that the autistic voice has a vexed and disidentificatory relationship with language, since, according to Lacan, even this other scene is structured like a language. For this reason, any equation of the autistic voice with the realm of unconscious impulses would also be overly simplistic.
45. See Baggs, "Up in the Clouds."

46. Baggs et al., "What We Have to Tell You."

47. Prince, "The Silence Between."

48. See Grandin, *Emergence*, 9–10; 25–30.

49. Mukhopadhyay, *Beyond the Silence*, 52.

50. See Savarese, "Cultural Commentary: Communicate with Me." Savarese is the writer, co-producer, and protagonist of the television documentary *Deej*. The film, directed by Robert Rooy, and co-produced by ITVS (Independent Television Service), is in production as of November 2016.

51. Manning, *Always More Than One*, 152.

52. Manning, *Always More Than One*, 161.

53. Barthes, "Grain of the Voice," 182. In an astute comparative analysis of Barthes and Dolar, Dominic Pettman has noted that Dolar is thoroughly unsympathetic to Barthes's anchoring of the grain of the voice in the organic, insisting that the voice cannot be pinned to the singular uniqueness of bodies. Pettman argues that Dolar's insistence on the alien impersonality of the voice is equally unhelpful and neglects to confront the enigmatic manner in which the voice is both singular and plural at once. See Pettman, "Pavlov's Podcast," esp. 155.

54. See Grandin, *Emergence*, 25.

55. Frances Dyson has written at length on this topic in relation to the hegemonic voices encountered on mainstream radio programs. Dyson proposes that the apotheosis of inner speech is achieved in certain paradigmatic instances of the radio voice, where the anechoic dead space of the studio invokes the anaerobic space of the mind's inner chamber. The disembodied, omniscient voice, especially that of an older, white male, behaves as the perfect medium of language severed from the interference of the body. The "proper" voice must be human but not *too* human — a mechanical voice devoid of intonation, accent, emotive clues, or involuntary sounds (laughter, coughing, clicking, sneezing) can be uncanny to encounter, but an excess of these idiosyncrasies can distract from the missive of the mind. This is why voices that audibly announce their difference are habitually excluded from mainstream radio, unless they modulate their vocal inflections to accord with the ideal male voice. See Dyson, "Genealogy of the Radio Voice," 177–82.

56. See Ruoff, "Conventions of Sound in Documentary," 222.

57. See Heath, translator's note in *Image, Music, Text*, 10.

58. Barthes, "Grain of the Voice," 181.

59. Adriana Cavarero expresses a similar sentiment when she describes the pleasures of the "voice as voice," or a horizon of experience that permits one to concentrate on the vocal, liberated from the interpretive obligations of the phonemic, semantic realm. See Cavarero, *For More Than One Voice*, 12. I do not discuss Cavarero's important book *For More Than One Voice* in this chapter not only because space does not allow but mainly because her interpretation of this vocal horizon in terms of individual human uniqueness runs counter to Baggs's and Manning's suggestion that the human, understood as the ground of uniqueness, is a counterproductive framework through which to understand voicing, which actually reveals

that the human is both "more and less than one," as the title of Manning's book suggests.

60. See Kozloff, *Invisible Storytellers*, 6; see also 8–22. Sarah Kozloff provides historical and transmedial context for a variety of widely held prejudices against voice-over narration from the emergence of sound film onward. In addition to those I have mentioned, she addresses the literary and theatrical associations of the voice-over, concerns regarding narrative redundancy, and the subjective shadings of speech.

61. Nichols, *Representing Reality*, 18.

62. Nichols, *Representing Reality*, 21.

63. Nichols, *Representing Reality*, 21.

64. Nichols, *Representing Reality*, 116; and Nichols, *Introduction to Documentary*, 88.

65. Dolar, *Voice and Nothing More*, 15.

66. Nichols, "Voice of Documentary," 18.

67. Nichols, *Introduction to Documentary*, 72. When Nichols does focus on speech in its specificity, his analyses are limited to the rhetorical devices and evidentiary conventions through which speech endows its contents with the impression of truth (such as metaphor, metonymy, arrangement, refutation, delivery, style, and so on). In the brief paragraph or two where he turns to the nonlinguistic, fleshly dimensions of speech, such as gesture or affect, these too are turned into a mode of the articulate, as supports that reinforce the conviction of speech, rather than a portal onto a parallel, autistic spectrum of voicing that might operate at odds with a documentary's voice (77–93). Although Nichols has written elsewhere about rhetoric and excess, he does not write about the grain of speech in these terms. See, for instance, the chapter "Sticking to Reality: Rhetoric and What Exceeds It," in *Representing Reality*, 134–64.

68. Nichols, "Voice of Documentary," 20.

69. See Nichols, "Voice of Documentary," 17–18. Also see Nichols, *Introduction to Documentary*, 162–66, 199–209.

70. Bruzzi, *New Documentary*, 3.

71. See, for instance, Renov, *Subject of Documentary*; Beattie, *Documentary Display*; and Smaill, *Documentary*.

72. Renov, *Subject of Documentary*, esp. 104–19; Rascaroli, "Essay Film"; Russell, "Autoethnography"; Lebow, *First Person Jewish*; and Lebow, introduction to *Cinema of Me*.

73. Russell, "Autoethnography," 277.

74. See Lebow, *First Person Jewish*, xii.

75. Chion, *Voice in Cinema*, 5–6.

76. Silverman, *Understanding Autism*, 15.

77. Pinchevski, "Displacing Incommunicability," 171.

78. Hacking, "Kinds of People."

79. Stuart Murray offers a comprehensive and accessible account of recent debates surrounding the causes of autism in his book *Autism*. See Murray, *Autism*, 77–89.

80. See Eyal, Hart, Onculer, Oren, and Rossi, *Autism Matrix*, esp. chaps. 1 and 4.

81. See Nadesan, *Constructing Autism*; Silverman, *Understanding Autism*; Eyal et al., *Autism Matrix*, esp. chap. 10; Murray, *Autism*, esp. chaps. 11 and 12; Fisher, "No Search, No Subject?"; Murray, "Hollywood"; Murray, *Representing Autism*; and Evans, "Making Up Disabled People." Evans offers a persuasive reading of the structures of splitting and projection embedded in the "impairment" cipher of representing autism, which, she notes, derives from a Judeo-Christian cosmology in which biological wholeness is seen as divine.

82. See, for instance, Osteen, "Autism and Representation," 3–4.

83. McRuer, *Crip Theory*, 1.

84. McRuer, *Crip Theory*, 2.

85. McRuer, *Crip Theory*, 18.

86. See Murray, "Hollywood."

87. McRuer, *Crip Theory*, 57.

88. Muñoz, *Disidentifications*, 4, 12–31.

89. Serres, "Geometry of the Incommunicable," 41.

90. Butler writes that "heterosexuality offers normative sexual positions that are intrinsically impossible to embody, and the persistent failure to identify fully and without incoherence with these positions reveals heterosexuality itself not only as a compulsory law, but as an inevitable comedy." *Gender Trouble*, 166; also see McRuer, *Crip Theory*, 9–10.

91. Serres, "Geometry of the Incommunicable," 42.

92. To quote the introduction to a recent issue of *Disability Studies Quarterly* entitled "Autism and the Concept of Neurodiversity," in which Baggs is a contributor, hir aim is to "remain attentive to a different sensibility—indeed a different way of being in, and perceiving, the world—while at the same time reminding us of the need to construct the category of the human in the most capacious manner possible." Savarese and Savarese, "'Superior Half of Speaking.'" The authors also discuss the origins of and debates around neurodiversity at length.

93. Serres, "Geometry of the Incommunicable," 51.

Chapter 4: The Documentary Art of Surrender

1. See "Original Elephant Painting."

2. One of the objections most frequently mentioned by skeptics is the idea that the mahout's hand guides the elephant's trunk, and that the author of these paintings is therefore the human and not the animal. Although I cannot address this more substantially here, the perception of manipulation of the animal by the mahout, and the possibilities of interspecies collaboration, are worth thinking through in relation to Lisa Cartwright's discussion of the analogous perception of autistic children as being manipulated by their facilitators, and the skepticism regarding the interpersonal bond between the two as the basis of a legitimate, trustworthy mode of communication (also discussed in chapter 3). See Cartwright, *Moral Spectatorship*, 7–9, and chap. 3 ("'A Child Is Being Beaten': Disorders of Authorship, Agency, and Affect in Facilitated Communication").

3. Melamid, quoted in Komar and Melamid, with Fineman, *When Elephants Paint*, 51; also see 19–60.

4. See the Asian Elephant Art and Conservation Project website, especially the pages "Mission Statement," "Artist Statement," and "History" under "About AEACP," at http://www.elephantart.com.

5. See Exotic World Gifts, "Mission Statement" (the site has been discontinued, but Exotic World Gifts continues to operate under the name Gifts with a Cause).

6. See Nichols, *Representing Reality*, 69.

7. Nichols, *Representing Reality*, 69–75.

8. Nichols, *Representing Reality*, 65.

9. Nichols, *Representing Reality*, 64; also see Lesage, "Political Aesthetics."

10. Nichols, *Representing Reality*, 59. Nichols frames this "bipolarity of reflexive strategies"—formal and political—in terms of two different approaches to materialism that focus, respectively, on the cinematic signifier and on social practices (65–66).

11. See Agre, "Surveillance and Capture."

12. See chapter 2; and Keenan, "Mobilizing Shame," 438.

13. Fassin, "Heart of Humaneness," 271. Fassin offers a detailed historical analysis of the relationship between modern humanitarianism and discourses of humanity in pre- and post-Revolutionary France.

14. Fassin, "Heart of Humaneness," 272.

15. Bentham writes, "The question is not, Can they [animals] *reason*? nor, Can they *talk*? but, Can they *suffer*?" *Introduction to the Principles*, 311.

16. See Calarco, *Zoographies*, 7; see also 5–10, 103–49.

17. Foucault, *Discipline and Punish*, 200. Foucault writes, "Full lighting and the eye of a supervisor capture better than darkness, which ultimately protected. Visibility is a trap." Rey Chow notes this passage in her analysis of the figure of the trap in literary and artistic representations of capture and imprisonment; see Chow, "On Captivation." This chapter is greatly indebted to Chow's argument that "captivation . . . is the deranged remainder that is unassimilable to the metanarratives of freedom that underlie both capitalist consumerism . . . and socialist revolution" (52).

18. Lippit has argued that Edison's filming of the electrocution of Topsy the elephant—sentenced to death for having allegedly murdered three men—served as a medium not only for demonstrating the deathly "liveness" of electricity but also for animating what André Bazin would later refer to as film's "profane" capacity for animating the "elusive passage" from life to death. See Lippit, "Death of an Animal," 12–13; Bazin, "Death Every Afternoon." Lippit writes, "The dying animal in Edison's film is survived by the film; Topsy lives on and survives as the film, which transfers the anima of the animal, its life, into a phantom archive, preserving the movement that leaves the elephant in the technology of animation" (13). As Dominic Pettman has more recently pointed out, Topsy was executed by electricity (allegedly the more humane option) rather than hanging as a result of a

humanitarian intervention by the American Society for the Prevention of Cruelty to Animals. Pettman, "Zooicide," 60.

19. Editor Alfred Appel, Jr. notes that Nabokov's anecdote about encountering a newspaper article about this ape's drawing in the late 1930s may in fact be fictitious. Nabokov, *Annotated Lolita*, 311. Also see Pettman, *Love and Other Technologies*, 66.

20. Berger, "Why Look at Animals?," 23.

21. See, for instance, Elephant Art Gallery, "Are Paintings?" This organization denounces the realistic portraits sold on competing websites as being unnaturally coerced rather than products of the elephants' "own volition." Examples of nonfigurative elephant brushstroke paintings can be seen in the sale section of this online gallery.

22. See Lacan, "Mirror Stage."

23. Thomas A. Sebeok notes that within discourses of biology, only the draining of an entire species's gene pool is considered to have an impact in communicational terms, being conceptualized as "the elimination of a unique communicative code." "'Animal,'" 68.

24. Agamben, *Open*, 26.

25. Agamben, *Open*, 25; see Linnaeus, *Systema naturae* (1735). Agamben notes that Linnaeus changes *Homo* to *Homo sapiens* in the tenth edition of this book.

26. Cartwright, *Moral Spectatorship*, 2, 22–36.

27. Later in the chapter, I return to this topic and describe the form of visual orientation implied by this structure of (mis)recognition in terms of Laura U. Marks's notion of optical visuality.

28. Melamid, quoted in Komar and Melamid, with Fineman, *When Elephants Paint*, 94.

29. Grosz, *Chaos, Territory, Art*, 69–70. Grosz explains: "In being rendered functional . . . all excess and redundancy are eliminated; sexual selection is reduced to natural selection" (67). She continues: "In the case of battling birds, many territorial struggles are primarily theatrical, staged, a performance of the body at its most splendid and appealing, rather than a real battle with its attendant risks and dangers. . . . It is not clear that the skills the male displays are those that attract females, even if they are successful in various battling spectacles" (68). Grosz concludes the section: "Art is of the animal precisely to the degree that sexuality is artistic" (70).

30. See Fineman, "Elephant Painting in Thailand."

31. Sebeok and Ingold have both deliberated on the status of animal autopoiesis, as a way of unsettling the anthropocentric questions guiding semiotic and anthropological inquiries about labor and art. See Sebeok, "'Animal,'"; and Ingold, "Architect and Bee."

32. See Chow, *Protestant Ethnic*, 100.

33. See Agre, "Surveillance and Capture."

34. Cary Wolfe, *What Is Posthumanism?*, 127; also see 124–26.

35. Cary Wolfe, *What Is Posthumanism?*, 126.

36. Cary Wolfe, *What Is Posthumanism?*, xv–xvi.

37. Cary Wolfe, *What Is Posthumanism?*, esp. 127–28 in chap. 5 ("Learning from Temple Grandin: Animal Studies, Disability Studies, and Who Comes after the Subject").

38. Cary Wolfe, *What Is Posthumanism?*, 131. See also chap. 6 ("From Dead Meat to Glow-in-the-Dark Bunnies: The Animal Question in Contemporary Art").

39. See Parikka, *Insect Media*, 67. Parikka synthesizes the work of many other important contemporary scholars who have written on the animal question but whom I don't discuss, including feminist scholars Rosi Braidotti and Donna Haraway, media theorists Akira Mizuta Lippit and Eugene Thacker, and, for their theoretical contributions, Charles Darwin, Jacques Derrida, Henri Bergson, Gilbert Simondon, and Gilles Deleuze and Félix Guattari, among others.

40. Parikka, *Insect Media*, ix.

41. Uexküll, *Foray into the Worlds*, 43.

42. Uexküll, *Foray into the Worlds*, 43.

43. Uexküll, *Foray into the Worlds*, 43.

44. Parikka, *Insect Media*, 74, 77; see all of chap. 3 ("Technics of Nature and Temporality: Uexküll's Ethology").

45. Deleuze, *Foucault*, 52.

46. Caillois, "Mimicry and Legendary Psychasthenia," 93–94.

47. Caillois, "Mimicry and Legendary Psychasthenia," 98–99, 101.

48. Caillois, "Mimicry and Legendary Psychasthenia," 100.

49. Lacan, "Mirror Stage," 5.

50. As Grosz has noted elsewhere, Lacan adopts Caillois's ideas regarding embodiment and space as the basis of his theory of the centrality of the gaze of the other for the formation of subjectivity. She writes, "The primacy of the subject's own perspective is replaced by the gaze of another for whom the subject is merely *a* point in space, not *the* focal point organizing space." *Architecture from the Outside*, 38.

51. Caillois, "Mimicry and Legendary Psychasthenia," 99.

52. Autism and schizophrenia share a diagnostic history. Before its modern classification as a separate syndrome by Leo Kanner in 1943, the term *autism* was first used by the Swiss psychiatrist Eugen Bleuler in 1911 to refer to "severe cases of schizophrenia (another term he coined) manifested in detachment or escape from reality." Kanner subsequently concluded that autism was a separate disorder from schizophrenia owing to "the lack of common characteristics, such as early onset, hallucinations, and precedents in family history" and "withdrawal from preexisting relationships." Pinchevski, "Displacing Incommunicability," 165.

53. Caillois, "Mimicry and Legendary Psychasthenia," 96.

54. Caillois, "Mimicry and Legendary Psychasthenia," 101–2.

55. Caillois, "Mimicry and Legendary Psychasthenia," 97. Caillois himself dismisses the relation between his "instinct of renunciation" and the Freudian death drive as an issue of "secondary interest" (103n40). This may be because Caillois wanted to distance himself from Freudian psychoanalysis by turning to Janet (a psychother-

apist) and his notion of psychasthenia, or loss in ego strength, in lieu of Freud's death drive. Even if Caillois's intention was to find a less anthropocentric vocabulary, the shift from psychoanalysis to psychotherapy as a model hardly achieves this. I thank David Bering-Porter for this observation.

56. Lacan writes, "If a bird were to paint would it not be by letting fall its feathers, a snake by casting off its scales, a tree by letting fall its leaves?" "What Is a Picture?," 114.

57. See Caillois, "Mimicry and Legendary Psychasthenia," 94–97.

58. Spivak, "Can the Subaltern Speak?," 276.

59. Spivak, "Can the Subaltern Speak?," 307–8.

60. See Foucault, *Order of Things*, 17–77. Foucault traces the epistemic shift from classical to modern times through the disappearance of resemblance as a mode of knowledge production, and its replacement by epistemological approaches based on differences.

61. Chow argues that poststructuralist theoretical thinking—as well as the strains of cultural studies that it has informed—is suspicious of mimesis for the latter's affiliation with realist verisimilitude or connotations of a replica of an original, even as poststructuralism's trademark techniques of deconstruction (such as alternation, substitution, and differentiation) belong to a mimetic order of thinking. For this reason, she equates the vast majority of twentieth-century thinking with the antimimetic tradition. See Chow, "Sacrifice."

62. Caillois's essay begins:

Ultimately, from whatever angle one may approach things, the fundamental question proves to be that of *distinction*: distinctions between what is real and imaginary, between wakefulness and sleep, between ignorance and knowledge, and so on. These are all distinctions, in short, that any acceptable project must seek to chart very precisely and, at the same time, insist on resolving. Certainly, no distinction is more pronounced than the one demarcating an organism from its environment; at least, none involves a more acutely perceptible sense of separation. We should pay particular attention to this phenomenon, and more specifically to what we must still call, given our limited information, its pathology (although the term has a purely statistical meaning): namely the set of phenomena referred to as mimicry. "

Mimicry and Legendary Psychasthenia," 91.

63. Caillois, "New Plea."

64. For instance, see chap. 4 ("Metamorphosis, Intensity, and Devouring Space: Elements for an Insect Game Theory"). Parikka reads Caillois's portrait of the metamorphosis of mimetic insects into their milieu as a commentary on the immersive qualities of modern media cultures, and game environments in particular, which he characterizes as "engines of metamorphosis" (107).

65. See Chow, *The Protestant Ethnic*, esp. chap. 3 ("Keeping Them in Their Place: Coercive Mimeticism and Cross-Ethnic Representation"); Manning, *Always More Than One*; and Cartwright, *Moral Spectatorship*.

66. Nichols, *Representing Reality*, 60.
67. Chow, *Protestant Ethnic*, 101–3.
68. Marks, *Skin of the Film*, 132–33, 163. Also see Foster, *Vision and Visuality*.
69. Marks, *Skin of the Film*, 132.
70. Marks, *Skin of the Film*, 162.
71. Marks, *Skin of the Film*, 188.
72. Manning attributes a similar potentiality to touch in her book *Politics of Touch*. Focusing specifically on the improvisatory and transcultural engagements of tango, understood through the vocabularies of Deleuze and Simondon, she proposes that "sensing bodies in movement" gesture toward the individuating potentialities of touch. She writes, "Touch . . . invents by drawing the other into relation, thereby qualitatively altering the limits of the emerging touched-touching bodies. Touch is not graspable as a stable concept." *Politics of Touch*, xiv.
73. Marks, *Skin of the Film*, 162–63.
74. Marks, *Skin of the Film*, 170–87.
75. Marks, *Skin of the Film*, 141. Among other sources for tactile epistemology, Marks discusses Marxist scholars affiliated with the Frankfurt school (Walter Benjamin, Theodor Adorno, and Max Horkheimer), anthropologists (Michael Taussig and Paul Stoller), and feminist scholars (Luce Irigaray). To the charge that these scholars indulge in an unrigorous romanticization of foreign cultures and ages that goes hand in hand with a denigration of the "fallen" West, Marks urges caution, arguing, "It is possible to take up theories of tactile epistemology without adopting the dire diagnosis of complete cultural alienation on which these scholars' arguments rest. Sensuous forms of knowledge do not get wiped out as though by a plague. . . . The issue is that these are not necessarily valued in a given culture" (144; also see 138–45).
76. Peirce, *Philosophical Writings*, 102.
77. Doane, "Indexicality," 2.
78. See da Costa, "Reaching the Limit," 377.
79. See the *PigeonBlog* project page, especially the downloadable "Statement" at http://nideffer.net/shaniweb/pigeonblog.php (accessed October 7, 2016).
80. See Starling, "Simon Starling."
81. See *Animal Cams*, directed by Sam Easterson.
82. Easterson, "Sam Easterson, Video Artist."
83. See "Crittercam FAQs."
84. Animal studies scholar Cynthia Chris has argued that the editing conventions of nature television shows emphasize the eventfulness of animal life by "excising the tiresome bits of any real visit to a menagerie or zoo: animals that have hidden themselves out of view, sleeping or otherwise inactive animals, long walks between displays. Thus, animals on film are even better than animals in zoo enclosures, and surely better than animals in the wild: they are not only captive and visible at our whim, not their own, but they are at their very best." *Watching Wildlife*, xiii.
85. Paravel, in Castaing-Taylor, Paravel, and Rivers, "Cruel Radiance," 53.

86. Castaing-Taylor, Paravel, and Rivers, "Cruel Radiance," 54.
87. See Marks, *Skin of the Film*, 162–64.
88. Castaing-Taylor and Paravel, "The Wordless Sea." Also see Pavsek, "*Leviathan* and the Experience of Sensory Ethnography." Pavsek offers an extended critique of the immersive discourse of immediacy of which *Leviathan* partakes, arguing that Castaing-Taylor and Paravel's investment in the senses as an unmediated horizon of experience goes hand-in-hand with "a visceral distrust of words or discursivity, a *logophobia*" (4). This can be seen, he argues, in their "near-total eschewal of textual devices, be they in the form of explanatory or expository voiceover, intertitles or other textual framing devices, and in many cases even much comprehensible dialogue from its human subjects" (5).

Conclusion: The Gift of Documentary

1. Keenan, *Fables of Responsibility*, 39.
2. Keenan, *Fables of Responsibility*, 39, 35.
3. Keenan, "'Where Are Human Rights . . . ?,'" 65.
4. Fassin writes, "One has to be reminded that in the humanitarian ethics, the potential sacrifice of one's life reasserts the sacredness of others' lives, which is precisely denied by the military necessities." "Humanitarianism," 508.
5. Mauss, *Gift*, 13.
6. Douglas, Foreword, ix.
7. Mauss, *Gift*, 26.
8. Keenan, *Fables of Responsibility*, 24–27. James R. Martel offers a similar speculation in *The Misinterpellated Subject*, arguing that hails from authority are always vulnerable to unexpected and even radical possibilities.
9. Vaughan, "Let There Be Lumière," 5.
10. Vaughan, "Let There Be Lumière," 8.
11. Keenan, *Fables of Responsibility*, 16. Keenan quotes from Fish, "Force."

BIBLIOGRAPHY

Adynata. Directed by Leslie Thornton. New York: Women Make Movies, 1983. 16mm.

Agamben, Giorgio. *Homo Sacer: Sovereign Power and Bare Life*. Translated by Daniel Heller-Roazen. Stanford, CA: Stanford University Press, 1998.

Agamben, Giorgio. *The Open: Man and Animal*. Translated by Kevin Attel. Stanford, CA: Stanford University Press, 2004.

Agre, Philip E. "Surveillance and Capture: Two Models of Privacy." *Information Society* 10, no. 2 (1994): 101–27.

Althusser, Louis. "Ideology and Ideological State Apparatuses (Notes Toward an Investigation)." In *Lenin and Philosophy and Other Essays*, translated by Ben Brewster, 85–126. New York: Monthly Review Press, 2001.

American Psychiatric Association. "Autism Spectrum Disorders." 2013. http://www .dsm5.org/Documents/Autism%20Spectrum%20Disorder%20Fact%20Sheet.pdf.

Animal Cams. Directed by Sam Easterson. Chicago: Video Data Bank, 2008. DVD.

Ariès, Philippe. *Centuries of Childhood: A Social History of Family Life*. Translated by Robert Baldick. New York: Vantage Books, 1962.

Aristotle. "De Anima." In *The Basic Works of Aristotle*, edited by Richard McKeon, 535–603. New York: Modern Library, 2001.

Armatage, Kay. "About to Speak: The Woman's Voice in Patricia Gruben's *Sifted Evidence*." In *Take Two: A Tribute to Film in Canada*, edited by Seth Feldman, 298–303. Toronto: Book Society of Canada, 1984.

Arora, Poonam. "The Production of Third World Subjects for First World Consumption: *Salaam Bombay and Parama*." In *Multiple Voices in Feminist Film Criticism*, edited by Diane Carson, Linda Dittmar, and Janice R. Welsch, 293–304. Minneapolis: University of Minnesota Press, 1994.

Autism Is a World. Directed by Gerardine Wurzburg. 2004. Washington, D.C.: CNN Productions and State of the Art, 2005. DVD.

"'Autism Is a World' Nominated for Academy Award." State of the Art, January 25, 2005. http://www.stateart.com/news.php?newsItemId=24.

Autism Speaks. "I Am Autism." Vimeo video, 3.43. Posted by "Robert Stephens," 2015. https://vimeo.com/112235562.

Baggs, Amanda. "In My Language." YouTube video, 8:36. Posted by "silentmiaow," January 14, 2007. https://www.youtube.com/watch?v=JnylM1hI2jc.

Baggs, Amanda. "Up in the Clouds and Down in the Valley: My Richness and Yours." *Disability Studies Quarterly* 30, no. 1 (2010). http://dsq-sds.org/article/view/1052 /1238.

Baggs, Amanda, et al. "What We Have to Tell You: A Roundtable with Self-Advocates from AutCom." *Disability Studies Quarterly* 30, no. 1 (2010). http://dsq-sds.org /article/view/1073/1239.

Baggs, Mel. "A Bunch of Stuff That Needed Saying." *Ballastexistenz*, April 18, 2013. https://ballastexistenz.wordpress.com/2013/04/18/a-bunch-of-stuff-that-needed -saying/.

Baggs, Mel. "Glossary." Amelia Evelyn Voicy Baggs. Accessed November 20, 2014. https://ameliabaggs.wordpress.com/glossary/.

Barnett, Michael, and Thomas G. Weiss, eds. *Humanitarianism in Question: Politics, Power, Ethics*. Ithaca, NY: Cornell University Press, 2008.

Barthes, Roland. *Camera Lucida*. Translated by Richard Howard. New York: Hill and Wang, 1982.

Barthes, Roland. "The Grain of the Voice." In *Image, Music, Text*, translated by Stephen Heath, 179–89. New York: Hill and Wang, 1978.

Batchen, Geoffrey. *Burning with Desire: The Conception of Photography*. Cambridge, MA: MIT Press, 1999.

Bazin, André. "Death Every Afternoon." Translated by Mark A. Cohen. In *Rites of Realism*, edited by Ivone Margulies, 27–31. Durham, NC: Duke University Press, 2003.

Bazin, André. "The Ontology of the Photographic Image." Translated by Hugh Grey. *Film Quarterly* 13, no. 4 (1960): 4–9.

Beattie, Keith. *Documentary Display: Re-viewing Nonfiction Film and Video*. New York: Wallflower, 2008.

Bentham, Jeremy. *An Introduction to the Principles of Morals and Legislation*. Mineola, NY: Dover, 2007.

Berger, John. "Why Look at Animals?" In *About Looking*, 3–28. New York: Vintage Books, 1991.

Berlant, Lauren. *Cruel Optimism*. Durham, NC: Duke University Press, 2011.

Berlant, Lauren. "The Subject of True Feeling: Pain, Privacy, and Politics." In *Cultural Pluralism, Identity Politics, and the Law*, edited by Austin Sarat and Thomas R. Kearns, 49–84. Ann Arbor: University of Michigan Press, 1999.

Bernstein, J. M. "Bare Life, Bearing Witness: Auschwitz and the Pornography of Horror." *Parallax* 10, no. 1 (2004): 2–16.

Biever, Celeste. "'Poetic' Autism Film Divides Campaigners." *New Scientist*, September 29, 2009. https://www.newscientist.com/article/dn17878-poetic-autism-film -divides-campaigners/.

Biever, Celeste. "Voices of Autism 'Silenced' by Charity." *New Scientist*, January 30, 2008. https://www.newscientist.com/article/mg19726414.300-voices-of-autism -silenced-by-charity/.

Big. Directed by Penny Marshall. 1988. Los Angeles: Twentieth Century Fox, 2007. DVD.

Boltanski, Luc. *Distant Suffering: Morality, Media and Politics.* Translated by Graham Burchell. Cambridge: Cambridge University Press, 1999.

Born into Brothels. Directed by Zana Briski and Ross Kauffman. 2004. New York: ThinkFilm, 2006. DVD.

Briski, Zana. *Born into Brothels: Photographs by the Children of Calcutta.* New York: Umbrage, 2004.

Broomberg, Adam, and Oliver Chanarin. "Unconcerned but Not Indifferent." In *Documentary,* edited by Julian Stallabrass, 98–103. Cambridge, MA: MIT Press, 2013.

Brown, Kimberly Juanita. "Regarding the Pain of the Other: Photography, Famine, and the Transference." In *Feeling Photography,* edited by Elspeth H. Brown and Thy Phu, 181–203. Durham, NC: Duke University Press, 2014.

Brown, Lydia X. Z. "Responding to Autism Speaks." Autistichoya.com, March 22, 2012. http://www.autistichoya.com/2012/03/responding-to-autism-speaks.html.

Bruzzi, Stella. *New Documentary.* 2nd ed. New York: Routledge, 2006.

Burman, Erica. "Innocents Abroad: Western Fantasies of Childhood and the Iconography of Emergencies." *Disasters* 18, no. 3 (1994): 238–53.

Butler, Judith. *Gender Trouble: Feminism and the Subversion of Identity.* New York: Routledge Classics, 2006.

Butler, Judith. *Precarious Life: The Powers of Mourning and Violence.* London: Verso, 2004.

Caillois, Roger. "Mimicry and Legendary Psychasthenia." In *The Edge of Surrealism: A Roger Caillois Reader,* translated by Camille Nash and edited by Claudine Frank, 89–103. Durham, NC: Duke University Press, 2003.

Caillois, Roger. "A New Plea for Diagonal Science." In *The Edge of Surrealism: A Roger Caillois Reader,* translated by Camille Nash and edited by Claudine Frank, 343–47. Durham, NC: Duke University Press, 2003.

Calarco, Matthew. *Zoographies: The Question of the Animal from Heidegger to Derrida.* New York: Columbia University Press, 2008.

Calhoun, Craig. "The Idea of Emergency: Humanitarian Action and Global (Dis) Order." In *Contemporary States of Emergency: The Politics of Military and Humanitarian Interventions,* edited by Didier Fassin and Mariella Pandolfi, 29–58. New York: Zone Books, 2010.

Campbell, Timothy, and Adam Sitze. "Introduction: Biopolitics: An Encounter." In *Biopolitics: A Reader,* edited by Timothy Campbell and Adam Sitze, 1–40. Durham, NC: Duke University Press, 2013.

Cartwright, Lisa. "Images of Waiting Children: Spectatorship and Pity in the Representation of the Global Social Orphan in the 1990s." In *Cultures of Transnational Adoption,* edited by Toby Alice Volkman, 185–212. Durham, NC: Duke University Press, 2005.

Cartwright, Lisa. *Moral Spectatorship: Technologies of Voice and Affect in Postwar Representations of the Child.* Durham, NC: Duke University Press, 2008.

Castaing-Taylor, Lucien, and Véréna Paravel. "The Wordless Sea: An Interview with Directors Lucien Castaing-Taylor and Véréna Paravel." By Jason Ward. *OhComely,*

November 29, 2014. http://www.jasonward.co.uk/film-writing/lucien-castaing
-taylor-and-verena-paravel/.

Castaing-Taylor, Lucien, Véréna Paravel, and Ben Rivers. "The Cruel Radiance of
What Is: Lucien Castaing-Taylor, Véréna Paravel, and Ben Rivers in Conversation."
In *Documentary across Disciplines*, edited by Erika Balsom and Hila Peleg, 40–78.
Cambridge, MA: MIT Press, 2016.

Castelli, Elizabeth. "Theologizing Human Rights: Christian Activism and the Limits
of Religious Freedom." In *Nongovernmental Politics*, edited by Michel Feher, with
Gaëlle Krikorian and Yates McKee, 673–87. New York: Zone Books, 2007.

Cavarero, Adriana. *For More Than One Voice: Toward a Philosophy of Vocal Expression*.
Stanford, CA: Stanford University Press, 2005.

Chalfen, Richard. "Afterword to the Revised Edition." In *Through Navajo Eyes: An
Exploration in Film Communication and Anthropology*, by Sol Worth and John Adair,
275–341. Albuquerque: University of New Mexico Press, 1997.

Chion, Michel. *The Voice in Cinema*. Translated by Claudia Gorbman. New York: Columbia University Press, 1999.

Chouliaraki, Lilie. *The Ironic Spectator: Solidarity in the Age of Post-humanitarianism*.
Cambridge, UK: Polity, 2013.

Chouliaraki, Lilie. *The Spectatorship of Suffering*. London: Sage, 2006.

Chow, Rey. "After the Passage of the Beast: 'False Documentary' Aspirations, Acousmatic Complications." In *Rancière and Film*, edited by Paul Bowman, 34–52. Edinburgh: Edinburgh University Press, 2013.

Chow, Rey. "On Captivation: A Remainder from the 'Indistinction of Art and Nonart'
(written with Julian Rohrhuber)." In *Entanglements, or Transmedial Thinking about
Capture*, 31–58. Durham, NC: Duke University Press, 2012.

Chow, Rey. *Primitive Passions: Visuality, Sexuality, Ethnography, and Contemporary Chi-
nese Cinema*. New York: Columbia University Press, 1995.

Chow, Rey. *The Protestant Ethnic and the Spirit of Capitalism*. New York: Columbia
University Press, 2002.

Chow, Rey. "Sacrifice, Mimesis, and the Theorizing of Victimhood." In *Entanglements,
or Transmedial Thinking about Capture*, 81–105. Durham, NC: Duke University
Press, 2012.

Chris, Cynthia. *Watching Wildlife*. Minneapolis: University of Minnesota Press, 2006.

Chun, Wendy Hui Kyong. "Crisis, Crisis, Crisis, or Sovereignty and Networks."
Theory, Culture, and Society 28, no. 6 (2011): 91–112.

City of God. Directed by Fernando Meirelles. 2002. Santa Monica, CA: Miramax
Lionsgate, 2011. DVD.

Classen, Steve. "'Reporters Gone Wild': Reporters and Their Critics on Hurricane
Katrina, Gender, Race, and Place." *Journal of E-Media Studies* 2, no. 1 (2009).
http://journals.dartmouth.edu/cgi-bin/WebObjects/Journals.woa/1/xmlpage/4
/article/336.

CNN. "CNN Live Today: Hurricane Katrina." *American Morning*. Aired August 29,
2005. Transcript 1. http://www.cnn.com/TRANSCRIPTS/0508/29/lt.01.html.

CNN. "CNN Live Today: Hurricane Katrina." *American Morning*. Aired August 29, 2005. Transcript 2. http://www.cnn.com/TRANSCRIPTS/0508/29/lt.02.html.

CNN. "CNN Live Today: Hurricane Katrina." *American Morning*. Aired August 29, 2005. Transcript 3. http://www.cnn.com/TRANSCRIPTS/0508/29/lt.03.html.

Cohen, Stanley, and Bruna Sue. "Knowing Enough Not to Feel Too Much: Emotional Thinking about Human Rights Appeals." In *Truth Claims: Representation and Human Rights*, edited by Mark Philip Bradley and Patrice Petro, 187–201. New Brunswick, NJ: Rutgers University Press, 2002.

Cooper, Anderson. *Dispatches from the Edge: A Memoir of War, Disasters, and Survival*. New York: HarperCollins, 2006.

Corner, John. *The Art of Record: A Critical Introduction to Documentary*. Manchester: Manchester University Press, 1996.

Cotter, Holland. "Out of Ruins, Haiti's Visionaries." *New York Times*, March 13, 2010. http://www.nytimes.com/2010/03/18/arts/artsspecial/18HAITI.html?_r=2& pagewanted=1.

Cowie, Elizabeth. *Recording Reality, Desiring the Real*. Minneapolis: University of Minnesota Press, 2011.

"Crittercam FAQs." National Geographic. Accessed November 11, 2010. http://animals .nationalgeographic.com/animals/crittercam-faqs/.

Cullen, Holly. "Child Labor Standards: From Treaties to Labels." In *Child Labor and Human Rights*, edited by Burns H. Weston, 87–115. Boulder, CO: Lynne Rienner, 2005.

Cussans, John. "From the Archives: Tele Geto: Interview with John Cussans." By Kirsten Cooke. London Fields Radio, May 20, 2010. http://www.londonfieldsradio .co.uk/2010/05/20/from-the-archive-tele-geto-2/.

Cussans, John. "Tele Geto Project at the Portman Gallery." *Zombi Diaspora*, June 11, 2010. https://codeless88.wordpress.com/2010/06/11/tele-geto-project-at-the -portman-gallery/.

da Costa, Beatriz. "Reaching the Limit: When Art Becomes Science." In *Tactical Biopolitics: Art, Activism, and Technoscience*, edited by Beatriz da Costa and Kavita Philip, 365–85. Cambridge, MA: MIT Press, 2010.

Dayan, Daniel, and Elihu Katz. *Media Events: The Live Broadcasting of History*. Cambridge, MA: Harvard University Press, 1994.

Deleuze, Gilles. *Foucault*. Minneapolis: University of Minnesota Press, 1988.

Didi-Huberman, Georges. *Images in Spite of All*. Translated by Shaun B. Lillis. Chicago: University of Chicago Press, 2008.

Doane, Mary Ann. "Indexicality: Trace and Sign: Introduction." *differences* 18, no. 1 (2007): 1–6.

Doane, Mary Ann. "Information, Crisis, Catastrophe." In *Logics of Television: Essays in Cultural Criticism*, edited by Patricia Mellencamp, 222–39. Bloomington: Indiana University Press, 1990.

Dolar, Mladen. *A Voice and Nothing More*. Cambridge, MA: MIT Press, 2006.

Douglas, Mary. Foreword to *The Gift: The Form and Reason for Exchange in Archaic*

Societies by Marcel Mauss, translated by W. D. Halls, vii–xviii. New York: Norton, 2000.

Dyson, Frances. "The Genealogy of the Radio Voice." In *Radio Rethink: Art, Sound, and Transmission*, edited by Daina Augaitis and Dan Lander, 167–86. Alberta: Banff Center Press, 1994.

Easterson, Sam. "Sam Easterson, Video Artist." Artbabble. Accessed July 31, 2012. http://www.artbabble.org/video/ima/sam-easterson-video-artist.

Ebert, Roger. Review of *Born into Brothels*, directed by Zana Briski and Ross Kauffman. Roger Ebert, February 10, 2005. http://www.rogerebert.com/reviews/born-into-brothels-2005.

Edelman, Lee. *No Future: Queer Theory and the Death Drive*. Durham, NC: Duke University Press, 2004.

The Elephant Art Gallery. "Are Paintings by Elephants Really Art?" Accessed July 31, 2012. http://www.elephantartgallery.com/learn/authentic/are-elephant-paintings-art.php.

Engber, Daniel. "The Strange Case of Anna Stubblefield." *New York Times Magazine*, October 20, 2015. http://www.nytimes.com/2015/10/25/magazine/the-strange-case-of-anna-stubblefield.html.

Engelbrecht, Kate. *Please Read (If At All Possible): The Girl Project*. New York: Rizzoli International Publications, 2011.

Evans, Jessica. "Making Up Disabled People." In *Visual Culture: The Reader*, edited by Stuart Hall and Jessica Evans, 274–88. Thousand Oaks, CA: Sage, 1999.

Exotic World Gifts. "Mission Statement." Accessed July 31, 2012. http://www.exoticworldgifts.com (site discontinued).

Eyal, Gil, Brendan Hart, Emine Onculer, Neta Oren, and Natasha Rossi. *The Autism Matrix: The Social Origins of the Autism Epidemic*. Cambridge, UK: Polity, 2010.

Fabian, Johannes. *Time and the Other: How Anthropology Makes Its Object*. New York: Columbia University Press, 2002.

Fassin, Didier. "Heart of Humaneness: The Moral Economy of Humanitarian Intervention." In *Contemporary States of Emergency: The Politics of Military and Humanitarian Interventions*, edited by Didier Fassin and Mariella Pandolfi, 269–93. New York: Zone Books, 2010.

Fassin, Didier. "Humanitarianism as a Politics of Life." *Public Culture* 19, no. 3 (2007): 499–520.

Fassin, Didier, and Mariella Pandolfi. "Introduction: Military and Humanitarian Government in the Age of Intervention." In *Contemporary States of Emergency: The Politics of Military and Humanitarian Interventions*, edited by Didier Fassin and Mariella Pandolfi, 9–25. New York: Zone Books, 2010.

Fassin, Didier, and Paula Vasquez. "Humanitarian Exception as the Rule: The Political Theology of the 1999 'Tragedia' in Venezuela." *American Ethnologist* 32, no. 3 (2005): 389–405.

Feher, Michel. "The Governed in Politics." In *Nongovernmental Politics*, edited by Michel Feher with Gaëlle Krikorian and Yates McKee, 12–27. New York: Zone Books, 2007.

Feitosa, Monica. "The Other's Visions: From the Ivory Tower to the Barricade." *Visual Anthropology Review* 7, no. 2 (1991): 48–49.

Feuer, Jane. "The Concept of Live Television: Ontology as Ideology." In *Regarding Television: Critical Approaches—an Anthology*, edited by E. Ann Kaplan, 12–22. Frederick, MD: University Publications of America, 1983.

Fineberg, Jonathan. *The Innocent Eye: Children's Art and the Modern Artist*. Princeton, NJ: Princeton University Press, 1997.

Fineman, Mia. "Elephant Painting in Thailand." Asian Elephant Art and Conservation Project. Accessed July 31, 2012. http://www.elephantart.com/catalog/thailand .php.

Fish, Stanley. "Force." In *Doing What Comes Naturally: Change, Rhetoric, and the Practice of Theory in Literary and Legal Studies*, 503–24. Durham, NC: Duke University Press, 1990.

Fisher, James T. "No Search, No Subject? Autism and the American Conversion Narrative." In *Autism and Representation*, edited by Mark Osteen, 51–64. New York: Routledge, 2008.

Fleetwood, Nicole R. "Failing Narratives, Initiating Technologies: Hurricane Katrina and the Production of a Weather Media Event." *American Quarterly* 58, no. 3 (2006): 767–89.

Foster, Hal, ed. *Vision and Visuality*. New York: New Press, 1999.

Foucault, Michel. *Discipline and Punish: The Birth of the Prison*. Translated by Alan Sheridan. New York: Vintage Books, 1991.

Foucault, Michel. *History of Sexuality*. Vol. 1, *An Introduction*. Translated by Robert Hurley. New York: Vintage Books, 1990.

Foucault, Michel. *Madness and Civilization: A History of Insanity in the Age of Reason*. Translated by Richard Howard. New York: Vintage Books, 1988.

Foucault, Michel. *The Order of Things: An Archaeology of the Human Sciences*. New York: Vintage Books, 1994.

Foucault, Michel. *"Society Must Be Defended": Lectures at the Collège de France, 1975–1976*. Translated by David Macey. New York: Picador, 2003.

Frota, Monica. "Taking Aim: The Video Technology of Cultural Resistance." In *Resolutions: Contemporary Video Practices*, edited by Michael Renov and Erika Suderburg, 258–82. Minneapolis: University of Minnesota Press, 1996.

Fuqua, Joy. "'That Part of the World': Hurricane Katrina and the 'Place' of Local Media." *Journal of E-Media Studies* 2, no. 1 (2009). http://journals.dartmouth.edu /cgibin/WebObjects/Journals.woa/1/xmlpage/4/article/337.

George, Ivy. *Child Labour and Child Work*. New Delhi: Ashish, 1990.

Ghosh, Bishnupriya. "The Subaltern at the Edge of the Popular." *Postcolonial Studies* 8, no. 4 (2005): 459–74.

Ginsburg, Faye. "Indigenous Media: Faustian Contract or Global Village?" *Cultural Anthropology* 6, no. 1 (1991): 92–112.

Ginsburg, Faye. "Shooting Back: From Ethnographic Film to Indigenous Production/ Ethnography of Media." In *A Companion to Film Theory*, edited by Toby Miller and Robert Stam, 295–322. Malden, MA: Blackwell, 1999.

Giroux, Henry A. "Reading Hurricane Katrina: Race, Class, and the Biopolitics of Disposability." *College Literature* 33, no. 3 (2006): 171–96.

Giroux, Henry A. *Stormy Weather: Katrina and the Politics of Disposability*. London: Paradigm, 2006.

Grandin, Temple. *Emergence: Labeled Autistic*. New York: Grand Central Publishing, 2005.

Grierson, John. "The Documentary Idea: 1942." In *Grierson on Documentary*, edited by Forsyth Hardy, 248–58. Berkeley: University of California Press, 1966.

Grierson, John. "The Documentary Producer." *Cinema Quarterly* 2 (1933): 7–8.

Grosz, Elizabeth. *Architecture from the Outside: Essays on Virtual and Real Space*. Cambridge, MA: MIT Press, 2001.

Grosz, Elizabeth. *Chaos, Territory, Art: Deleuze and the Framing of the Earth*. New York: Columbia University Press, 2008.

Guerin, Frances, and Roger Hallas. Introduction to *The Image and the Witness: Trauma, Memory and Visual Culture*, edited by Frances Guerin and Roger Hallas, 1–22. London: Wallflower, 2007.

Hacking, Ian. "Kinds of People: Moving Targets." *Proceedings of the British Academy* 151 (2007): 285–318.

Hardt, Michael, and Antonio Negri. *Commonwealth*. Cambridge, MA: Harvard University Press, 2009.

Hardt, Michael, and Antonio Negri. *Empire*. Cambridge, MA: Harvard University Press, 2000.

Hardt, Michael, and Antonio Negri. *Multitude: War and Democracy in the Age of Empire*. New York: Penguin, 2005.

Hardy, Forsyth. Introduction to *Grierson on Documentary*. Edited by Forsyth Hardy, 13–39. Berkeley: University of California Press, 1966.

Hartl, John. "*Trouble the Water* Captures Katrina through a Survivor's Point of View." *Seattle Times*, October 16, 2008. http://www.seattletimes.com/entertainment/movies/trouble-the-water-captures-katrina-through-a-survivors-point-of-view/.

Heath, Stephen. Translator's note in *Image, Music, Text*, by Roland Barthes, translated by Stephen Heath, 7–11. New York: Hill and Wang, 1977.

Hertz, Leba. "Children from Immigrant and Refugee Families Point Cameras at Their Communities and the World Beyond." *SFGate*, March 26, 2005. http://www.sfgate.com/entertainment/article/Children-from-immigrant-and-refugee-families-2690045.php.

Hesford, Wendy S. *Spectacular Rhetorics: Human Rights Visions, Recognitions, Feminisms*. Durham, NC: Duke University Press, 2011.

Higonnet, Anne. *Pictures of Innocence: The History and Crisis of Ideal Childhood*. London: Thames and Hudson, 1998.

Hobbes, Thomas. *Leviathan*. London: Penguin, 1985.

Honig, Bonnie. "Three Models of Emergency Politics." *Boundary 2* 41, no. 2 (2014): 45–70.

"I'm Autistic: Parody of Autism Speaks Video 'I Am Autism.'" YouTube video, 3:33. Posted by "thAutcast," September 24, 2009. http://www.youtube.com/watch?v=SXYN5kZrgyo.

Ingold, Tim. "The Architect and the Bee: Reflections on the Work of Animals and Men." *Man* 18, no. 1 (1983): 1–20.

Invisible Children. Directed by Jason Russell, Bobby Bailey, and Laren Poole. San Diego CA: Invisible Children, Inc., 2006. DVD.

Jam Jar. Directed by Simon Everson. London: Fresh Film, 1995. DVD.

Juhasz, Alexandra, and Jesse Lerner, eds. *F Is for Phony: Fake Documentary and Truth's Undoing.* Minneapolis: University of Minnesota Press, 2006.

Kahana, Jonathan. *Intelligence Work: The Politics of American Documentary.* New York: Columbia University Press, 2008.

Karunan, Victor. "Working Children as Change Makers: Perspectives from the South." In *Child Labor and Human Rights,* edited by Burns H. Weston, 293–317. Boulder, CO: Lynne Rienner, 2005.

Keenan, Thomas. *Fables of Responsibility: Aberrations and Predicaments in Ethics and Politics.* Stanford, CA: Stanford University Press, 1997.

Keenan, Thomas. "Mobilizing Shame." *South Atlantic Quarterly* 103, no. 2/3 (2004): 435–49.

Keenan, Thomas. "Publicity and Indifference (Sarajevo on Television)." In "Mobile Citizens, Media States," special issue, *PMLA* 117, no. 1 (2002): 104–16.

Keenan, Thomas. "'Where Are Human Rights . . . ?' Reading a Communiqué from Iraq." In *Nongovernmental Politics,* edited by Michel Feher with Gaëlle Krikorian and Yates McKee, 57–71. New York: Zone Books, 2007.

Keller, Marjorie. *The Untutored Eye: Childhood in the Films of Cocteau, Cornell, and Brakhage.* Teaneck, NJ: Fairleigh Dickinson University Press, 1986.

Komar, Vitaly, and Alexander Melamid, with Mia Fineman. *When Elephants Paint: The Quest of Two Russian Artists to Save the Elephants of Thailand.* New York: Harper-Collins, 2000.

Kozloff, Sarah. *Invisible Storytellers: Voice-Over Narration in American Fiction Film.* Berkeley: University of California Press, 1988.

Kramer, Sina. "Judith Butler's 'New Humanism': A Thing or Not a Thing, and So What?" *philoSOPHIA* 5, no. 1 (2015): 25–40.

Lacan, Jacques. "The Mirror Stage as Formative of the I Function, as Revealed in Psychoanalytic Experience." In *Ecrits: A Selection,* translated by Bruce Fink, 3–9. New York: Norton, 2002.

Lacan, Jacques. "What Is a Picture?" In *Four Fundamental Concepts of Psychoanalysis,* book 11 of *The Seminar of Jacques Lacan,* translated by Alan Sheridan, 105–19. New York: Norton, 1998.

Laqueur, Thomas. "Mourning, Pity, and the Work of Narrative in the Making of 'Humanity.'" In *Humanitarianism and Suffering: The Mobilization of Empathy,* edited by Richard Ashby Wilson and Richard D. Brown, 31–57. Cambridge: Cambridge University Press, 2009.

The Last Movie. Directed by Dennis Hopper. 1971. Charlotte, NC: United American Video, 1993. VHS.

Lavallee, Dave. "The Making of *Born into Brothels*." *Quad Angles*, June 10, 2005. http://advance.uri.edu/quadangles/sum2005/story9.htm (site discontinued).

Lazzarato, Maurizio. "Immaterial Labor." Translated by Paul Colilli and Ed Emory. In *Radical Thought in Italy: A Potential Politics*, edited by Paolo Virno and Michael Hardt, 132–47. Minneapolis: University of Minnesota Press, 1996.

Lebow, Alisa. *First Person Jewish*. Minneapolis: University of Minnesota Press, 2008.

Lebow, Alisa. Introduction to *The Cinema of Me: Self and Subjectivity in First Person Documentary*, edited by Alisa Lebow, 1–11. New York: Wallflower, 2012.

Lesage, Julia. "The Political Aesthetics of the Feminist Documentary Film." *Quarterly Review of Film Studies* 3, no. 4 (1978): 507–23.

Leviathan. Directed by Lucien Castaing-Taylor and Véréna Paravel. 2012. New York: Cinema Guild, 2013. DVD.

Levinas, Emmanuel, and Richard Kearney. "Dialogue with Emmanuel Levinas." In *Face to Face with Levinas*, edited by Richard A. Cohen, 13–34. Albany: SUNY Press, 1986.

Linnaeus, Carolus. *Systema naturae, sive, Regna tria naturae systematice proposita per classes, ordines, genera, & species*. Lugduni Batavorum: Haak, 1735.

Linné (Linnaeus), Carl von. *Systemae naturae*. 13th ed. Leipzig, 1788.

Lippit, Akira Mizuta. "The Death of an Animal." *Film Quarterly* 56, no. 1 (2002): 9–22.

MacDonald, Scott. *Avant-Doc: Intersections of Documentary and Avant-Garde Cinema*. New York: Oxford University Press, 2014.

Malkki, Liisa. "Children, Humanity, and the Infantilization of Peace." In *In the Name of Humanity: The Government of Threat and Care*, edited by Ilana Feldman and Miriam Ticktin, 58–85. Durham, NC: Duke University Press, 2010.

Manning, Erin. *Always More than One: Individuation's Dance*. Durham, NC: Duke University Press, 2013.

Manning, Erin. *Politics of Touch: Sense, Movement, Sovereignty*. Minneapolis: University of Minnesota Press, 2007.

Margesson, Rhoda, and Maureen Taft-Morales. "Haiti Earthquake: Crisis and Response." *Congressional Research Service Report for Congress*, February 2, 2010. http://www.fas.org/sgp/crs/row/R41023.pdf.

Marks, Laura U. *The Skin of the Film: Intercultural Cinema, Embodiment, and the Senses*. Durham, NC: Duke University Press, 2000.

Martel, James R. *The Misinterpellated Subject*. Durham, NC: Duke University Press, 2017.

Mauss, Marcel. *The Gift: The Form and Reason for Exchange in Archaic Societies*. Translated by W. D. Halls. New York: Norton, 2000.

McLagan, Meg. "Human Rights, Testimony, and Transnational Publicity." In *Nongovernmental Politics*, edited by Michel Feher with Gaëlle Krikorian and Yates McKee, 304–17. New York: Zone Books, 2007.

McRuer, Robert. *Crip Theory: Cultural Signs of Queerness and Disability*. New York: New York University Press, 2006.

"Mess O'Slightly-to-the-Left O'Potamia: Pro-Mubarak Demonstrators." *The Daily Show* with John Stewart video, 3:29. Comedy Central, February 2, 2011. http://www.cc.com/video-clips/eh7noh/the-daily-show-with-jon-stewart-mess-o-slightly-to-the-left-o-potamia---pro-mubarak-demonstrators.

Michaels, Eric. "The Social Organisation of an Aboriginal Video Workplace." *Australian Aboriginal Studies* no. 1 (1984): 26–34.

Mirzoeff, Nicholas. "The Shadow and the Substance: Race, Photography, and the Index." In *Only Skin Deep: Changing Visions of the American Self*, edited by Coco Fusco and Brian Wallis, 111–27. New York: Harry N. Abrams, 2003.

Mizen, Phillip, Christopher Pole, and Angela Bolton. "Why Be a School-Age Worker?" In *Hidden Hands: International Perspectives on Children's Work and Labour*, edited by Phillip Mizen, Christopher Pole, and Angela Bolton, 37–54. New York: RoutledgeFalmer, 2001.

MMadmin. "AspieWeb Being Bullied by Autism Speaks." Aspieweb.net. Accessed November 20, 2013. http://aspieweb.net/aspieweb-being-bullied-by-autism-speaks/ (site discontinued).

Moeller, Susan. *Compassion Fatigue: How the Media Sell Disease, Famine, War, and Death*. New York: Routledge, 1999.

Moore, Rachel. "Marketing Alterity." In *Visualizing Theory: Selected Essays from Visual Anthropology Review, 1990–1994*, edited by Lucien Taylor, 126–42. New York: Routledge, 1994.

Moore, Rachel O. *Savage Theory: Cinema as Modern Magic*. Durham, NC: Duke University Press, 2000.

Morel, Daniel. "Showcase: This Isn't Show Business." By Robert A. Harris. *New York Times*, January 27, 2010. http://lens.blogs.nytimes.com/2010/01/27/showcase-117/.

Morogiello, Vanessa Lynn. "A Content Analysis of Anderson Cooper 360°'s Coverage of Hurricane Katrina: Politically Slanted or Objective Reporting on a National Crisis." Master's thesis, Seton Hall University, 2007. http://scholarship.shu.edu/cgi/viewcontent.cgi?article=1700&context=dissertations.

Morse, Margaret. "The Television News Anchor and Credibility: Reflections on the News in Transition." In *Studies in Entertainment: Critical Approaches to Mass Culture*, edited by Tania Modleski, 55–79. Bloomington: Indiana University Press, 1986.

Mosquera, Daniel O. "Media, Technology, and Participation: Life in Its Duration, toward a New Evanescence?" *Journal of Latin American Cultural Studies* 22, no. 1 (2013): 41–56.

Mukhopadhyay, Tito Rajarshi. *Beyond the Silence: My Life, the World and Autism*. London: Crowes of Norwich, 2002.

Muñoz, José Esteban. *Disidentifications: Queers of Color and the Performance of Politics*. Minneapolis: University of Minnesota Press, 1999.

Murray, Stuart. *Autism*. New York: Routledge, 2012.

Murray, Stuart. "Hollywood and the Fascination of Autism." In *Autism and Representation*, edited by Mark Osteen, 244–55. New York: Routledge, 2008.

Murray, Stuart. *Representing Autism: Culture, Narrative, Fascination*. Liverpool: Liverpool University Press, 2008.

My *Classic Life as an Artist: A Portrait of Larry Bissonnette*. Directed by Douglas Biklen. 2004. Syracuse, NY: Syracuse University Video Production Unit. 2005. DVD.

Nabokov, Vladimir. *The Annotated Lolita*. Edited by Alfred Appel, Jr. New York: Vintage Books, 1991.

Nadesan, Majia Holmer. *Constructing Autism: Unravelling the "Truth" and Understanding the Social*. New York: Routledge, 2005.

Ne'eman, Ari. "Disability Community Condemns Autism Speaks." Autistic Self Advocacy Network, October 7, 2009. http://autisticadvocacy.org/2009/10/disability-community-condemns-autism-speaks/.

Nichols, Bill. *Introduction to Documentary*. 2nd ed. Bloomington: Indiana University Press, 2010.

Nichols, Bill. *Representing Reality*. Bloomington: Indiana University Press, 1991.

Nichols, Bill. "The Voice of Documentary." *Film Quarterly* 36, no. 3 (1983): 17–30.

Nieuwenhuys, Olga. "The Paradox of Anthropology and Child Labor." *Annual Review of Anthropology* 25 (1996): 237–51.

Ophir, Adi. "The Sovereign, the Humanitarian, and the Terrorist." In *Nongovernmental Politics*, edited by Michel Feher with Gaëlle Krikorian and Yates McKee, 161–82. New York: Zone Books, 2007.

"Original Elephant Painting." YouTube video, 8:28. Posted by "ExoticWorldGifts," March 7, 2008. http://www.youtube.com/watch?v=He7Ge7Sogrk&feature=fvw.

Osteen, Mark. "Autism and Representation: A Comprehensive Introduction." In *Autism and Representation*, edited by Mark Osteen, 1–48. New York: Routledge, 2008.

Pack, Sam. "Indigenous Media Then and Now: Situating the Navajo Film Project." *Quarterly Review of Film and Video* 17, no. 3 (2000): 273–86.

Pack, Sam. "Uniquely Navajo? The Navajo Film Project Reconsidered." *Visual Ethnography* 1, no. 2 (2012): 1–20.

Parikka, Jussi. *Insect Media: An Archeology of Animals and Technology*. Minneapolis: University of Minnesota Press, 2010.

Parks, Lisa. "Digging into Google Earth: An Analysis of 'Crisis in Darfur.'" *Geoforum* 40, no. 4 (2009): 535–45.

Pavsek, Christopher. "*Leviathan* and the Experience of Sensory Ethnography." *Visual Anthropology Review* 31, no. 1 (2015): 4–11.

Peckham, Linda. "Not Speaking with Language/Speaking with No Language: Leslie Thornton's *Adynata*." In *Psychoanalysis and Cinema*, edited by E. Ann Kaplan, 181–87. New York: Routledge, 1990.

Peirce, Charles Sanders. *Philosophical Writings of Peirce*. Edited by Justus Buchler. Mineola, NY: Dover, 1955.

Peterson, Leighton C. "Reclaiming Diné Film: Visual Sovereignty and the Return of *Navajo Film Themselves*." *Visual Anthropology* 29, no. 1 (2013): 29–41.

Pettman, Dominic. *Human Error: Species-Being and Media Machines*. Minneapolis: University of Minnesota Press, 2011.

Pettman, Dominic. *Love and Other Technologies: Retrofitting Eros for the Information Age*. New York: Fordham University Press, 2006.

Pettman, Dominic. "Pavlov's Podcast: The Acousmatic Voice in the Age of MP3s." *differences* 22, no. 2/3 (2011): 140–67.

Pettman, Dominic. "Zooicide: Animal Love and Human Justice." In *Human Error: Species-Being and Media Machines*, 59–110. Minneapolis: University of Minnesota Press, 2011.

Pinchevski, Amit. "Displacing Incommunicability: Autism as an Epistemological Boundary." *Communication and Critical/Cultural Studies* 2, no. 2 (2005): 163–84.

Plan International. "Bangladesh Street Children Launch Photo Exhibition." Accessed March 10, 2010. https://plan-international.org/news/2010-03-10-bangladesh-street -children-launch-photo-exhibition.

Popplewell, Georgia, and Nicholas Laughlin. "Global Voices in Haiti: The Grand Rue Artists, after the Earthquake." Global Voices, February 1, 2010. https:// globalvoices.org/2010/02/01/global-voices-in-haiti-the-grand-rue-artists-after-the -earthquake/.

Post, David M. "Conceiving Child Labor in Human Rights Terms: Can It Mobilize Progressive Change?" In *Child Labor and Human Rights*, edited by Burns H. Weston, 267–92. Boulder, CO: Lynne Rienner, 2005.

Prince, Dawn. "Cultural Commentary: The Silence Between: An Autoethnographic Examination of the Language Prejudice and Its Impact on the Assessment of Autistic and Animal Intelligence." *Disability Studies Quarterly* 30, no. 1 (2010). http://dsq -sds.org/article/view/1055/1242.

Rancière, Jacques. "Who Is the Subject of the Rights of Man?" *South Atlantic Quarterly* 103, no. 2/3 (2004): 297–310.

Rascaroli, Laura. "The Essay Film: Problems, Definitions, Textual Commitments." *Framework: The Journal of Cinema and Media* 49, no. 2 (2008): 24–47.

Reassemblage. Directed by Trinh T. Minh-ha. New York: Women Make Movies, 1982. 16mm.

Redfield, Peter. "Sacrifice, Triage and Global Humanitarianism." In *Humanitarianism in Question: Politics, Power, Ethics*, edited by Michael Barnett and Thomas G. Weiss, 196–214. Ithaca, NY: Cornell University Press, 2008.

Renov, Michael. "Introduction: The Truth about Non-fiction." In *Theorizing Documentary*, edited by Michael Renov, 1–11. New York: Routledge, 1993.

Renov, Michael. *The Subject of Documentary*. Minneapolis: University of Minnesota Press, 2004.

Rieff, David. *A Bed for the Night: Humanitarianism in Crisis*. New York: Simon and Schuster, 2003.

Rony, Fatimah Tobing. "Taxidermy and Romantic Ethnography: Robert Flaherty's *Nanook of the North*." In *The Third Eye: Race, Cinema and Ethnographic Spectacle*, 99–126. Durham, NC: Duke University Press, 1996.

Rony, Fatimah Tobing. *The Third Eye: Race, Cinema and Ethnographic Spectacle*. Durham, NC: Duke University Press, 1996.

Rose. "So, What's the Problem with Autism Speaks?" *I Am. I Am. I Am.* Accessed November 14, 2013. http://goldenheartedrose.tumblr.com/post/17644810872/so -whats-the-problem-with-autism-speaks.

Rosen, Marc. "Autism Speaks PSA 'I Am Autism' Faces Major Backlash." *Examiner* .com, September 26, 2009. http://www.examiner.com/article/autism-speaks-psa-i -am-autism-faces-major-backlash (site discontinued).

Rosen, Philip. "Border Times and Geopolitical Frames." *Canadian Journal of Film Studies* 15, no. 2 (2006): 2–19.

Rousseau, Jean-Jacques. *The Social Contract and The First and Second Discourses.* Edited by Susan Dunn. New Haven, CT: Yale University Press, 2002.

Ruoff, Jeffrey K. "Conventions of Sound in Documentary." In *Sound Theory, Sound Practice*, edited by Rick Altman, 217–34. New York: Routledge, 1992.

Russell, Catherine. "Autoethnography: Journeys of the Self." In *Experimental Ethnography: The Work of Film in the Age of Video*, 275–314. Durham, NC: Duke University Press, 1999.

Salaam Bombay. Directed by Mira Nair. 1988. Beverly Hills, CA: Metro-Goldwyn-Mayer, 2003. DVD.

Savarese, D. J. "Cultural Commentary: Communicate with Me." *Disability Studies Quarterly* 30, no. 1 (2010). http://dsq-sds.org/article/view/1051/1237.

Savarese, Emily Thornton, and Ralph James Savarese. "'The Superior Half of Speaking': An Introduction." *Disability Studies Quarterly* 30, no. 1 (2010). http://dsq-sds .org/article/view/1062/1230.

Scarry, Elaine. *Thinking in an Emergency.* New York: Norton, 2011.

Schalk, Sami. "Metaphorically Speaking: Ableist Metaphors in Feminist Writing." *Disability Studies Quarterly* 33, no. 4 (2013). http://dsq-sds.org/article/view/3874 /3410.

Sebeok, Thomas. "'Animal' in Biological and Semiotic Perspective." In *What Is an Animal?*, edited by Tim Ingold, 63–76. New York: Routledge, 1994.

Serres, Michel. "The Geometry of the Incommunicable: Madness." Translated by Felicia McCarren. In *Foucault and His Interlocutors*, edited by Arnold Davidson, 36–56. Chicago: University of Chicago Press, 1997.

Shah, Svati. "Born into Saving Brothel Children." *Samar Magazine* 19 (July 2005). http://samarmagazine.org/archive/articles/190.

Shape of a Right Statement. Directed by Wu Tsang. 2008. New York: Museum of Modern Art Department of Media and Performance Art, 2016. Video.

Silverman, Chloe. *Understanding Autism: Parents, Doctors, and the History of a Disorder.* Princeton, NJ: Princeton University Press, 2012.

Simpson, Richard L., with Sonja R. de Boer-Ott, Deborah E. Griswold, Brenda Smith Myles, Sara E. Byrd, Jennifer B. Ganz, and Katherine Tapscott Cook. *Autism Spectrum Disorders: Interventions and Treatments for Children and Youth.* Thousand Oaks, CA: Corwin, 2004.

Sliwinski, Sharon. *Human Rights in Camera.* Chicago: University of Chicago Press, 2011.

Slumdog Millionaire. Directed by Danny Boyle and Loveleen Tandon. 2008. Century City, CA: Fox Searchlight, 2009. DVD.

Smaill, Belinda. *The Documentary: Politics, Emotion, Culture.* Basingstoke, UK: Palgrave Macmillan, 2010.

Smith, Katherine. "Atis Rezistans: Gede and the Art of Vagabondaj." In *Obeah and*

Other Powers: The Politics of Caribbean Religion and Healing, edited by Diana Paton and Maarit Forde, 121–45. Durham, NC: Duke University Press, 2012.

Socrates. "I Am Autism Speaks (Now with Added Sub-titles)." YouTube video, 2:42. Posted by "MisterZonkerHarris," September 24, 2009. http://www.youtube.com /watch?v=yU2paLv1MGE.

Sontag, Susan. *Regarding the Pain of Others.* New York: Picador, 2003.

Spivak, Gayatri Chakravorty. "Can the Subaltern Speak?" In *Marxism and the Interpretation of Culture*, edited by Cary Nelson and Lawrence Grossberg, 271–316. Urbana-Champaign: University of Illinois Press, 1988.

Starling, Simon. "Simon Starling." By Edoardo Bonaspetti. *Mousse Magazine* 13, March 2008. Accessed July 31, 2012. http://www.moussemagazine.it/simon-starling -edoardo-bonaspetti-2008/.

Sterne, Jonathan. MP3: *The Meaning of a Format*. Durham, NC: Duke University Press, 2012.

Sturken, Marita. "Desiring the Weather: El Niño, the Media, and California Identity." *Public Culture* 13, no. 2 (2001): 161–89.

Sturken, Marita. "Weather Media and Homeland Security: Selling Preparedness in a Volatile World." *Understanding Katrina: Perspectives from the Social Sciences,* Social Science Research Council, June 11, 2006. http://understandingkatrina.ssrc.org /Sturken/.

Taussig, Michael. *Mimesis and Alterity: A Particular History of the Senses.* New York: Routledge, 1993.

Teitel, Ruti G. "For Humanity." *Journal of Human Rights* 3, no. 2 (2004): 225–37.

"Tele Geto 1." YouTube video, 10:05. Posted by "John Cussans," July 23, 2010. https:// www.youtube.com/watch?v=UbJuDaPfGHo.

"Tele Geto 2." YouTube video, 7:53. Posted by "John Cussans," July 25, 2010. https:// www.youtube.com/watch?v=wyLUkFYNTSk.

"Tele Geto 3." YouTube video, 7:48. Posted by "John Cussans," July 24, 2010. https:// www.youtube.com/watch?v=xi22RomHXpQ.

"Tele Geto 4." YouTube video, 9:45. Posted by "John Cussans," August 6, 2010. https:// www.youtube.com/watch?v=WRKe81t5HF4.

"Tele Geto 5." YouTube video, 10:08. Posted by "John Cussans," August 8, 2010. https://www.youtube.com/watch?v=HKNoj2bMKeQ.

"Tele Geto 6." YouTube video, 7:47. Posted by "John Cussans," August 7, 2010. https:// www.youtube.com/watch?v=FPGpFBlxcao.

"Teleghetto—Election Part 2." YouTube video, 2:33. Posted by "Students Rebuild," December 14, 2010. https://www.youtube.com/watch?v=knxjgenyySs.

"Tele Ghetto: Guerilla Media in Haiti." YouTube video, 7:43. Posted by "Students Rebuild," February 9, 2011. https://www.youtube.com/watch?v=p9IyeP-XS78.

"Tele Ghetto: One Year Anniversary." YouTube video, 2:37. Posted by "Students Rebuild," March 29, 2011. https://www.youtube.com/watch?v=SoJ290Df5ys.

"TeleGhetto Pre-elections Interview." YouTube video, 2:56. Posted by "Global Nomads Group," November 4, 2010. https://www.youtube.com/watch?v= SFMzczOBk1Q.

Ticktin, Miriam. *Casualties of Care: Immigration and the Politics of Humanitarianism in France.* Berkeley: University of California Press, 2011.

Torchin, Leshu. *Creating the Witness: Documenting Genocide on Film, Video, and the Internet.* Minneapolis: University of Minnesota Press, 2012.

Trinh T. Minh-ha. "Mechanical Eye, Electronic Ear, and the Lure of Authenticity." In *When the Moon Waxes Red: Representation, Gender, and Cultural Politics,* 53–62. New York: Routledge, 1991.

Trinh T. Minh-ha. "'Speaking Nearby': A Conversation with Trinh T. Minh-ha." By Nancy N. Chen. *Visual Anthropology Review* 8, no. 1 (1992): 82–91.

Trinh T. Minh-ha. "The Totalizing Quest of Meaning." In *When the Moon Waxes Red: Representation, Gender, and Cultural Politics,* 29–50. New York: Routledge, 1991.

Trouble the Water. Directed by Tia Lessin and Carl Deal. 2008. New York: Zeitgeist Films, 2009. DVD.

Turan, Kenneth. "The Eyes of the Storm: A New Orleans Couple's Raw Hurricane Footage Gave Two Filmmakers a New Focus." *Los Angeles Times,* January 21, 2008. http://articles.latimes.com/2008/jan/21/entertainment/et-trouble21.

Turner, Terrence. "Defiant Images: The Kayapo Appropriation of Video." *Anthropology Today* 8, no. 6 (1992): 5–16.

Uexküll, Jakob von. *A Foray into the Worlds of Animals and Humans with A Theory of Meaning.* Translated by Joseph D. O'Neil. Minneapolis: University of Minnesota Press, 2010.

Valentine, Gill. "Angels and Devils: Moral Landscapes of Childhood." *Environment and Planning D: Society and Space* 14, no. 5 (1996): 581–99.

Van Meter, Jonathan. "Unanchored." *New York Magazine,* September 19, 2005. http://nymag.com/nymetro/news/features/14301/.

Vaughan, Dai. "Let There Be Lumière." In *For Documentary: Twelve Essays,* 1–8. Berkeley: University of California Press, 1999.

Virno, Paolo. *A Grammar of the Multitude.* Los Angeles: Semiotext(e), 2004.

Walker, Janet. "Rights and Return: Perils and Fantasies of Situated Testimony after Katrina." In *Documentary Testimonies: Global Archives of Suffering,* edited by Bhaskar Sarkar and Janet Walker, 83–114. New York: Routledge, 2010.

Wall, John. "Fallen Angels: A Contemporary Christian Ethical Ontology of Childhood." *International Journal of Practical Theology* 8, no. 2 (2004): 160–84.

Wallis, Claudia. "'I Am Autism': An Advocacy Video Sparks Protest." *Time,* November 6, 2009. http://content.time.com/time/health/article/0,8599,1935959,00.html.

Warner, Marina. "Little Angels, Little Monsters: Keeping Childhood Innocent." In *Six Myths of Our Time: Little Angels, Little Monsters, Beautiful Beasts, and More,* 43–62. New York: Vintage Books, 1995.

When the Levees Broke: A Requiem in Four Acts. Directed by Spike Lee. Brooklyn: 40 Acres and a Mule, 2006. DVD.

The Wild Child. Directed by François Truffaut. 1970. Beverly Hills, CA: United Artists, 2001. DVD.

Winston, Brian. *Claiming the Real II: Documentary: Grierson and Beyond.* New York: Palgrave Macmillan, 2008.

Wolfe, Cary. *What Is Posthumanism?* Minneapolis: University of Minnesota Press, 2010.

Wolfe, Charles. "Historicising the 'Voice of God': The Place of Vocal Narration in Classical Documentary." *Film History* 9, no. 2 (1997): 149–67.

Worth, Sol, and John Adair. *Through Navajo Eyes: An Exploration in Film Communication and Anthropology*. Albuquerque: University of New Mexico Press, 1997.

Yousef, Nancy. *Isolated Cases: The Anxieties of Autonomy in Enlightenment Philosophy and Romantic Literature*. Ithaca, NY: Cornell University Press, 2004.

Zelizer, Barbie. *About to Die: How News Images Move the Public*. New York: Oxford University Press, 2010.

Žižek, Slavoj. "Have Michael Hardt and Antonio Negri Rewritten the *Communist Manifesto* for the Twenty-First Century?" *Rethinking Marxism* 13, no. 3/4 (2001): 190–98.

INDEX

autism (*continued*)
of disorders of, 106, 125, 212n35; as term 219n52
Autism Is a World (Wurzburg, 2004), 21, 107, 110, 114–18; documentary voicing and, 109; stills from, 115, 117, 119; voice-over commentary in, 112, 140, 193
Autism Speaks, 21, 103–9, 143–44, 210n1, 210n3, 210n5, 210n6. *See also* "I Am Autism"
autistic counterdiscourse of voicing, 108, 130–31, 133, 134, 157
autistic perception, 17, 130, 162, 166, 175
autistics: on autism cure, 210–11n9; in *Autism Is a World*, 114–18; conflated with children, 112; in films, 107–8, 145–46; first-person voice-over of, 4, 9, 21; high-functioning, 147; in hypervisuality of, 166; object to "I Am Autism," 104–5; as passive, 144; as poets and writers, 129–30, 131, 133; as primitive, 107; stereotypes of, 210n5
Autistic Self Advocacy Network, 103
autistic speech, autistic voice, 2, 18, 21, 131, 133, 147–48, 210n6, 213n44; Baggs on, 125–26, 131, 133, 148–49, 213n44; documentary voice and, 109, 140; first-person voice-over and, 139; human rights and, 125–26; recognizable mode of personhood and, 141
autobiography, 113, 138, 139
Avijit, 33, 189; career of, 48–49; photographs by, 32, 47; self-portrait of, 43, 44

Baggs, Mel (Amanda), 17, 214n59, 216n92; on autism, 128–29; autistic voice and, 125–26, 131, 133, 148–49, 213n44; communication by, 121–22; first-person voice-over and, 124, 141; gender pronouns and, 211n14; "In My Language" (2007), 21, 108–9, 110, 118–24, 194
Bailey, Bobby, *Invisible Children* (2006), 36
bare life, bare liveness, 72, 93, 98, 186; Agamben on, 20, 95; discourse of, 94; humanitarian emergency and, 75; Hurricane Katrina and, 76; politics vs., 70; as racist

technique, 101; representatives of, 65–66; Roberts and, 68, 101, 193; unmediated reality of, 89
Barthes, Roland, 34, 47, 108, 124, 214n53; on grain of voice, 131–33
Batchen, Geoffrey, 45, 201n36
Baton Rouge, 75, 77–78
Bazin, André, 64, 217n18
Benjamin, Walter, 201n34, 221n75
Bentham, Jeremy, 159, 217n15
Berger, John, 160
Berlant, Lauren, 31, 92, 200n11
Bernstein, J. M., 96
Bettelheim, Bruno, 212n34
Bhutto, Benazir, 46
Bicêtre state asylum, 23–24, 199n4
Biklen, Douglas, *My Classic Life as an Artist: A Portrait of Larry Bissonnette* (2004), 110
bio-documentary, 28, 54–55. *See also* Navajo Film Themselves Project
biopolitics, biopoliticization, 99, 158, 159, 182; biopolitical emergence and, 93–101; communicative, 16, 67, 99; of disposability, 94, 95; Emmett Till murder and, 209n69; Foucault and, 101, 144; Hardt and Negri on, 96–98; of humane reform, 160; oppositional, 96; racism and, 94, 97; vocabulary of, 93. *See also* biopower
biopower, 67, 92; Giroux on, 94–98; racism and 7, 93, 101
bios, 70, 95
Bissonnette, Larry, 113, 114, 212n27; *My Classic Life as an Artist* (Biklen, 2004), 110
Boat Leaving Harbor, A (Lumière Brothers, 1895), 194, 195, *196*
body, bodies: black, 91, 94–96, 100; materiality of, 133
Boltanski, Luc, *Distant Suffering*, 15
Born Hustler Records, 83
Born into Brothels (Briski and Kauffman, 2004), 2, 5, 19–20, 26–37, 49, 153, 189, 193, 195, 200n12; cinematography in, 31; funders of, 199–200n70; opening montage of, 31–32, 33; mise-en-scène in, 34, 41; stills from, 33, 34, 40, 41, 42, 44
Boyle, Danny, *Slumdog Millionaire* (2008), 32

Brecht, Bertolt, 168
Briski, Zana, 19, 83, 144, 189; *Born into Broth-els*, 26–37, 195, 200n12; Hope House and, 37; photographs by, 40; as photojournalist, 199n7; students of, 35–36, 145, 193
Brokaw, Tom, 73–74
Broomberg, Adam, 46
Brown, Aaron, 207n32
Brown, Kimberly Juanita, 36
Brown, Lydia X. Y., 210–11n9
Brown, Michael D., 89
Bruzzi, Stella, 137–38
Burman, Erica, 35, 200n18
Bush, George W., 89, *90*
Butler, Judith, 13–14, 139, 147, 198n33, 198n35, 216n90

Caillois, Roger, 21, 166, 219n50, 219–20n55, 220n62; on mimesis, 17, 173, 176; on mimetic insects, 169–76, 220n64; on mimetic surrender, 156–57
Calarco, Matthew, 159
Calcutta, 42, 200n16; children of sex workers in, 5, 11, 19–20, 26–37
Calhoun, Craig, 3, 10
camera, 18, 119; handing over, 189, 154–55. *See also* giving the camera to the other; video cameras
Cameron, Betsy, 47
Campbell, Timothy, 210n86
capture apparatus: Agre on, 158, 164–65; humane-itarianism as, 157–65
Cargol, Jean-Pierre, 23, 27
Carter, Kevin, 36
Cartwright, Lisa, 10–11, 14, 15–16, 105–6, 116, 162, 175, 200–201n18, 216n2
Castaing-Taylor, Lucien, 188, 222n88; *Leviathan*, 187
Castelli, Elizabeth, 208n59
catastrophe, 20, 65, 67, 81, 85, 94, 95, 207n30; Doane on, 73–74; television and, 66–67, 75, 84
Cavarero, Adriana, 214–15n59
Céleur, Jean-Hérard, 205n3
Chalfen, Richard, 202n46
Challenger explosion (1986), 72, 73–74

Chanarin, Adam, 46
Charleston Kids with Cameras, 49
child, children: as active social actors, 203n50; agency of, 51–52; autistic, 103–4, 111, 216n2; childhood and, 7, 14, 20, 46–47, 200n18, 203n52, 211n23; conflated with autistics, 112; as emblem of innocent and pure humanity, 4–5, 7, 23, 24, 31, 35; feral, 23–26; in fiction films, 32; humanitarian imaginary of, 27; media and, 19, 49–54; photographs by, 38–49; portrayed as victims, 34–35; rights of, 27–28, 50, 53; as savages, 38; of sex workers, 5, 11, 19–20, 26–37; as soldiers, 28, 36, 39; street, 32, 33, 49; taboo, 41; trafficking of, 202n49; voice of, 50. *See also* child labor
child labor, 14, 27–28, 202n49, 203n50, 203n52; child work vs., 50–52; dematerialized, 49–54
Chion, Michel, 111, 140
Chouliaraki, Lilie, 11, 15
Chow, Rey, 59, 175; on benevolent gaze, 164; on captivation, 217n17; on ethnic as term, 6; on mimesis and poststructuralism, 177, 220n61; on voice-over, 111
Chris, Cynthia, 221n84
Chun, Wendy Hui Kyong, 81
citizen journalists: CNN's call for, 80, 80–81, 84; Hurricane Katrina victims as, 72
City of God (Meirelles, 2001), 32
civil rights, 65, 95–96
Classen, Steve, 74
close reading, 17, 18
close-ups: in *Autism Is a World*, 117; in *Born into Brothels*, 32
CNN, 73, 75; *American Morning*, 75, 76, 77, 80; autism documentary of, 21, 116; coverage of Hurricane Katrina by, 20, 72, 74–80, 77, 80; television documentaries of, 107–8
coevalness, 107, 118, 211n12. *See also* Fabian, Johannes
commodity fetish, 47–48
communication: autism and, 125; by autistics, 105–9, 114, 118; democratic communities and, 98; enunciation and, 133; lin-

formal reflexivity, 155, 165, 176, 217n10
Foucault, Michel, 6, 149, 156, 158, 168, 174, 199n4, 217n17, 220n60; autism and, 141–42; biopolitics and biopower and, 7, 67, 93, 94, 144, 161; *Discipline and Punish*, 101, 159–60; *Madness and Civilization*, 109, 141–42, 143, 146; on racism, 94, 95, 208n61; on surveillance society, 101, 164–65
Frankfurt School, 221n75
Freud, Sigmund, death drive and, 173, 219–20n55
Full Frame Documentary Film Festival, 83
Fuqua, Joy, 96

gaze, 40, 84, 164, 219n50
Geddes, Anne, 47
Gede, 62, 205n3
George, Ivy, 203n50
Ghetto Biennale, 62–63, 64, 205n10
Ghosh, Bishnupriya, 99
gift giving, 191–93
Ginsburg, Faye, 56–57
Girl Project, 50
Giroux, Henry, 67, 94, 100, 101, 209n69; on biopower, 94–98
giving the camera to the other, 22, 191; in *Born into Brothels*, 29–37; children and, 49–50; as hailing, 193–94; mediation and, 9; in participatory documentary, 1–2, 5, 7
Global Nomads Group, 61, 69; YouTube videos of, 61–68, 62, 65
Gour, 32, 33
governance, 27, 29, 65, 93; of emergency, 68–72; governmentality and, 159
grain, of voice, 131–32, 132–33, 214n53
Grandin, Temple, 108, 129, 131–32, 166
Grierson, John, 3, 109; on documentary, 2–3, 197n2, 197n3; on expository voice-over, 135, 137, 138–39; narration and, 110, 114
Grosz, Elizabeth, 163, 218n29, 219n50
Gruben, Patricia, 123, 124
Guattari, Félix, 219n39
Guerin, Frances, 209n72
Guha, Ranajit, 99

Hacking, Ian, 143–44
hail, hails, 192, 193. *See also* counterhail
Haiti: art of, 62; disenfranchised youth in, 205n3; hurricane relief for, 63, 68–69; 2010 earthquake in, 20, 61–68, 205n7, 205n8, 205n10
Hallas, Roger, 209n72
hapticity, 121, 171, 177; haptic image and, 157, 176–79, 190
Haraway, Donna, 219n39
Hardt, Michael, 93, 99, 209n76; *Common-wealth*, 98, 209n76; on communicative biopolitics, 16, 67, 93–94, 95, 100; *Empire*, 98; view of biopolitics of, 96–98. *See also* Negri, Antonio
Heidegger, Martin, 167
Hesford, Wendy S., 16, 35; on *Born into Brothels*, 37, 200n16
heterosexuality, 145, 147, 216n90
Hetherington, Tim, 207n45
Higonnet, Anne, 41, 46–47
Hobbes, Thomas, 199n2
Hollywood films: autistics in, 145–46; feminist experimental film and, 123, 124
Homo sapiens, 8, 162, 218n25; *Homo sapiens ferus*, 24
Honig, Bonnie, 10, 11
Hope House, 37, 201n21
Hopper, Dennis, *The Last Movie*, 205n5
Horkheimer, Max, 221n75
humane-itarianism: as capture apparatus, 157–65; humane-itarian approach and, 155–56
humaneness, 158–59; biopolitics of, 160; humane reform and, 156, 158; humane societies and, 159; humanitarianism and, 159
humanism, 158; ethics after, 12–15; as ideological glue, 9
humanitarian emergency, 20; bare life and, 75; brothels as, 35; depoliticizing logic of, 98; discursive space of, 69; documentary codes of, 20; as live media event, 66; real time of, 81; spectacle of, 101; subjects of, 93; testimonial codes of, 91, 92, 100
humanitarian impulse: in documentary, 1–22; in participatory documentary, 6, 176; priorities of, 3; to salvage childhood, 20

humanitarian intervention: critiques of, 70–71; discourses of, 68; documentary tropes of, 123; myth of childhood innocence and, 26; politics of, 93; principles of, 69–70

humanitarianism, 65; aesthetic of, 53; apparatus of, 37; autistic discourse of, 141–49; crisis of contemporary, 69; discourses of, 15, 217n13; elephant painting and, 153; ethics of, 1, 7, 13, 14, 154, 222n4; fantasy of, 27, 53; in governance of emergency, 68–72; human rights and, 71; imaginary of, 27; merges with humane reform, 159; myth of, 25–26; organizations of, 206n21; principles of, 173; reason of, 156; state of, 24; testimony of, 65; vision of, 26; visual culture of, 38–39; voice of, 146; volunteers of, 92; witnessing of, 158

humanitarian media: interventions of, 11, 53, 158; live media as, 81, 85; voice-over in, 112

humanity: of animals, 164; appeal to, 5; Baggs and, 149; child as symbol of, 7; community of, 193; of dehumanized, 4; discourses of, 217n13; of elephants, 154; human beings and, 152; human condition and, 7, 106; *humanité* and, 158–59; humanization and, 155; humankind and, 158; human sensorium and, 166, 167; as imperative, 6; lineage of, 159; markers of, 138; as signifier, 7; speaking voice and, 134; of suffering others, 17; Teitel on, 198n15, 198n17; as ultimate imagined community, 7; of wild child, 1

human rights, 65, 198n17, 208n59; advocacy for, 68; autistic voice and, 125–26; biopolitical struggle for, 67; claims of, 82, 100, 125–26, 191; discourse of, 11–12, 69; in governance of emergency, 68–72; Hardt and Negri on, 99; humanitarianism and, 71; logic of, 26; organizations for, 96; sentimentalist thesis of, 198n26; speech acts of, 71, 98; testimonies of, 210n84; universal, 50

Hurricane Katrina, 2, 96, 208n47; aftermath of, 66; CNN coverage of, 20, 72, 74–80, 77, 80; Giroux on, 209n69; media doc-umentations of, 95; New Orleans and, 82–93, *88*

Hurricane Katrina victims, 11, 81, 94, 208n48; as citizen journalists, 72; vulnerability of, 79–80

Hurricane Tomas, 68

"I Am Autism" (Cuarón, 2009), 145, 210n3; documentary voicing and, 109; dominant voice and, 143; expository voice-over narration in, 135, 140; first-person voice-over in, 107; objections to, 210n1; parodies of, 109–10; stills from, 104, 105

"I Am Autism Speaks" ("Socrates," 2009), 109–10

icon, index and, 179

identification: dis-, 146; empathetic, 175; haptic mode of, 172; projective, 200–201n18

illumination, 159, 169

"I'm Autistic: I Can Speak," 110

immaterial labor and production, 97, 99; Hardt and Negri on, 209n76; neoliberalism and, 52–53

immediacy: in *Born into Brothels*, 34; discursive, 115; of dispossessed, 93–94; documentary and, 2, 27; humanitarian discourse of, 54; humanitarian mandate and, 3; ideology of, 99–100; raw documentary, 79; rhetoric of, 11, 67–68, 107; of *Trouble the Water*, 82, 85. *See also* documentary immediacy

immediation, immediations, 2; aesthetics of, 114; discourse of, 58; documentary, 107; documentary as discourse of, 190; documentary logic of, 73; documentary tropes of, 6, 148; ethic of, 9; examples of, 4; feral innocence as, 27; humanitarian discourse of, 157; as optical devices, 8–9; televisual strategies of, 83; traumatic, 74; vicious circle of, 155. *See also* documentary immediation

inclusion, 7, 101, 156, 210n86. *See also* exclusion

index, indexicality, 177, 187; icon and, 179; indexical sign and, 180; live eyewitness as, 72–82

India, 35, 173–74; child laborers in, 203n50; female infanticide in, 199n7
Ingold, Tim, 164, 218n31
"In My Language" (Baggs, 2007), 21, 107–8, 118–24, 155; autistic voice in, 148–49; documentary voicing and, 109; first-person voice-over in, 110; re-performance of, 132; soundtrack of, 119, 121; stills from, 120, 123
innocence: humanitarian aesthetic of, 145; photographic aesthetic of, 4. *See also* feral innocence
innocence: childhood, 38; discourse of, 37, 46–47, 59; myth of, 25–26, 31, 41
insects: behavior of, 21; biology of, 167; mimesis of, 169–76, 220n64
interactive mode of documentary, 137. *See also* participatory documentary
interiority, 105, 108, 124, 142, 146; subjugated, 113, 148. *See also* exteriority
International Labour Organization Convention C182 (1999), 50–51
interview, in documentary genre, 108
invisibility, 169, 209n69; of black bodies, 94, 96
Invisible Children (Russell, Bailey, Poole, 2006), 36
Irigaray, Luce, 221n75
Itard, Jean-Marc Gaspard, 1–2, 24, 25, 27, 37, 49, 189

Jacques, Frantz (Guyudo), 205n3
Jameson, Fredric, 127
Jam Jar (Everson, 1995), 110, 114, 212n27; Williams as protagonist in, 112–13
Janet, Pierre, 170, 220n55

Kac, Eduardo, 166
Kagan, Daryn, 76, 77
Kahana, Jonathan, 3, 197n6
Kanner, Leo, 212n34, 219n52; autism research of, 125, 143
Kant, Immanuel, 159, 163
Karunan, Victor, 203n50
Katz, Elihu, 80
Kauffman, Ross, *Born into Brothels*, 26–37, 200n12

Keenan, Thomas, 71, 96, 158, 195; *Fables of Responsibility*, 191; on gift giving, 191–93; on human rights discourse, 11–12, 16, 98
Kids with Cameras, 27, 37, 48, 50, 83, 201n21, 202n46; website of, 40, 41, 45
Kids with Destiny, 37
Klein, Jonathan, 75
Klein, Melanie, 200n18
Kline, Franz, 163
Kochi, 31, 32, 35
Kold Madina. *See* Roberts, Kimberly Rivers
Komar, Vitaly, 163; elephant art academy of, 152–53; *When Elephants Paint*, 153. *See also* Melamid, Alexander
Kozloff, Sarah, 215n60
Kramer, Sina, 198n35

Lacan, Jacques, 213n44, 220n56; on mirror stage, 161–62, 169, 171
language: acquired by feral children, 24–25; Baggs's, 121–22; conflated with speech and voice, 125–26; encounter between voice and, 132–33; mimetic encounter with, 129
Laqueur, Thomas, 198n17
Last Movie, The (Hopper, 1971), 205n5
Lazzarato, Maurizio, 28, 52–53
Lebow, Alisa, 113, 138, 139, 141
Lee, Spike, *When the Levees Broke* (2006), 82
Lesage, Julia, 155
Lessin, Tia, 144; *Trouble the Water*, 20, 84, 91, 99, 100, 195. *See also* Deal, Carl
Leviathan (Castaing-Taylor and Paravel, 2012), 187, 188, 222n88
Levinas, Emmanuel, 139, 192, 198n33, 198n35; ethical turn of, 12–14
liberalism, internal violence of, 6
life, as ultimate humanitarian principle, 173
liminality, 7, 19
Linnaeus, Carl, 8, 218n25; *Systema naturae*, 24, 161–62
Lippit, Akira Mizuta, 160, 217n18, 219n39
live eyewitness, as performance and index, 72–82
liveness: definition of, 72–73; as documentary idiom of humanitarian testimony, 65; as humanizing attribute, 7; perfor-

mance of, 91; of Roberts, 148; sensation of, 73; televisual discourse of, 73; televisual performance of, 82; as televisual rhetoric, 20; televised code of, 4; televisual tropes of, 89; testimonial codes of, 86; theater of, 66

logocentrism, 138; autistic voice and, 139; of documentary studies, 134

logophobia, 222n88

logos, as inner speech, 108, 126

long take, 30

looping effect, 143–44

Louis, Alex, 205n1

Lumière Brothers, *A Boat Leaving Harbor*, 194–96

Madame Guérin, 24–25, 26

madness, 148; Foucault on, 146–47

Maetaman Elephant Camp, 154

Malkki, Liisa, 38–39

Manik, 32, 34, 35; as child photographer; photos by, 39–40, 40, 41, 42, 42–43, 47, 59, 194

Manning, Erin, 14, 17, 175, 214–15n59, 221n72; on autistic perception, 130, 162

March of Time, The, 110, 211n22

Margulies, Julianna, 116, 117, 118, 140

Marie of Champagne, 24

Marks, Laura U., 14, 218n27, 221n75; on haptic, sonic eye, 121, 157; on mimesis, 17, 176–79

Martel, James R., 222n8

Marxism, autonomist tradition of, 28, 52

Mauss, Marcel, 192–93

McElwee, Ross, 30

McLagan, Meg, 209–10n84

McRuer, Robert, 145–46, 147, 148

Médecins Sans Frontières (Doctors without Borders), 69

media: cultures of, 220n64; as discursive reality, 91; empowerment and, 28, 50, 100; mainstream, 94; news, 15; scholars of, 13; surrender of, 22; theory of, 154; visibility in, 101

mediation, 9, 190; beyond, 15–17; of biopolitical emergence, 93–101; Briski's, 29; emergency and, 10–11; as field of action,

190; new vistas of, 17; theories of, 99; witnessing by, 158

Meirelles, Fernando, *City of God* (2001), 32

Melamid, Alexander, 162–63; elephant art academy of, 152–53; *When Elephants Paint*, 153. *See also* Komar, Vitaly

Meserve, Jeanne, 76

methodology of book, 17–19

Michael, Eric, 57

mimesis, 17, 176; Caillois on, 157, 173; Chow on, 177, 220n61; coercive mimeticism and, 175; of insects, 169–76, 220n64; language and, 129, 131; logic of, 175; Marks on, 176–79; mimetic ethic of surrender and, 22, 169–70; mimetic indistinction and, 165–76; mimetic insects and, 172–73, 174; mimetic surrender and, 21, 156–57; mimicry and, 220n62; Platonic repudiation of, 178; spectacle of, 151

mirror stage, 161–62, 171

Mirzoeff, Nicholas, 209n83

Moana (Flaherty, 1926), 197n2, 197n6

Moore, Henry, *Warrior with Shield*, 183

Moore, Rachel, 57–58

Morel, Daniel, 63–64, 205n7, 205n8

Morris, Errol, 30

Morse, Margaret, 73, 84, 143

Mosquera, Daniel O., 33

Mubarak, Hosni, 79

Mukhopadhyay, Tito Rajarshi, 108, 129

Muñoz, José Esteban, 146

Murray, Stuart, 145–46

mussels, zebra, 183–85

Muybridge, Eadweard, 185

My Classic Life as an Artist (Biklen, 2005), 110, 114, 212n27; voice-over commentary in, 112

Myers, Chad, 76, 207n38

Nabokov, Vladimir, 160, 218n19

Nagin, Ray, 89

Nair, Mira, *Salaam Bombay* (1988), 32–33

National Geographic, *Crittercam*, 186

National Press Photographers Association, 199n7

natural man, nature, state of, 24, 199n2. *See also Homo sapiens ferus*; wild child

political reflexivity, 155, 165, 176, 217n10
politics: bare life vs., 70; of documentary voicing, 21; humanitarianism vs., 69; paradox of, 12
Pollock, Jackson, 153, 163
Poole, Laren, *Invisible Children* (2006), 36
Port-au-Prince, Haiti, 62, 64, 68, 205n7, 205–6n10
postcolonialism and postcolonialist scholars, 14, 54
posthumanism, 156, 165, 175
postmodernity, postmodernization, 50, 97, 145
poststructuralism, 54, 177, 220n61
primitivism, primitives, 58–59, 107, 163, 168, 174–75
Prince, Dawn, 108, 130, 129
prison, modern, 159, 168
projective identification, 36–37
propaganda, 3, 111
prostitution, prostitutes, 37, 200n17; children as, 51, 202n49. *See also* sex workers
proximity, mimetic relations of, 177. *See also* mimesis
pseudoliberation, 147, 149
pseudoparticipatory documentary, 19–20, 29–37, 58, 59; of *Born into Brothels*, 26
psychasthenia, 170–71, 175, 220n55
psychoanalysis, 139, 171, 212n34, 220n55
psychotherapy, 220n55. *See also* Janet, Pierre
public, 16
public sphere theory, 96
Puja, 32, 33, 34; photograph of, 39–40, 40
punctum, in Briski's footage, 34

queer, 145; queer studies and, 162; queer theory and, 146

race and racism, 5, 35, 67, 80, 91, 92, 95, 209n83; bare liveness and, 101; biopolitical, 94, 97; biopower and, 93, 95, 101, 208n61
Rancière, Jacques, 11, 98
Rascaroli, Laura, 138, 141
Rather, Dan, 74
realism, 32, 73, 166
reality, 10, 15, 46, 89, 91

reality television, 33
reason, 126, 143, 146, 149, 156
Red Cross, 69, 83, 158
Redfield, Peter, 93
referentiality, 66, 75, 89
reflexive mode of documentary, 137, 138
reflexivity, 155, 176; act of self-knowledge and, 162; documentary and, 109; formal, 28; gestures of, 154; humane-itarian approach to, 165; new techniques of, 157; posthumanist approach to, 156, 167–68, 169, 175; reflexive critique and, 19; reflexive gaze and, 164
refugeehood, refugees, 7, 97, 98, 208n48
Renov, Michael, 50, 138, 197n9, 202n47
reporters, privilege of, 66
rhetoric, 195, 196, 207n30
rights: of children, 27–28; discourse of, 175. *See also* civil rights; human rights
Roberts, Kimberly Rivers, 83, 91–92, 87, 94, 145; bare life and liveness of, 68, 101, 193; Hurricane Katrina footage of, 81–92, 99, 100; as Hurricane Katrina survivor, 20, 66–67
Roberts, Scott, 82, 91
Roma, 23, 27
romanticism: aesthetics of, 46; humanitarian photography and, 47–48; romantic naturalism and, 5
Romel Jean Pierre, 204–5n1
Rony, Fatimah Tobing, 5–6, 7, 107
Rooy, Robert: *Deej*, 214n50
Rorty, Richard, 198n26
Rouch, Jean, 30
Rousseau, Jean-Jacques, 24, 199n2
Royal Humane Society, 159
Rubin, Sue, 21, 110, 130, 145, 193; in *Autism Is a World*, 108, 113, 114–18, 117, 140
Russell, Catherine, 138, 139, 141
Russell, Jason, *Invisible Children* (2006), 36

Salaam Bombay (Nair, 1988), 32
Sanlaap, 37
Savarese, D. J., 129–30, 214n50
Scarry, Elaine, 3, 10
schizophrenia, autism and, 219n52
science and technology studies, 109

Sebeok, Thomas, 164, 218n23, 218n31
self-actualization, child labor as, 28
self-effacement, 143
self-formation, 161
selfhood, 162, 172; of animals, 21, 152, 154, 161; of elephants, 154, 158, 161; liberal, 164, 176
selfies, as genre, 43
Serres, Michel, 146–47, 148, 149
sexuality, 218n29; sexual fetish and, 47–48
sex workers, 2, 35, 200n16
Shah, Svati, 200n17
Shanti, 32, 34, 40; Manik and, 42–43
Shape of a Right Statement (Tsang, 2008), 132
sign, signs, 76, 89, 106, 174, 197n9, 202n47; of agency, 92, 100; indexical, 179–80
signifier, signifiers, 7, 36, 72, 130, 184–85, 187, 197n9; elephant self-portrait as, 160–61; of interiority, 118; slippage of, 133; speech as, 136–37; television and, 75–76, 79; voice and, 122, 127–28, 131–33, 136
Silverman, Chloe, 142; *Understanding Autism*, 212n34
similitude, 174. *See also* index, indexicality; icon
Simondon, Gilbert, 219n39, 221n72
Sitze, Adam, 210n86
slippages, 133, 173; in *Born into Brothels*, 34–35
Sliwinski, Sharon, 15
Slumdog Millionaire (Boyle and Tandon, 2008), 32
Smith, Katherine, 205n3
social problems, 3, 10
Socrates, 126
Sontag, Susan, 46
speaking and speaking out, 105, 108, 146, 212n31
spectacle. of bare life, 72, 89; black bodies at risk as, 11, 78, 91, 101, 123, 151, 160
spectator, spectatorship, 15, 25, 53, 73, 85, 207n30
speech, 130, 136–37, 215n67; acts of, 67, 71, 106, 107; conflated with language and voice, 125–26; inner, 108, 214n59; spoken word and, 20–21. *See also* voice, voicing

Spivak, Gayatri Chakravorty, 175; "Can the Subaltern Speak?," 14, 173–74
spontaneity, 27, 42, 43, 46, 195
Starling, Simon, 177, 180, 189; *Infestation Piece (Musselled Moore)*, 183–85, 184
Steevens, Simeon, 205n1
Sterne, Jonathan, 211n21
Stewart, Jon, 79
Stoller, Paul, 221n75
Sturken, Marita, 79
subaltern, subalterns, 36, 47, 97, 99, 100
subjectivity, 50, 113, 116, 138, 140, 161, 172, 202n47, 219n50; autistic, 109, 139
subtitles, 121, 132
Suchitra, 32, 35; photographs by, 43–44, 44, 45, 47
suffering, spectatorship of, 15
suicidal mimesis, 174. *See also* Caillois, Roger
Sundance Documentary Film Program, 45
Sundance Film Festival, 83
Superdome, 76, 89
surrender, surrendering, 17, 21, 22; *Animal Cams* and, 186; documentary, 157, 176–90, 194
surveillance, 186, 101, 164–65
sympathetic magic, 205n5
symptomatic reading, 18

taboos, 56
tactile epistemology, 179
Tandon, Loveleen, *Slumdog Millionaire* (2008), 32
Tapasi, 32, 35, 41; photos by, 40–41, 41, 47, 59, 194
Taussig, Michael, 205n5, 221n75
Teitel, Ruti, 7, 198n15, 198n17
Tele Geto ("Ghetto TV"), 204–5n1, 205–6n10; bearing witness by, 68; celebrated, 71–72; fake cameras of, 205n5; ironic mimicry of, 100; videos of, 61–68, 62, 65
teleplasty, 172
television: news on, 11; televised code of liveness and, 4; televisual images and, 15
temporality, 29, 107, 111; of emergency, 10, 69
testimonial acts, 71; of human rights, 210n84

voice-of-God narration, 30, 138, 211n22; in "I Am Autism," 110–12

voice-over, 111, 112, 143, 215n60; in *Autism Is a World*, 117; in *Born into Brothels*, 29, 30, 31; in documentary genre, 107, 108; in films on autism, 112–13, 134–35

voicing, 138; autistic counterdiscourse of, 108, 124, 130–31

vulnerability, 41, 76, 86, 159, 222n8; of the other, 12–13; of reporter's body, 77, 78–79

Walker, Janet, 84

Warner, Marina, 38

Weather Channel, 79, 86, 87

West, 23, 27, 28, 33, 47, 142, 221n75; childhood in, 51, 203n52; philosophy of, 126, 127

Weyerman, Diane, 45

wide-angle shot, 30

Wild Boy of Aveyron, 23. *See also* Victor of Aveyron

wild child, 19; humanity of, 1–2; taming of, 23–29

Wild Child, The (L'Enfant Sauvage) (Truffaut, 1970), 1, 23–26, 26, 49

Williams, Brian, 74

Williams, Donna, 110, 114, 212n27; in *Jam Jar* (1995), 112–13

Winston, Brian, 3

witnessing and bearing witness, 13, 68, 71, 158

Wittgenstein, Ludwig, 127

Wolfe, Cary, 165–67, 175

Wolfe, Charles, 111–12, 211n22

World Press Photo, 46, 48–49, 63

World Press Photo Foundation: awards from, 199n7

Worth, Sol, 54, 168, 204n75; Navajo Film Themselves Project, 16–17, 54–59, 204n65, 204n67; *Through Navajo Eyes*, 28, 54, 202n46

Wurzburg, Gerardine, 116, 144; *Autism Is a World*, 21, 117, 118

Wynter, Kareen, 78

Yazzie, Sam, 56–57

YouTube, 61, 108, 110, 206n11; elephants painting on, 151, 154, 161, 188; of Global Nomads Group, 61–68, 62, 65

Zarrella, John, 76, 207n38

zebra mussels, 183–85

Zelizer, Barbie, 75

Žižek, Slavoj, 98

zoë, 69, 70, 95

ZoomUganda, 49

zoos, 160, 164